37 LIES
and Counting
OF PRESIDENT
DONALD J. TRUMP

𝔚e the ~~People~~ Trumps

As told by William George Houraney, Jr.

Published by

American Dream Entertainment Corporation

www.37lies.com

———————

Copyright © 2017 by William George Houraney, Jr.

ISBN: 978-0-692-90450-3

Editor: Paul Kurzweil

Printed in the United States of America

For additional copies or more information, visit **37Lies.com**

The people who helped me produce this book were not asked or requested to voice or endorse any opinion as to the book's content. Being professionals, I expected them to remain neutral—unless there comes a time they wish to voice their opinions. I do thank them for being the professionals they have been in carrying out what they do best in their profession. —William George Houraney

Contents

Editor's Note

When I was introduced to George Houraney through a longtime client of mine who happens to be one of George's closest friends, I wasn't quite sure what I might be getting into, but with the prospect of having a hand in bringing such material to the world (all of which is provable by eyewitness accounts, court documentation and sworn depositions), I made the decision that I shouldn't resist the opportunity.

Mr. Houraney has achieved a monumental undertaking. I was given the task of collating, proofreading and editing all of George's writings, which were extensive.

It has been our attempt to give you, dear reader, only the facts. Everything you read will be straight from the horse's mouth, with no hearsay, assumptions or exaggerations. We will leave it up to you to make your own informed decisions concerning the information that will be revealed here.

In addition, there are "op-ed" essays included after the facts have been revealed that contain George's many ideas for rescuing the country he and I so love. Keep in mind that if I'd had even the slightest inkling that the facts presented here were questionable in the least, I never would have agreed to sign on and put my name to it. I was truly honored to be chosen and trusted with this material, and my hope is that it has been presented in a way that is accessible, informative and enjoyable.

The length of this book has also been kept in check to avoid bogging the reader down with unnecessary details. George could have easily written an entire book on just the lawsuit, which took two years. Finally, please note that we have printed this book in slightly larger text in the hope that it will be easier to read for those who wear glasses.

Paul Kurzweil
July 2017

About the Author

It was fate that this book had to be written.

The truth about Donald J. Trump was predicted twenty-five years ago by someone he tried to destroy. While the world saw Trump as a great and powerful businessman all those years ago, our good friend George predicted that someday the world would see the real Donald Trump, a man who is without feelings or concern for others, except for his own family, and, even then, *he* comes first. He is a man who judges people by their wealth, not their heart and soul, and who does not like the word *no*, that is, unless he's the one who says it.

He is man who, no matter how much he denies it, feels that women, blacks, Muslims and the poor are all beneath him. We saw this firsthand. We saw how cold and calculating he can be, and how nothing is more important to him than what *he wants*. At first, we were all Trump supporters just like our dear friend George, but then gradually we started to see, as George pointed out, that Trump is not the genius we all believed him to be. Even worse, other than himself (and at times his family), he cared about no one.

After our friend George worked personally with Donald Trump there was a two-year court battle between them, one which the media described as a "David and

Goliath" story. George was the small businessman fighting the all-powerful Donald Trump in federal court. We will never forget what he told us at the end of that trial. "Trump thinks he's indestructible, that he can do anything he wants and get away with it. But someday he will get into a situation where he will not be able to do anything he wants, there will be people who will say no to him, and for once in his life, 'no' will be a word he must finally face. If he goes along with this, he will survive, however, if he fights, it will finally be his downfall. I'm not talking about money; I'm talking about his reputation, the respect most of the world has for him, and his place in history as either a smart and great man whom people look up to, or the exact opposite."

After Trump won the Presidency, George said, "Unbelievable, if Trump won over Clinton, something's terribly wrong." We replied, "You said he's the luckiest guy on Earth—he can get away with anything. This time he got the biggest prize in the world and got away with it." George then said, "Yes, I did say he's all that, but did you forget I also said that someday he will get into a situation where if he fights it, thinking it's his world, the 'Donald Trump World' where he always gets what he wants, that it will be his downfall? Well, this is it! If he tries to control the government, even as president, it will be the end of the great Donald Trump as the world knows him."

Amazingly, George had Trump figured out long before anyone else, but then again, he went through hell for years to reach that conclusion.

Since our friend George worked with Trump, going

through some of his life's most terrible times, we and others have constantly been on him to write a book so people could see the *real* Trump. Although he started to write about his experiences with Trump, he refused to finish his book, saying, "Who will believe me over the famous Donald Trump? When I say what he's really like, they'll think I'm crazy." So, we all felt bad thinking George's book would never happen.

Here is where fate stepped in. When Trump actually won the Presidency, George said, "It's time, now I can finally finish writing the book about Trump." We asked him, "Why now? As president, people will not believe you over Trump." George laughed and said, "You don't get it. Now, Trump will do all of the things I've wanted to write about him, and he will verify everything I will write. He's his own worst enemy, and his acts as president will once and for all prove what I found out years ago. You'll see." And so, we did.

How can William "George" Houraney write a first-of-its-kind book about Donald Trump? Not only has he never written a book like this before, but with all due respect to others who have written books about Trump, none of them went through what George did, which included Trump pursuing his wife for years. Because George was not a wealthy man, to Trump he was a "loser"—a term he used on George's wife when trying to win her over. Because of this, Trump never took George seriously and let his guard down, which allowed George to see the *real* Donald Trump, the person most people never see.

We are three of his closest friends who have known George since he was twelve years old. From the time his father moved the family to New York, from George's musical days, photography and racing days, to his meeting Trump, to his days in court, we saw George go through what most people never could, and survive. Accordingly, we saw that George knew Trump better than Trump knew himself.

We know you are anxious to read about Trump, but first you must know more about George to fully appreciate what he has written here, and to understand how only someone that has been through what he has, both in life and in dealing with Trump, could ever write a book with so much truth about the man who is now president of the United States.

George Houraney was born in Altoona, Pennsylvania, as were his mother and father. Both his parents were accomplished musicians. His father was so good he actually had a radio show during the 1950s that was broadcast live from his home, playing dinner music over the air five days a week. Although we weren't there, George says he remembers they all had to go upstairs and be very quiet when his dad was on-air. Another big thing his parents did was to put on concerts featuring twenty-one organs, with all their students playing at the same time. From what George showed us, they were amazing concerts.

At the age of six, George started his musical career. At age ten, his parents dressed him up in a Davy Crockett outfit, and at a concert they were producing with five thousand people watching, he walked onstage and played Davy Crockett, which was a famous Disney hit show at the time, on a Hammond Organ.

At age twelve, his parents moved to Long Island because his father was offered a job at Macy's. At thirteen, George became the youngest member of the Musician's Union Local 802, playing in a band with his father in New York City and around Long Island.

At sixteen (he looked and dressed older so he told clients he was twenty-one), besides the music, he was so good at photography that a friend asked him to photograph his sister's wedding because they could not afford a professional. Although hesitant because he had never photographed a wedding before, his friend talked him into it, telling him if he didn't take photos his sister would not have any wedding pictures. The photos he took turned out so well he got two other offers to shoot weddings. Before he knew it, he was in such demand that he opened a photo studio working from his parents' home while still playing in his father's band.

At seventeen, between the band and weddings he was making more money than most adults at that time. He was always very generous, buying us movie tickets, pizza and drinks (even though we would constantly pressure him to buy us beers, Coke was the strongest drink he would ever buy). However, he also saved all he could, and by his seventeenth birthday he had enough money to buy one of the most sought-after cars at the time—a Chevy 409. This car was so fast that it took him to the world of racing and motorsports. With his 409, George won so many trophies that you could barely get into his bedroom. Then one day, after he had survived his car crashing and rolling over several times, he decided it was time to quit racing.

He loved racing so much, he used his photography skills to win a job as the official photographer at a brand-new Super Speedway that had opened on Long Island. Called New York National Speedway, it was one of the first professional drag strips ever built from scratch.

One day when we went with him to the speedway, he was dropping off some photos for the owner when he overheard the owner saying that they needed someone to help publicize the big race coming up and to get the track some free exposure on TV and in the newspapers. George said to the owner, "I can do that. I've done it for some local car dealers and other businesses here, and I know all the newspapers and local media." We were surprised that he was telling the owner he did all that kind of work, since we knew he'd never done it before. We wondered why he was putting himself out on a limb because he could lose the photography job he liked so much. Then we were even more surprised when the owner said to him, "Okay, George, you've done such good photography work, let's see what you can do with public relations and marketing."

Driving home we said, "Are you crazy? You're not a marketing or PR director. How are you going to get the racetrack on TV and in the newspapers?" He said, "I don't even know why I offered to do it, but now I'm committed, so I have to try." We never did figure how he did it, but he ended up getting the speedway on television and in local New York newspapers, the toughest media in the country. So the next thing we knew he was made the Marketing Director and official photographer of one of the first Super Racetracks of its kind in the world. Just a few months later, he came up with an idea to sell N.Y. National Speedway shirts, hats and patches. Again, the owner loved the idea, and before we knew it we were all working in souvenir booths selling all types of Speedway souvenirs. We did have to admit it was really fun, and we made money that we never would've made at that age otherwise.

Now as Marketing Director, official photographer and also Souvenirs Director, he had no time to play in a band and photograph weddings, so he stopped those entirely. The owner of the New York raceway also owned the then-famous Detroit Dragway, the Bakersfield, California, Raceway and the Kansas City International Raceway, so he put George in the same positions at those racetracks as well. Talk about being busy!

On top of his motorsports operations, with the money he saved he and a friend opened up a nightclub for kids who couldn't go to a regular club because they were underage. At the time, surfing was just catching on, so they called it the Surfers' Club, which worked because it was only a mile or so from the famous Jones Beach. It was also within walking distance of the local high school. George knew that kids get in trouble when they have nothing to do, so he and Rich used their club to give kids a place to hang together, but they took it even further. You had to have a membership card to get in, and if you were failing any subject at school, you could not have a membership card, which he coordinated with the principal of the high school. Naturally the principal loved this, so they ended up with a good working arrangement. Parents loved the club too because it kept the kids off the streets and out of trouble and because they always knew where they could find their children.

Because of the age of the kids, no alcohol was served. Instead they had hamburgers, fries, milk shakes and Coca-Cola. Kids would go there after school for a burger or snack and at night they had music for dancing. They were doing very well and making good money, until one night their world changed. Some kids from another high school tried to get in. George and his partner explained to them that they had to have a membership card. To get one, they had to bring their current report card from school and not be failing even one subject. A group of about six kids argued with them—it was a stupid policy, so why not just let them in? It was obvious these boys were troublemakers, so George and his partner were happy they had the membership program and did not have to let them in. An hour later, they closed the club and were cleaning up when they heard a loud crash outside. When George went out to see what the noise was, he saw three kids laying in the street. It turns out the six boys from another school intentionally ran down the three kids with their car. George called the police, and he spent the night at the hospital worrying about the two girls and one boy he knew from the club who had been hurt. The girls had minor injuries, but shockingly, the boy died.

The next day George was inundated with calls from local newspapers and TV about the death of the 16-year-old boy. The next thing he knew, parents were blaming his club for the boy's death, even though it was closed at the time and he and his partner had nothing to do with it.

Despite all the good George tried to do by keeping kids off the streets at night and working with the school so kids did not fail any subjects, everyone still blamed the club, and they would no longer allow their kids to go. Within just a few weeks, George and Rich had to close the club for lack of business.

After that George opened a disco club with his best friend; only this one was for adults and they served alcohol. It was successful, but it became too much of a workload, so he sold his share of the disco to his partner.

George loved photography, public relations, marketing work and motorsports so much that he started a company in those fields. He produced calendars and photos of some of the top motorsports champions in the world. At the time, color pictures were very costly, so no one in the motorsports industry produced calendars or a national magazine in full color like George did. His motorsports calendar was so popular that for years, Petersen Publishing (which owned over twenty top magazines) offered George's National Motorsports Calendar if you subscribed to *Hot Rod, Motor Trend* or *Car Craft Magazine*. It was a tremendous accomplishment, considering Petersen was a giant in the publishing industry, yet they offered the items George published.

He started getting requests from soldiers in Vietnam for his calendar and postcards, saying, "We can't afford much but we love your calendars and postcards of racing champions, because they remind us of being back home. We will pay, but could you give us military men a special price?" Being the type of person he is, he didn't feel right charging these men who were risking their lives for America, so he sent the calendars to them for free. Of course, he was at draft age, so he too was waiting to be drafted at any time.

Because so many men were being drafted into the war and the demand for his calendars became so great, he created The National Armed Forces Club. Through this club, George sent servicemen free calendars, stickers and other items. The mail poured in by the thousands, then in the tens of thousands. The demand got so high it ate up every dollar he was making. Then one day he sat there with thousands of requests from servicemen all pleading for a calendar of racing's top champions, postcards or anything that reminded them of their days back home— days without war and death. George could not disappoint the thousands who were risking their lives, and for what? Because their government ordered them to.

With all the profits already being used to send soldiers free National Armed Forces Club items, he turned to the banks for a loan. They refused him, despite his explanation that the money would be used to send simple items to boost the morale of those risking their lives every day, so those very same banks could remain operating in a free country.

Having read many of the thousands of letters these soldiers had sent him, George just could not disappoint them, so he made what we feel is the kind of sacrifice that Donald Trump would never make. He gave up what took him years to save for, two special items he had dreamed of since he was just six years old that to this day he has not been able to replace. In order to raise the money to send those thousands of soldiers free motorsports items, he sold both of his most prized possessions, a beautiful Harley Davidson motorcycle, and a car he had just bought just 6 months before—a 1963 Corvette, deep green with tan leather interior. We had never seen him so upset, but he felt he had no choice, being the caring and honest person he is. With thousands of letters sitting in his office from soldiers waiting for their motorsports items, his conscience would not let him disappointment them.

Afterward, we wrote to our Congressman, sending samples of the letters that soldiers fighting in Vietnam sent to George, and we told him what George was doing. The Congressman told us he would make sure George was never drafted, because of the morale he was building for hundreds of thousands of American soldiers, and he wanted that to continue.

Donald Trump was awarded the #1 Jersey from the Air Force, despite the fact that he *evaded* the draft during the Vietnam War and did nothing but make promises to the military. Yet here was George, barely out of his teens, who gave up his most prized possessions plus tens of thousands of dollars of income he was making, just so the American servicemen risking their lives for their country would know that there were still some back home who cared about them. Just read the sampling of the hundreds of thousands of letters George received, showing just how much good the sacrifice of his most prized possessions did. These are actual letters from American soldiers written while they were in Vietnam. Some of these letters are shown in the color photos at the center of this book.

Donald Trump was a draft evader and never did anything to help our soldiers, even though he had the money to do it, yet he was honored by the United States Air Force, while George basically went broke helping thousands of our military men by doing what no others had done at that time. Talk about an injustice! And now Trump is our president?

George did all of this before his twenty-first birthday, totally on his own, with no help from a rich father like Trump's. What good did Donald Trump accomplish before his twenty-first birthday?

GEORGE'S TRIBUTE TO SEPTEMBER 11

If it wasn't enough that George gave up his two most prized possessions to help build American soldiers' morale during the Vietnam War, when our country let them down, he kept this National Armed Forces Club going for every war thereafter, including Iraq. Wanting to make sure America knew the "real" Donald Trump, George turned down the opportunity to make big money from a publishing company because they wanted to retain the right to change parts of the book, which meant bending the truth—something Trump does but not our friend George who mortgaged his home to pay for this book. On top of these two life-altering sacrifices, when the Twin Towers were destroyed, George did what no others we know of did. Because he worked in New York City most of his life, George had spent a lot of time at the Twin Towers from the day they broke ground, to opening day, to the years he went in and out of the Towers for meetings. With all this, the Towers became a part of George's life. When he saw those planes hit the Towers, and, worse yet, the Towers crumbled—something no one thought would happen—George was so affected that he felt he just had to do something to pay tribute to those who lost their lives. George once again "sacrificed" far more than most and did something Trump would never do. He cleaned out his savings account and, using his music background, he and his good friend Glen Grayson, the musical director for Steve Wynn, a Las Vegas legend, wrote an incredibly moving CD tribute to all who had lost their lives that day, and then sent thousands of copies FREE worldwide. Their tribute CD was so moving that it met with immediate success and was played on radio stations around the world and in many other venues. Thereafter each year he continues to send copies free to the media. On the following pages are just a few of the many letters George received. For a scan of the CD case, see the color insert in the center of the book.

So Donald Trump, George Houraney, the man who you constantly told his wife was a "loser," gave up his two most prized possessions, which he's never been able to replace, to boost our military's morale, many of whom, during the Vietnam War, felt deserted by their own government. He used up his life savings to create an incredible 9-11 tribute to those who lost their lives on 9-11 and, finally at the end of his life while fighting cancer and an auto accident so bad that he could not work anymore, still gave up a large sum of money and mortgaged his home so his fellow Americans could see the TRUTH about Trump as our president.

THE WHITE HOUSE

Mr. George Houraney
American Dream Enterprises

33433+1045

Thank you for your kind gift and caring words of support and prayer. I am pleased that you would think of me in such a special way, and I appreciate your generosity.

With warm wishes,

Laura Bush

THE VICE PRESIDENT
WASHINGTON

August 28, 2002

Dear Mr. Houraney:

Thank you for giving me a CD of the song, "We're Stronger Than Before," composed by you and Glenn Grayson. I very much appreciate your thoughtfulness.

Lynne joins me in sending our best wishes to you.

Sincerely,

Dick Cheney

Mr. George Houraney
American Dream Enterprises

OFFICE OF THE DEPUTY COMMISSIONER
FOR COMMUNITY AFFAIRS

1 Police Plaza — Room 200 ● New York, N.Y. 10038-1497
(646) 610-5323

RAYMOND W. KELLY
Police Commissioner

FREDRICK J. PATRICK
Deputy Commissioner

August 16, 2002

George Honraney, Founder
American Dream Enterprises
Box 273527
Boca Raton, FL. 33427

Dear Mr. Honraney:

On the morning of September 11, 2001 New York City and our nation experienced an unthinkable terrorist attack that resulted in a terrible loss of human life. In a matter of minutes our lives and our world was changed.

On that day while thousands of people were fleeing for their lives, New York City Police Officers and other emergency service workers put others before themselves and heroically undertook the greatest rescue mission in our history. Unfortunately, twenty-three of New York's Finest made the ultimate sacrifice entering into harm's way to save others. Their dedication, bravery and heroism will never be forgotten. Their legacy is an inspiration to all, making New York and America strong, determined and resilient.

On behalf of Police Commissioner Raymond W. Kelly and all the members of the New York City Police Department, thank you for your CD tribute *We're Stronger Than Before*. Please continue to keep the men and women of the New York City Police Department, as well as other emergency service workers and all affected by this great tragedy in your thoughts and prayers.

Sincerely,

Fred J. Patrick
Fredrick J. Patrick
Deputy Commissioner

FJP:kc

DEPARTMENT OF DEFENSE
ARMED FORCES RADIO AND TELEVISION SERVICE BROADCAST CENTER
1363 Z Street, Bldg. 2730
March ARB, California 92518-2073

September 20, 2002

LTC Curry W. Krider (Ret.)
World Dream Network
220 Krider Drive
Salisbury, NC 28144

Dear LTC Krider:

I wanted to assure you that we received "We're Stronger Than Before." It has been sent it via satellite to AFRTS' 35 affiliated radio stations overseas for their use among a special category of "military salute/patriotic/inspirational" songs.

Some stations air a smattering of songs from this category, others do so only rarely.

And I hope you understand, but we lack the ability to track the use any song gets. Our affiliated stations—and even our Broadcast Center at March Air Reserve Base—are spartanly staffed. We have had to be ruthless in limiting the time we devote to administrative tasks that are not mission-critical.

I greatly appreciate receiving "We're Stronger Than Before." It is exactly the type of song our "military salute/patriotic/inspirational" song category was meant to put in the hands of our affiliates. I trust they will recognize its quality and expose it to their local audiences.

Sincerely,

Manny Levy
Chief, AFRTS Radio

ONE OF MANY RECEIVED

FROM NEW YORK

FIRE DEPARTMENTS

Subject: Hello from FDNY
Date: Mon, 2 Sep 2002 12:41:35 EDT
From: FDNYL
To:

Dear George & The Team of "We're Stronger Than Before"

Received and appreciated the CD Tribute that your organization has sent us. It is indeed inspirational and well written and recorded.

Please do not take the lack of response from FDNY as callousness, as that is very far removed from any of our intentions. The fact is that the firehouses have been inundated with CD's and recordings, and while every one of these is appreciated, it is mentally tough to listen to them all. While intentions are always good, some are downright depressing. Thankfully, yours was deeply touching and appreciated.

In my firehouse, we have lost .   at the WTC. I am the liaison for the family, and am constantly being asked to drop off things at   house from all over the country and the world. The fact is that many of these things are all now cluttered in a small room at   house, where, eventually,   might build up the fortitude to go through them all.

While the rest of the country continues to fight and go forward with resiliency, we are still stuck in a situation where our emotions and mental toughness are put to the test every day. The outpouring of support from the regular citizen, the corporations (the ones that aren't cooking the books), and our firehouse neighborhood has been nothing short of outstanding. However, the politicians, city government, and the Fire Department itself, seems only interested in praising us with words, and leaving us in our own despair. The families are, and should be, taken well care of. The guys in the firehouse seem to be a totally different story.

On September 11th, we will be having a plaque dedication,
The Department has NOT done anything for us that day. Each member of the firehouse here will probably have to chip in and lay money out of our pockets to "do the right thing." Last I heard we are catering for 300 people.

I am sorry to have gotten off of the point. My whole and only reason to be telling you this, is that on that day, the firehouse will be flooded with people with concerns so varied as to be unimaginable. However, I will be working here that day. As you requested, I will play the CD

I will be thankful to listen to it, and can only hope that my emotions will be controlled that day. Stay well, and stay safe!

Sincerely,

FDNY

Three life altering sacrifices were made, one even before his 21st birthday, for his country and fellow Americans; this is Trump's version of a loser.

What have you sacrificed Donald Trump? Already president for over half a year and in your seventies, healthcare and many other serious programs you promised to fix for Americans still have not happened. Even more lies: you stated you would be too busy working as president to take vacations, then YOU TOOK A SEVENTEEN-DAY VACATION after just months in office. That's some sacrifice.

With this it's easy to see who should really be America's president, he who sacrifices, NOT HE WHO TAKES VACATIONS.

George had three brothers and a sister. His sister Melody was a wonderful person, however, her father's early death devastated her. She married a man who never really got her the help she needed, so she died in her early fifties. Although one brother remained neutral, the two others were jealous of George. Their mother was the type of woman everyone loved. When her husband died prematurely, she was lost. She and her husband were both in the entertainment business, so when he passed it left a void. She lost not only the man she adored but also her life in the entertainment business they ran together and loved so much. Once George brought her into the events he was running in Vegas, it was like she was reborn. She loved everything about what he was doing. His mother became a permanent fixture at his events, working with the contestants for his model contests on- and offstage. Everyone just loved her, and in over thirty years she never missed an event. Tragically, as she got older, she started to lose her memory, and one of her sons moving in with her made it worse.

As she became so ill she could barely talk, George went to see her one day, bringing her some money. His brother "M," who was always jealous of George, actually pulled a gun on George, his wife and young son, which really set their mother off. They left, not wanting to upset her anymore. When we heard, we told him he should call the police, but his mother was so sick he didn't want to make her worse, unlike his brother who pulled out a gun, making her almost pass out.

Toward the end of his mother's life, M and another brother, both broke and trying to get money from George, actually filed a lawsuit against George, saying he had stolen his mother's equity in her home. The lawsuit was signed by his mother. She could barely talk and had no real memory, so even the judge saw right through it. Plus, we were ready to testify on his behalf. Yes, George did take over his mom's house one day over fifteen years ago. Why? One of us was with him the day he stopped by to give his mom her plane ticket to their next event. When we walked in, she was laying on the couch crying. She saw me and ran into her bedroom. Her house was small, so I could hear them talking. She was upset because she was going to lose her home. She only received $550 per month in Social Security, and even with the money George and his one brother Bill gave her, it was not nearly enough. George did not make enough to take care of his family plus her home but told her not to worry, that he would make sure she didn't lose her home. George took over her home for her, and for ten years she never paid taxes, homeowner's insurance, mortgage payments, etc., and when she needed money for new carpets or for other things she wanted, or to give money to her daughter and son, George he made sure she got it. How? He borrowed against his own home.

Then when M, the gun brother, moved in, his mom and M decided they wanted her home in M's name and that they were getting a reverse mortgage. George agreed, but he had kept track of the money he had borrowed against his own home, and, since the house would now be in his brother's name, he wanted this money back so he could pay back what he had borrowed against his own home.

His mother, who was extremely alert at this time, got a lawyer and made sure everything was legal. She went over everything with her own attorney and made sure the money George had borrowed in order to make her mortgage payments and all other bills went to George's bank. Now the house and money left over after the reverse mortgage was in his brother M's name. All 100 percent legal, yet his brother M had the nerve to file a court document stating that George had taken his mother's equity.

Since George and his mom had done everything legally for years before M made the court filing, it didn't hold any water. Just the opposite, the cash left over after the reverse mortgage went to M, and he lived off his mother until she died. It amazed us that his brother tried to say that George took advantage of his mom, etc. His mother would tell everyone at the events that she would have died years ago, but George gave her reasons to live.

At every event, he made sure she had a suite, that she could charge anything she wanted, got picked up by a limo, even gave her money because she loved playing the slot machines. She used to tell us she felt like a queen. He always brought her onstage and made sure she got recognition for helping at the events, and that she had everything she wanted. She loved him for always making sure she was treated like number one.

Making this mess even worse, his other brother, "B," was working with M to try to get money out of George. Years before, the two brothers, B and M had a very successful business. Then one day M took $90,000 from the business account and moved from Florida to New York. His brother B was ready to kill him. They never talked or saw each other for over ten years, which devastated their mom. Then, one day as a Christmas present for his mom, B forgave M for stealing the money, and they spent Christmas together as a family for the first time in a decade. When B, who knew M was the crook, worked with M against George, it was obvious he only did it because they both needed money and they made up the ridiculous story that George had taken advantage of his mom by trying to take her money when she had but a few months to live. The judge saw through their scam and, in fact, had suggested that George press charges against them because in Florida the law goes after anyone who takes advantage of an elderly person.

We still believe George should have taught them a lesson and put them in jail. Just how low can you go, taking advantage of your own mother during the last days of her life, and trying to turn her against her eldest son, who for forty years had given her the kind of life she had dreamed of? To show how sick these brothers were, they never even told him when their mother died, making it impossible for him to come to her funeral. Luckily weeks before she passed, George got to see his mom when she was in the hospital, even though his brother M tried to get him banned from the hospital by telling security that George was there to hurt his mother.

Just imagine what scum these guys were, knowing she was sick and dying, yet trying to turn her against the son that took care of her after her husband died, having her sign a court document accusing her eldest son of taking money from her, when during the ten years George took care of all her bills, neither of them helped her. It was constantly hard for George. Her only income was $550 Social Security, which he allowed her to keep 100 percent. He borrowed against his own home and made sure she never had to pay for anything but her electric. We know this to be true because with accounting knowledge, one of us was constantly helping him figure out how to borrow money to pay all her bills, from mortgage to home insurance to home taxes. It's just too bad this never went to court, as we saw all the documents George had, including many in his own mother's handwriting from years ago when she was very healthy and in full frame of mind. He would have buried those two lowlifes. Besides us, there were hundreds, if not thousands, of people over the years with whom she had worked or become friends at his events and she would tell them that George gave her reasons to live—her dream life.

Although she was in terrible pain and her memory

was mostly gone, that last time he saw her in the hospital she held his hand, and with what little energy she had left squeezed it, then held the hand of his eight-year-old son, her grandchild. Despite all that M and B did to try to turn her against him during her last days, at least for a few moments her mind came together, and for the last time she thanked him for all the years that he had given her a dream life.

We included this to show that, unlike Trump, George has a strong conscience, as thousands saw how he treated his mother over the years. Also, we added this because last year his brother M had the nerve to do an interview with news media, calling George the black sheep of the family. Of course, luckily, they didn't just take M's word for it, and upon researching it just a little, the media found out that everything M had said about George was an outright lie, and so they killed that interview. They found out from attorneys that George was never going to make his mom pay back all the money he borrowed against his own home, which was in the six figures over ten years, but once the home was going in his brother M's name, the freeloader who lived off his dying mom, George has cancer and there was no way he was going to leave his wife and son owing all the borrowed money while M took title of his mom's home. Anyway, as we said, we included this for two reasons. First, so you can see this is a man with a real, loving and caring conscience. Second, if his brothers try to lie again and the story that George is the black sheep in the family, hopefully the media would find out the truth first. These two brothers, who were so evil they actually tried to turn their dying mother against her firstborn, the son that for forty years made her so happy, a happiness only working in the entertainment business could have brought her after her beloved husband died so suddenly, they could have cared less. They were lazy bums who needed money and stooped this low trying to get it.

Now back to George and Trump. The Motorsports Calendar George had created led to the casino events that started his work with some of the largest casinos in Las Vegas, the first being the casinos owned by the Howard Hughes company. George was so successful that the Hughes company kept him on for ten years, until they sold their casinos.

Eventually George felt he could do more than what was going on in Vegas at the time, and that's when he was finally able to meet Donald Trump—a meeting that would change his life forever. Trump was a man that George first thought was the greatest person on Earth. In fact, all he did was rave about Trump. But that would change, and unfortunately not just for him, but for our country.

The night Trump won, George said, "The country has no idea what it is in store for. Now we're about to see the worst president in the history of our country." We said, "From what you told us when you worked with him, we knew Trump was not an ethical or caring person, but do you think he would really be that bad as president?" He answered, "Absolutely! Trump does not care about anything except himself. He has no conscience, no feelings; he's like an empty shell of a man when it comes to the important things in life. He will lie to the people and to the government. He will do whatever it takes to get what he wants, even if he's wrong. You will see. Trump is one of the most spoiled human beings on Earth. He has always gotten whatever he wants his entire life, and he doesn't care what it takes or who he hurts. He will lie, mislead and get rid of anyone in his way to get what he wants. Despite becoming president, for the first time in his life Trump will have others he will have to answer to, and that's when the trouble will start. Unfortunately, we the people will suffer."

Wow, was George ever right! Everything he predicted since then has happened, and in fact it's a little unnerving how well he knows Trump. Before any of us knew it, he predicted that Trump would use Air Force One like it's his own private jet, with no regard to the cost to taxpayers. George told us unless the media backs him, Trump will tear the media apart. To him the White House will be like a second home, not the home of our president. Trump will do what he wants, not what's good for our country and its people. And his wife is just like him."

As we've watched the news since Trump won, everything George predicted has happened. It really has been amazing how accurate George has been.

He took on Trump in court, which we all felt took tremendous courage. Now he's taking on not only Trump, but the President of the United States. Hopefully this book will do some good for the people of our great country. Too many men and women have died, and too many Americans have worked their entire lives to make this country what it is today. As George said, "Trump can ruin all of that in just a few years." He's right on track to be absolutely correct about Trump.

Most of us make mistakes in our life, but Trump is the king of mistakes. He had so many great businesses he lost because they just did not matter to him. Trump had a terrific, beautiful and very smart first wife and a wonderful family most men would kill for and he gave it all up for sex with a younger girl, a girl he eventually dumped. George had thought that Trump was a hero, a genius at business and a good person. George was someone who did what none of Trump's million-dollar executives could do: George sold out Trump's casino in the dead of winter and cost Trump a fraction of what others would have spent and even then, they would have never sold out Trump's casino. With his decades of success in the casino world, George could have even saved Trump's casinos, but Trump threw all of this away because he never cared how smart George was, or what George had done for his casino because Trump was only focused on trying to have sex with George's wife. In fact, if he had kept George with him, not only would George have saved his Atlantic City casinos, but George could have led Trump down a far better path as president because George does have a conscience. George cares and knows how to get things done. In fact, by now there would have been a healthcare program for all Americans. As to George's ex-wife Jill, it was bad enough Trump totally misled her just to have sex.

Trump had promised Jill a job as part of his con and even though he had seen what a smart and hard worker she was, and George had told him that she does the work of three others, Trump dumped her too.

So as George pointed all this out to us, it was clear

to us that Trump is not the genius everyone thinks he is. We looked at what George had pointed out. Trump threw away a terrific wife, seven great businesses, a man who could have saved his casinos and probably made him a great president and a woman who in time could have easily been the head of one of his businesses. Why? No matter how much money Trump has, all these not only could have made him far wealthier but also happier. Then again, as George also pointed out, to want to save all this, to see its potential, to want the happiness it would bring, you have to have a heart, soul and conscience. All things Trump clearly does not have.

Read this book carefully, and read it again. You will see that what George predicted is true. It's truly incredible what damage Trump has already done to our country. Imagine the damage he will do if he serves a full term. We were not that worried about what George had told us because we thought only a few things would happen and then everything would start working, but evidently it is getting worse, not better, and now we're all quite worried about our country.

The *real* Donald Trump, the one our friend George saw years ago but could not write about because he felt no one would believe him, is emerging, but unfortunately, we Americans are paying the price. In just a few months he and his estranged wife have wasted hundreds of millions of dollars of our taxpayer money, not on government business but on themselves. Trump flies to his Florida mansion nearly every weekend, has pep rallies for himself, and his wife continued to live in New York, costing taxpayers a $140,000.00 a day. Imagine $140,000.00

PER DAY, just so Trump's wife could stay in New York. Just think of how many hours we the Taxpayers have to work to pay that $140,000 a day. Or better yet, how many hours to pay for the $4,200,000 (that's four million two hundred thousand dollars) required to pay for Trump's wife to live in New York for just one month, instead of Washington, like all previous first ladies have done. And this is just her costs to us taxpayers. Add to this the millions Trump wastes using Air Force One and the security costs on his mini-weekend vacation trips and pep rallies. Unbelievable that this is our president, this is the man that is supposed to be helping US, NOT himself.

Read this book carefully, and then read it again. You will see that what George predicted is really happening, and that we all must come together to save our country. It's truly incredible what Trump has already done to damage our country's reputation. Imagine the damage he will do if he's allowed to continue for four years. Originally, we were worried about what George had told us because we thought only a few things would happen and then everything would start working, but evidently again George was right. He predicted that with someone like Trump it will get worse, not better.

Despite all the amazing things George accomplished, writing this book is his biggest accomplishment by far. Not only did it take courage to write about someone like Trump as president, but George is fighting tremendous pain from cancer and a bad auto accident, and is having to take the most powerful kind of pain medication, which may ease the pain but unfortunately never takes it totally away. Making this even worse, because it is so expensive, he cannot afford enough each month so George suffers even more pain making it hard to function at times. Imagine living like that? George says every day is a fight just to get out of bed. So, writing such a book is hard normally, but facing this kind of daily pain has made it close to impossible.

However, wanting to make sure the truth about just who Trump really is gets out, once again George has done what most never thought possible and we are very glad he did. The good people of America deserve to know the truth about their president—the truth that only someone like George is able to tell.

As we have said, if you love your country, please read this book carefully, for it reveals what Donald Trump is truly like in real life, not the façade he shows the world.

As George says, you can bend the truth but you can't change it, and what is written in this book is most assuredly the truth.

Introduction

Although I have done marketing and public relations work since the 1960s, I am not a reporter, a politician or a professional writer trying to make money. What I am is your basic American businessman, one who was able to work *with*, *not for*, many top CEOs, executives and billionaires long before I started working with Donald J. Trump. This afforded me the opportunity to not only work with them, but to get close to them. I also wrote about a few of them in this book to prove I have experience with these types of people and not just Donald Trump, because without such experience there was no way I could compare other wealthy and well-connected people to someone like Trump. Although they can throw their power around, make false promises and lie, this behavior is extremely mild compared to how Donald Trump operates.

Being in business for fifty years, having the experiences I had with so many billionaires, and working alongside Donald Trump, seeing him in a light most never do are exactly why no other person could write this book the way I have. For them to do so, they would have had to have gone through *decades* of working closely with billionaires, working with Trump not as an employee but as a sort of partner, spending years in court with Trump, and having Trump try to seduce their wife during the time they worked with him.

What is written herein is based on my experiences with Trump, a man who for decades I felt should be our president, until I actually worked with him and saw the *real* Donald Trump. I will prove from my experiences with him why I went from a total believer in Trump to the exact opposite, finally concluding that he should *not* be our president. That was based on seeing how he operates, what type of person he really is and the fact that he's NOT the man most think he is. It's easy to conclude that Trump could become the worst president in American history.

Knowing what I had gone through with Trump, my friends had wanted me to write this book for years, but I refused, saying "No one will believe me, he's the famous Donald Trump, one of the best businessmen in the country, worth billions, and I'm just your average American businessman."

However, fate stepped in when he shocked the world and became president of our great nation. Only then could I write about the *real* Donald Trump. What America and the world are experiencing is what I had experienced years ago while working with him, and I also saw how he operated in a United States federal court. Finally, people that don't know what I went through with him, who would not believe what I experienced and would think I was exaggerating, or even outright lying, can now see the truth for themselves. Within the pages of this book is the truth of just who this man called Donald Trump really is.

The United States of America seeks to beat a path of progress through this new century, improve our lifestyle, protect the environment, foster better relations with our allies, and bequeath to our children a better world. This can only be done when decisions are made through a process of *cooperation, knowledge and research* that filters out the irrelevant and produces the *facts* that lead to *results*. Unfortunately, with Trump as president, rather than achieve all of this, he could set America back fifty years or more.

Donald Trump is by far the biggest hypocrite and liar America has ever seen in the White House.

For example, for someone whose money allowed him to avoid the draft during Vietnam while thousands died, he has a unbelievable amount of nerve wanting to ban transgendered people who are willing to enlist and risk their lives for their country, especially since he had promised in one of his campaign speeches to protect the rights of gays, women, etc., saying there is no one to protect these people's rights more than Donald Trump. Here is an exact quote from Trump during his campaign:

"As your president, I will do everything in my power to protect our LGBT citizens from the violence and oppression of a hateful foreign ideology."

He has also stated that, if elected, "Sexual orientation would be meaningless. I'm looking for brains and experience. If the best person for the job happens to be gay, I would certainly appoint them."

Here are a couple of other relevant quotes from Trump:

"If a gay person can be a doctor or a lawyer or a teacher or take another position of responsibility, why can't they serve this country in the military?"

"'Don't ask, don't tell' has clearly failed. Gay people

serve effectively in the military in a number of European countries. There is no reason why they can't serve in the United States."

Now as president he's constantly seeing what he can get away with, like this transgender issue. With no military experience at all, without consulting with any of the four branches of our Armed Forces, Trump sent a tweet stating that the transgendered cannot serve in America's military, making his decision *based on his opinion* and sending a presidential "decree" over Twitter. Truly scary.

He's fired some of America's best talent, made decisions without any experience, put his family into very important positions in the White House, despite the fact that they have no experience. Trump is the first president in decades to refuse to release his tax returns. He has said again and again that only those who have something to hide keep it hidden. I'll guarantee you his tax records would reveal things that would shock everyone, including those that support him. That is why he refuses to release them. So, we now have one man making some of America's most important decisions basically on his own and based on nothing but his opinion. What title best describes these actions? Anyone think of the word *DICTATOR*?

Besides seeing how much he can get away with, he's pushing the Office of the President into a dictatorship. Am I wrong? Am I exaggerating even a little? He's even trying to limit *free speech* by constantly demeaning the media and not answering official questions posed by them. Am I the only one that sees he is chipping away at America's Constitution bit by bit, curtailing Americans' rights, getting rid of *anyone* that opposes him, while demanding loyalty to *him* over America's supreme law, the Constitution? WAKE UP CONGRESS!

On top of all this, we have a president that sides with one of our country's biggest adversaries, Russia, over his own country and its expert people. Worldwide, America and its government are losing their credibility and influence all because of one man. Just one man is flying in the face of everything that millions of its citizens have given their lives for.

Despite all the evidence uncovered that Russia tainted America's 2016 election, Trump continues to deny Russia was involved. However, Putin wanted Trump to be president—what better competition than an opponent with no experience. Trump had no experience at all and Putin felt Trump was no threat compared to the decades of experience Hillary had.

To try to save face, because he's been president for seven months and has accomplished very little, he will take credit whenever possible for the things *others* make happen. For example, Apple announced its new plant in Wisconsin, and Trump makes it look like *he* did it. When the job rate or stock market is up, he acts like he caused it when in fact it was those that work in these areas who made it happen. Does anyone really believe that, in a matter of days or even weeks, things like new factories, new labor contracts and such just happen that fast? It takes months, even years for anything major to happen. Ever see a major new building being built in a few weeks? That's what Trump tries to convince people *he* did.

I must admit, I'm very surprised that Congress and the media have not caught on to Trump and how he operates, but in time they will. From the day I met him, he liked to see how far he could go when making decisions. With me, it was on just my second day with him when he hit me with the fact that he wanted to sleep with my wife.

I have no doubt that what you will read here is the most truthful, logical and complete knowledge of Donald J. Trump ever written. Call it the Trump Encyclopedia.

Some, mostly those brainwashed by Trump, will argue that what I've written here is not the truth. First, none of them were around when I experienced what I did with Trump so they have absolutely NO KNOWL-EDGE of what I experienced; obviously, they cannot accurately say anything. Second, when working with Trump, he never remembered what he said to me or my staff just a day or so before, nor did he or his staff ever take notes, whereas I took notes EVERY DAY I SPENT WITH TRUMP, just as I did with every billionaire or CEO I personally worked with. Why? Was it because I didn't trust them? The answer is NO! I took notes because with all that business executives have to deal with (one once told me he has 27,000 people on payroll every week), it is very easy for them to forget things. However, by taking notes, I was always on top of things—rarely making mistakes. How else could I last up to ten years working closely and personally with billionaires and CEOs? They had a conscience and thought with their brains, NOT with their other thought process—the one between their legs.

But if you read very carefully what is written, and take

everything into consideration and actually think—does what you read *make sense, or not*? If you have put clear thought into this, not allowing anything Trump says to influence your decision (since he lies and deceives so much), then and only then will you reach the *truth*.

I've fought many battles in my life against some of the most powerful people and companies in the world. Each time my friends would say, "George, are you crazy? You don't have the power to go up against such powerful opponents." This especially rang true when I fought Trump in federal court. Even my own attorneys thought I was crazy. After all, Trump had as many of the best attorneys as he needed. Money was no object, and just the threat of taking on a billionaire named Trump was enough to have most stop and never go through with it.

Despite all these powerful tools Trump could use in fighting me, I had but one. Can anyone guess what it was? The answer is:

THE TRUTH! A word that often escapes Trump's vocabulary.

I saw this in Trump's companies, and I am seeing it again now in the White House. His lies are making fools of the very Republicans that backed him. Despite all the negative things he's done, all the broken promises, the fact that he's not delivered even one of his major campaign promises and has embarrassed the White House and Office of the President, the worst is still yet to come, and when it does, there will not be another Republican president for *decades*.

Donald J. Trump does not believe in freedom of speech, unless it is the right to say what *he* wants. He believes *he* is the ultimate ruler, and everyone should listen to him. His main focus is always on what's best for him and his family. If one carefully adds up the *truths* in this book, the conclusion is what you just read. Truths that unless put in check will cause more damage to America's democracy and its citizens than any one president has ever done before.

One thing that should become more and more obvious to those that are willing to open their minds to the *facts* and *logic* written in this book, and what I've seen again and again with Trump, is that he can rarely be trusted to tell the truth.

I watched Trump lie again and again, not for days, weeks or months but for *years*. Here's another strong example of his lies—I along with dozens of promoters, media and family members watched him make American Dreams come true in a room filled with young people from over thirty countries, who had worked very hard, sacrificed and went through extreme emotional stress in order to win the Donald Trump American Dream events. Along with all the others, I listened to him make one of his very strong and emotional speeches, stating how impressed he was with the events, how they had turned out far better than he had ever expected. After all, his resort had sold out in the dead of winter, something that had never been done before. We all heard him *promise* that next year he would move the events to his larger Taj Mahal, with far more awards and sponsors, making them even bigger worldwide events, and making what all the winners had gone through worth it. Then, after weeks of everyone celebrating Trump's promise, out of nowhere and without warning, and with no reason why, came word from his office that he was *not* going to host the events next year as he had promised. This totally devastated the thousands involved in the events around the world, shattering their life's dreams. They had kept their promise to him, delivering a sold-out resort, but he couldn't care less about the agreement he had made to continue. Besides proving his outright lies, this also proves something just as bad—Trump has no conscience and no heart, and he just doesn't care about We the People.

One way Trump's presidency could finally get its business in order would be if he allows his newest chief of staff, John Kelly, to be in charge and not overpower Kelly's decision making. Kelly has to be allowed to operate without interference from Trump if the administration is ever to get their house in order.

Trump has pretty much proved he can't run the White House or be the kind of president America needs, because even before being sworn in, Trump caused nothing but turmoil. The White House has been so disorganized that all Trump has succeeded in doing has been spending millions and getting nowhere when it comes to promoting any polices that will help Americans and the country.

By now it's become obvious that the only way Trump will last the full four-year term is by allowing others, like John Kelly, to do their jobs. Why? Because if Trump has proved anything since taking office, it's that he is *not* equipped to be an efficient, productive and caring American president who will *serve the people*. However, I would bet Trump will be Trump and stay totally in charge. Trump will continue to keep up his lies and smoke screens to try to convince Americans he is a good president, so God help us with whatever damage Trump does to America and its people.

Knowing Trump the way I do, and knowing his lack of concern for people in general and how he only uses them to achieve *his* goals, I will present undeniable proof that "We the People" has and will continue to be "We the Trumps" until his very last day in office.

After reading this book, Americans must ask themselves: do we want America to be for "We the People" or "We the Trumps"?

Donald J. Trump had the world at his feet, yet he uses the great gift he was given to damage, even destroy, rather than build. Why else would America be so divided? Why else would so much presidential time and money be wasted?

To be a great American president one must dedicate his term in office first and foremost to serving We the People. Nothing can, nor should, come before this duty. If Trump has proved one thing it's what I found out years ago: what HE WANTS comes first. Next comes his family, and last is We the People. Because of this I believe, as many others I have spoken with, he will never be considered a great American president. The FACTS and TRUTH presented in this book prove once and for all Trump that is a man without a conscience, without a love for others because no one who has these traits, with zero experience as president, could take vacations every weekend the first months of his presidency and waste millions of taxpayers' dollars traveling in the world's most luxurious jet to locations to create pep rallies for himself, while not accomplishing one thing for We the People. He did not convince his wife to immediately move into the White House as first lady to be with her husband, but instead the president and first lady lived separately for months, which cost taxpayers $140,000.00 per day. Just these three items alone cost taxpayers enough millions to supply 50,000 American families with healthcare insurance for a year.

However, to Trump taking off weekends to get away from Washington's cold weather, making up pep rallies so people could cheer him on and boost his ego, and granting his wife her wish not to move into the White House despite the fact that it cost hardworking Americans $6,000.00 AN HOUR were far more important than American's healthcare.

With all he's done and continues to do for himself as president, he has changed We the People to WE THE TRUMPS. When I think of the millions Trump wastes on himself while millions of Americans still don't have decent healthcare, I am furious that anyone who has so much can use hard-earned taxpayer dollars on himself the way he does. Then I remember that I saw him do this to many others and it doesn't bother him at all because only someone without a conscience could be so selfish, so heartless.

Even more proof Trump not only lies but thinks about himself FIRST: HE PROMISED HE WOULD NOT TAKE A VACATION, THAT HE WOULD BE TOO BUSY WORKING HIS ASS OFF. Just months into his presidency, accomplishing literally nothing major, spending 20 percent of his time watching television and playing golf, spending every weekend for months flying to his mansion in Florida and wasting even more time and money, he then took a seventeen-day vacation.

Would not every American that works, and that's really not a word that describes Trump, like to take a seventeen-day vacation after just months of starting a new job? Furthermore, keep in mind that this is costing WE THE TAXPAYERS millions of dollars in security fees, costs, etc. Additionally, his behavior fits my description of a "man without a conscience," without even at least giving Americans the healthcare program he promised them he takes a seventeen-day vacation. I don't know about others, but I know my conscience would NEVER allow me to take a vacation while my fellow Americans badly need healthcare. That people may die while he's playing golf, IT'S AMAZING HOW TRUMP CAN LIVE WITH HIMSELF. Then again, I guess it's easy when you just don't care about others. And the best part is that he blames his inability to pass healthcare legislation on everyone but himself, the very one who PROMISED AMERICANS he would give them a better healthcare program. He expects his healthcare plans to be passed even though they are not good for Americans. Just as ridiculous is the fact that Trump has continuously attacked president Obama saying Obamacare is a "disaster," "terrible" and "must go." Yet in the years since it started, despite its flaws, Obamacare has given much needed jobs to over 3 million Americans, 3 million—that's a tremendous amount of families that have earned a paycheck every week for the last several years—given at least some healthcare to 20 million Americans and, more importantly, Obamacare has saved untold lives.

On the other hand, Trump had months during his campaign and more than half a year as president to put together a "workable" healthcare plan. Yet despite all this time, and without a new healthcare plan, he goes on a seventeen-day vacation, something he said he would not do as president—two more of Trump's broken promises. Of course he calls it a working vacation. The problem is, he didn't do much work while in the White House, so does anyone really think he will be working on a good healthcare plan that will pass? On vacation?

NORTH KOREA

In the early nineties, when Trump and I were on a very positive track, I valued his opinion, thinking that he was so smart. At that time, Iraq was becoming a serious issue for America. While having lunch at Mar-a-Lago the morning after a reception he had for some of our contestants, we discussed a few things. One thing I asked him was what he would do with Iraq, or "any country" that was becoming a threat to our country, if he were president. He said, "Dictators only understand one thing: Bomb the hell out of them. Talk is a waste of time. We have the most powerful military in the world. We should use it."

In this book, you will read about how Trump thrives on power, lives for it and has to be in charge. The fact that he "threatens" the dictator of North Korea—telling Kim Jong-un that he will face what no one has ever seen before—proves Trump's greed for power that will never change. It proves that he has to show the world that he is in charge, that he has the power. The statement he made to North Korea was not the way America normally handles things; "threatening" any dictator is declaring war. Yet Trump obviously does not care about that—he just has to show that he's the boss.

What Trump is doing threatening the leader of North Korea reminds me of when I moved from Pennsylvania to New York. I was just twelve years old and had a lot of good friends at school in Pennsylvania. However, I wasn't prepared for how the New York kids would accept me, or should I say *not* accept me. There were a few guys that, as the saying goes, were the leaders of the pack. They were the most popular, stars of their sports, and very good looking. I was basically a hick from the hills of Pennsylvania, and from day one they constantly made fun of me. Little did they know, especially the leader, that I was stronger and smarter than I looked. I had gotten that way from hiking in the mountains for miles. I even got lost in a cave once for twenty-four hours—all of which made me basically tougher and more clever than I looked or acted. Therefore, I could have easily taken care of the top guy, but I didn't believe "fighting" was the answer. So I handled it very diplomatically and—without all the details—the top guy became one of my best friends not only throughout high school but long after as well.

When it comes to North Korea, it is a similar situation—of course a million times more serious—but the scenario is the same. Just as I could have taken care of the top guy, America can easily defeat North Korea. Unfortunately, Trump has the power of America behind him and he's using America's power to "threaten" the leader of North Korea. This shows he has no diplomatic capabilities whatsoever, and diplomacy is a key characteristic we need for our president to have in order to avoid war.

If Trump was diplomatic and "cared" about the lives of America's military men and women, instead of first threatening North Korea with fire and brimstone he would approach it from a totally different angle. First, send a message to North Korea's president reading something like this:

> "Mr. President, you are the leader of North Korea. We respect you as the president and have no desire whatsoever to invade your country or remove you from power. However, by continuing to build nuclear weapons, you put not only our country but other countries in a terrible position.We hope you will cease building nuclear weapons, which would remove any threat from you America and other countries worry about. Of course, we cannot stop you from building nuclear arsenals, but if you insist on it, please understand you are the one causing unrest in the world and leaving the U.S. and other countries no choice but to be prepared if you ever try to use them. Rather than stay on a course that would be detrimental for everyone involved, America, Japan, China, and South Korea should all meet to

discuss working this out. I say again, we have no desire to remove you from power or attack your country, but we do have to prepare ourselves if you continue at the pace you are."

Of course this is rough, but basically the FIRST APPROACH any smart, caring president should take is NOT START OFF BY THREATENING someone who looks for a reason to use his power.

By Trump threatening the leader of North Korea instead of trying to work it out by taking a position as I outlined above, he's basically playing right into his hands—lighting a small fire which could become a nuclear one.

Threats do nothing but lead to trouble, and in this case could lead to a war where millions of people might die. I feel most people will agree that we do not need a president who threatens other countries—there are many other ways that must be approached long before the threat of military engagement.

I remind you that Trump, like Kim Jung-un, lives for power, and they both look for ways to use their power. Kim Jung-un is "baiting" Trump so if he uses his power he can blame America. Before America ever makes a threat that could lead to the death of millions, all avenues must be exhausted. However, Trump, by "threatening" Kim Jung-un, could create a situation in which thousands of men and women could die . . . from a single decision he makes. By his actions, Trump has again proved what I state throughout this book: Trump does what he wants first, even if it could lead to war and death.

With the mess Trump has created, this has become a real test for the Republicans. Will they do what's best for the Republican party or be true Americans and do what's best for their country and the American people? Time will answer this question.

Finally, what everyone should be worried about is what we are leaving to our children. I was amazed at how my son at just age ten knew everything there was about the Tesla electric cars. He talked about them day and night, telling us that we should get one as it's the safest and best car around. In fact, when we went to the dealer to look at them, he knew more about the car than the salesperson. Now at twelve, his mind has changed from positive, exciting thoughts about the Tesla car he wants to someday be driving to being worried about what's going to happen to our country with all the violence he sees now and having a president we can't trust. This is proof that Trump is already affecting our youth, who today are far more intelligent than in previous generations.

Now read more of the *truth* about the *real* Donald Trump, who, unfortunately, due to a flawed and centuries-old election process, was *not* elected by We the People but still carries the title President of the United States of America. He has divided the country, the White House and the rest of the government, like no other president in America's history.

To those who read this book and still feel Trump should be president, is doing a great job as president, does not lie, has done all he's promised, and truly CARES about We the People, it's obviously too late for you to help save America. However, I also say, "Thank God!" there are millions and millions more Americans who truly love their country and will not just stand by while Trump tries to change "We the People" to "We the Trumps." We must honor the sacrifice of the millions who died so that America would always belong to WE THE PEOPLE, and never allow a select few who feel America is "their country" to rule the way they wish and not for the benefit of all Americans.

No greater words have ever been written for our country than We the People. We must always make sure these words are the TOP PRIORITY of every member of Congress, every Senator, FBI, NSA, and every other government official; and most important of all, every president of the United States of America must always make his top priority WE THE PEOPLE, for WE THE PEOPLE are America.

The Caribbean Billionaire

This is about one of the billionaires I worked with the longest, almost ten years, a man who started with just five hundred dollars and became a multibillionaire all by himself. Here was a true self-made man and American Dream story, who at one time thought I was absolutely crazy for working with Donald Trump. He told me Trump was a terrible businessman who lost his yacht, his airline, the Plaza Hotel and more, and was only able to start out in business with a loan of millions from his father and by using his father's connections. Then years later, this person ended up being both partners and friends with Trump. Why? Because Trump had convinced even him, by far one of the most brilliant men I've ever met, that he, Donald Trump, was a smart businessman. That's how good Trump seems, until one gets to see the *real* Donald Trump.

For two years, struggling to expand our business, I had tried to convince a major casino in the Caribbean to sponsor one of my company's events because I had been so very successful in Las Vegas for over twenty years. These were events that dollar for dollar would draw more players than any event they had ever put on. I spent a tremendous amount of time making presentations to their marketing department. Then, after two years of being turned down because I could never get to their top executive, I simply stopped approaching them.

Then one night at a charity auction in Palm Beach,

Florida, I met the top executive at the very casino where I could never get past their marketing department. We hit it off, and when he asked me what I did and I explained, he immediately replied, "We're always looking for programs that draw players to our casino." I told him I had tried for two years but was constantly turned down by his marketing people. At the end of the night as we were leaving, he came up to me and gave me his phone number. He said, "Call me Monday and let's get together." I was very excited because I could now finally meet with the person I felt would see the potential of our events.

Monday came and I couldn't wait to call him, hoping he would be interested in our events. He asked if I could be there the following morning at 8 a.m. It was just what I was hoping for, so of course I said yes immediately!

Luckily, their main offices were in Miami, just forty minutes from my home. I had to leave very early because rush hour was really bad at that time of the morning, but I was hoping it would be worth it. When I walked into his office, there was no one there except him, which worried me a bit. I figured he would have his marketing and PR people there to hear about the event and see if it was worth doing. However, there was no one there but him. He said, "Give me a ten-minute presentation of what you do, how you started, how you would run it at our casino in the Caribbean, and what the cost would be." Ten minutes wasn't exactly much time to explain what had taken me over twenty years to create and learn how to operate, but I did my best, including showing him letters from the president of the Howard Hughes casinos praising how successful we were.

After what seemed like the longest ten minutes of my life, he said, "We've got a deal."

You see, this is the difference when dealing with the top people. If you have something good for them, they don't need days or weeks to figure it out. This is a perfect example of how Trump's bringing his daughter and son-in-law into the White House is *not* to help America and We the People, it's rather so *they* can make contacts with the world's top leaders, and you can't get any more "top" than presidents of countries like China. In effect, We the Taxpayers are paying for Trump's family to make contacts with people that very few other businesspeople in the world could ever meet.

Just imagine, you own a business that involves land, buildings, permits, copyrights, etc., with all the red tape you have to go through just to meet lower-placed officials like building inspectors, etc. To do this in foreign countries takes a tremendous amount of time, money and effort. Even then, you would be lucky to get anywhere. Now, imagine your dad is president of one of the most powerful countries in the world, and you're with him flying in Air Force One to Saudi Arabia, to meet their king. Now imagine that all of this doesn't cost you a single dollar! That's just what the president's daughter got from China, which could be worth hundreds of millions if not *billions* to her and her family.

Once I discussed such a situation with Trump, and of course he saw being in the position to meet the most powerful heads of state as president of the USA was a no-brainer. He believed it could make him wealthier than one could ever become any other way. However, as president you could not possibly approach the leaders of other nations—it would be too much of a conflict of interest. Yet if you had others with you whom you could trust, they could make contacts for you with little conflict. Better yet, have *family* with you as you travel around the world.

Yes, my fellow Americans, *your hard-earned tax dollars* are paying for Trump's family to travel in the most expensive jet in the world and make contacts that will earn them billions in the future. While after seven months Trump still has not created the better healthcare he promised to deliver if elected.

Now, back to this self-made billionaire. After I had presented my proposal to him in just ten minutes, he picked up the phone and told his secretary to call in his marketing and PR staff. I actually couldn't believe it—I had spent two years trying to sell our events to this casino, and in ten minutes I had made a deal, but only because I was able to talk to the top man there.

As I had learned from my years in business, it's not just what you know, it's who you know, which is something Trump and I had discussed more than once.

When the marketing and PR staff entered the room, it was a little awkward because these were all the same people who had turned me down for the past two years. Making it even more awkward, their boss said to them, "Why did you turn this man down? The events he runs are exactly what we need at the casino." Before they had a chance to say a word, he said, "We are going to do his events. I just made a deal with George, and I want you to cooperate completely with him and his people, since they must know what they're doing if his events lasted for years in Las Vegas, and he's still doing events there at the same casinos."

As excited as I was about having this deal, I was wondering how I could work with these people after they had turned me down for two years. Here I was with their boss, who had just made a deal with me in a way that made them look like they didn't know what they were doing, but I certainly wasn't going to lose this deal.

To make a long story short, in fear for their jobs, they cooperated completely with me and my staff, and we produced amazingly successful events, selling out every time. It turned out they also owned casinos in Freeport, Bahamas, and New Orleans. After just one event at the first casino, we ended up doing events at all three.

After about six years the owner decided to sell his casinos. I got the news from the head of marketing, who told me the new owner was a corporation owned by one man, who had told them he was not going to continue any programs they already had, which included us. I figured that we'd had a good run, and it was time to move on.

Later that day I was in the buffet having a late lunch. We were about to do what would be our last event there, starting in a few weeks. Most of the employees there knew me well and they were all coming over to me, including some casino executives, treating me like I was important. They wanted to know if I knew anything about the new owner. Then a man I didn't know came up to me and said, "You seem to know everyone here, and I'm going to be working here. What do you do?" I explained that we were producing these events, and that I understood the new owner was not going to do them anymore, but we still had one left in our contract, after which we would be leaving. He asked if I'd mind if he joined me. He had a few questions since I seemed to know so many employees at the resort, and I was happy to oblige. We ended up talking for over an hour and a half. I guess he saw I knew the place very well and that I was not an employee, but instead had a contract with the owner.

As we were getting up to leave, the vice president of the casino came over and said, "George, I see you've met the new owner." I looked over at the gentleman I had been speaking with for the past ninety minutes, and he started laughing and said, "I guess I should have told you, I just bought this place." I laughed too, and said, "I guess the joke's on me!"

He said, "I really didn't mean to mislead you, but you had so many interesting facts about this place which were of extreme interest to me, since I just put a lot of money into buying it." I said, "No problem, I understand." He said, "You know, I wasn't going to do anything that they're already doing here, and I know about your show and events, but now I've gotten to know you a little, and you seem to know this resort so well that I didn't say no immediately. I understand you have one more event coming up, so let me watch it and see how it goes, and then I'll decide whether I want to keep it or cancel it." I said, "Well that's fair." He then said, "Would you mind meeting me tomorrow at my office at 7 a.m.? I'd like to talk to you more," to which I replied, "Of course!"

I told my wife and many of my promoters that helped us produce our events what had happened, that I had met the new owner and we might even have a chance of keeping our events there. Everyone was very excited.

I met the new owner the next day, and several times after that, and we really hit it off, mainly because I was honest with him, plus I did know a lot about the resort, which were qualities he obviously liked.

Then came the time for our event, and of course he sat in the front row. We were all very nervous, but the event went well, and just like it had in the past we had a full house and the casino did well, so we thought we had a good chance of staying there. As our show was over and I was about to leave the showroom, the new owner's secretary came up to me and said that he would like to meet me in the boardroom upstairs in five minutes. I wondered if we were in or out.

I went upstairs and nervously entered the boardroom where he had all his new staff gathered together. I walked in and thought for a minute that I was in front of a firing squad—everyone had such a stern face, including the owner. The owner said to me, "I understand you do a similar event at another island in the Caribbean?" I said "Yes, we do the Summer Nationals event there." He said, "I really liked your event. It obviously brings players and guests to the casino and the resort, and it's a first-class production. I want to keep it, but I also want you to move the Summer Nationals here. I want both events." For a second I was excited because he wanted us to stay there, but then he also wanted me to move our Summer Nationals there, which were already running at another casino. I said, "Well, you did catch me off guard wanting both events, and luckily my contract is up for renewal with the other casino and we haven't signed it yet, but before doing two at the same resort and casino, I think I should talk to my promoters and decide what we should do." He said that was fine, and to let him know *in an hour*. Needless to say, I was both excited and shocked. It was an interesting idea—two events at the same resort—but I really needed to talk to my promoters and think about it, and he had given me only sixty minutes and wanted either both of the events, or none. Talk about stress!

This was indeed a very big decision. I was thoroughly exhausted from the whole week of producing our event and could barely think, and here I had to make a major decision—without a doubt one of my biggest decisions since starting in Las Vegas in the 1970s.

When I think back, I really got along well with this new owner. He told me he was going to do a lot of big things at his resort and casino. We were in a gambling establishment, so I figured I would roll the dice. I went back within forty-five minutes and told him we were going to do the deal. He said, "Now I know we're going to work well together. I gave you an hour and you made a big decision in less time, and you made the right one."

Although we knew he had money, he wasn't a billionaire—at least not yet. We ended up getting along so well that I did many projects for him at the resort. He wanted to rebuild the showroom since it was really run-down, and the estimates he had seen were very high. I told him that we could do it for him for 30 percent less than all of his other bids. He asked how I could do that, since I just produce events and shows. I told him I had a history of building experience; in fact I built my own house as well as several nightclubs in New York, plus I have an excellent crew that works for Universal Studios in Orlando and the best people from Las Vegas I've known for years.

The next day he called me up to his office and said, "Maybe I'm crazy, but for some reason I think you can do this, so you've got the job. You've got two months to rebuild the showroom." I was excited, but also nervous. I had just taken on something I had never done before. Then I thought about what I had told the owner —I had the best crew, and I did have building experience, but then this was a Vegas-style multimillion-dollar showroom!

We started the next week, ripping out the tables and seats and designing the new showroom. It was a beautiful theater with a Las Vegas–style stage, even though it was in the Caribbean. The owner tried a few times to see our progress but I told him no, you can only see it when it's done. I thought he would tell me I was crazy but he didn't, and he agreed to stay away until the showroom was ready.

My staff and I worked extremely hard day and night in order to finish on time. I brought the owner down to show him the finished product. When I opened the theater door and he walked in, his exact words were, "Holy s*** this is gorgeous, beautiful, I just don't believe how you did this in such short time. It's better than I ever expected!" And again, we had done it for 30 percent less than all the other bids from professional companies.

This created more faith between us, and we got along even better. I ended up doing several other projects for him, including building an 18-hole mini-golf course behind his casino and redesigning the entire casino entrance.

Then came the biggest project of all. He wanted to put on a full-blown Las Vegas–style show, of course from professional Las Vegas–type companies. We had now been together seven years, and again and again I had proven to him that my word was my bond. When I told him I would do something, I did it, and always on time and within the budget. By now he had enough faith in me that I convinced him I could produce a major stage production for his casino. I was going to do something really special, ranging from flying grand pianos from the ceiling to animatronic animals talking to the audience— the show would be like nothing they'd ever seen before.

While drawing up what would be the most important and largest contract of my life, my attorneys in New York put in certain clauses they said he would never agree to, but they wanted some bargaining power. I told them I didn't want to play games, just to put the agreement together. They said no, this is the biggest thing you've ever done, it's for five years and a multimillion-dollar show, and we have to be able to bargain a little. I finally agreed, as I knew the owner had one of the best lawyers in the Caribbean who would want certain things taken out of the contract that my lawyers had put in.

Then came the day of the contract signing. I gave the contract to his attorney who looked it over, and then the attorney asked the owner if there was anything he'd like to change. To my surprise, the owner said, "I've already done several deals with George. I trust him completely, and I'm not worried about anything he put in there. I know he's fair, and I don't say that about just anybody." The lawyer started to object, but then he was interrupted by the owner who grabbed the contract and signed it. I was surprised, but I was not going to take advantage of him by the things we had put into the contract thinking they would be taken out, and he was right that he could trust me. I called my lawyers and told them he had signed the contract without any changes. They were completely shocked, and I was told, "If he tries to screw you, you'll have an ironclad contract worth in the high six figures." It never even occurred to me that this could ever happen, so I put what they said out of my mind.

I started working on the show the following week. I flew in the best people from Orlando, Las Vegas and Hollywood with whom I had become friends over the years. Despite them all currently having important positions at the biggest resorts in the world, they were such good friends that they were willing to help me build my dream show. We all met to lay out the production. For the next eight months, we went to trade shows to pick out lighting and sound equipment, interviewed magicians and other performers, built waterfalls and sets for the theater, and the more we did, the more excited we got, knowing that this was going to be a one-of-a-kind production.

Then one day, out of nowhere the owner asked to talk to me. I went to his office where he explained that he'd decided to put on a Cuban-themed show in there. To say I was shocked would be an understatement. Not only did we have a signed contract, but I had pulled my best people together; some of the best in the business. I'd already spent several hundred thousand dollars of the owner's money buying equipment for the theater. We had worked day and night for months, for what would be the most spectacular show in the Caribbean. Anyone else I could believe would do this, but not him, not the only one I fully trusted.

I said, "But we spent all this money, we've done all this work, what do you mean you want to put a Cuban show in the showroom?" He said if he worked with the Cubans, once Cuba opened up, he could build one of the first resort casinos there, if he'd just put their show here. I told him that he was an American businessman, so it didn't matter that his resort was in the Caribbean. He was still an American doing business with Cuba, and that would violate the embargo the U.S. has against that country. He said he wasn't worried about that, and for me not to worry, he'd give me my salary for the year. I said I wasn't worried about a salary, because I was supposed to get much more than just a salary once the show opened, plus it was supposed to be for five years and we'd already done all of this work and spent so much money.

By this time, he had become a billionaire, and I had just witnessed the fact that it had totally changed him. He was no longer the honest, ethical man I had first met and worked with. I had no choice but to bring up the contract, to which he said, "Oh, come on, you're not going to sue me, let's just do this."

When I told my attorneys what had happened, they

told me that I had him—and big time—since he had personally signed that contract with those clauses. I could end up with high six figures or more for breach of contract, and that it wouldn't be a big case as it was an ironclad agreement that he had personally signed with his attorney present.

To say this was the most stressful time of my entire life would be an understatement. Here I was on the verge of producing the show I had dreamed of my entire life. I had worked so very hard and then had the rug pulled out from under me by a man I had trusted implicitly, more than any of the other billionaires I had worked with, especially Donald Trump.

My lawyers pressured me to sue him, saying I would get far more money than by staying there, and that my event was so successful we could put it anywhere—we did not have to stay.

I stressed over this so much that I became ill. I had really liked this man, and I had trusted him implicitly.

We had worked together perfectly for almost eight years and had done a lot of good together, but he didn't seem to care about any of that, and because of this Cuban show he insisted on, it was obvious he couldn't care less about our signed contract. With that attitude, I should have sued him, but I didn't—I just liked him personally too much. I believed him when he said that he would make it up to me. I learned the hard way that once a person becomes a billionaire, most lose their ethics.

As I had feared, the Cuban show was a total disaster. They had all kinds of trouble getting people there, and because it was in Spanish, many people didn't understand the show at all. Eventually the U.S. government sent them a notice to cease and desist because he was an American businessman doing business with Cuba, regardless of the fact that it was in the Caribbean, and he was given a short time to remove the show from his casino—just what I had tried to tell him would happen when he first mentioned it. He ended up losing at least a million dollars, most likely more.

At this point, we had the showroom but no show. His general manager (GM) asked me why I wouldn't put on a show there. I told him it could never be the same as the show I had originally planned because all the people that had worked with me didn't trust the owner anymore, so I could never get them back to work with me there. Plus, the owner had lost so much money on the Cuban show that he didn't want to put very much money into another one. However, the manager convinced me to put a small show in there, and that we could eventually make it a big production, and so I agreed.

As the show opened, I soon found out that the Cubans from the show had destroyed the reputation of the casino. To get tickets sold and people into the showroom, they had backstabbed every group from cab drivers to store owners to cruise ship operators, and none of them wanted to work with the casino now. I was counting on them to help sell tickets and bring people into the theater. It was extremely difficult, but we finally started to get people to come, however, the owner said he was going to cancel the show because it was losing too much money. I tried to convince him there was something wrong, that there was no way we could be losing that much money, but he listened to a new GM, a Caribbean man who did not like me to begin with simply because I was white, and he was a Bahamian that didn't like white men coming to his country, despite the fact this particular white man was employing thousands of his fellow countrymen and women. The show closed, and I later found out that when they sold the resort, money was funneled from the show into the food and beverage department, so we never got full credit for all the drinks and meals that were sold. I knew something was very wrong, but again, the owner was not the man I once knew. If he was, he would have allowed me to investigate this mess and find out the truth when I was running the show.

While I was producing this show, I had also been spending a year and a half working with Metro-Goldwyn-Mayer (MGM) to build a movie and sound studio on a small island the owner had behind his casino. I even brought the owner to a highly-placed executive at MGM, who told him this could be a great money maker because the Caribbean is a beautiful place to shoot movies, and when MGM was not shooting and using the studio we could rent it out. The deal was looking really good, but then the owner hired the people I had brought in to help build the studio in order to finalize the deal with MGM. They had somehow convinced him that because they had spent years in Hollywood, they could get a better deal. He paid them big money when I already had a deal in place, so instead of them finalizing it, they lost it because they got greedy, and MGM wanted nothing to do with the project anymore. For the second time, I was stabbed in the back by a man who at one time would never have done anything like this, costing me a year and a half of work and a deal that would have made us both a lot of money. Becoming a billionaire had cost him his integrity and his conscience. Normally I would understand how the ultra-rich can be, but this man was such a terrific human being to me for so many years that it was devastating to see him turn into this backstabbing, dare I say, Trump-like person.

My man at MGM, a top vice president, told me they had been ready to sign the deal, and asked me why on Earth the owner would take me out of this when I had put the whole thing together, and instead involve greedy men that no one at MGM wanted anything to do with? He said, "What you had presented convinced us it was a great deal for all involved, which is the only kind of deal we'd spend millions of dollars on. We were ready to spend that much because it was a win-win idea to create a soundstage on that island he owns, which apart from bringing in millions of dollars to his hotel from the movie studio's cast and crew, the soundstage would have created millions more in rental fees year-round. Plus, as you said it'd put his Resort & Casino on the map. You must be really depressed about all this, I know you worked hard at it."

Of course, it was bad enough that he had screwed me and lost money by insisting on the disastrous Cuban show, but then he had hired people who knew nothing about what I was doing. I tried to tell him that, especially since I was the one that brought him to MGM, but by now he was behaving like Donald Trump, a billionaire who does what he wants with no regard for anyone they might hurt, not even any regard for the money they could have made rather than lost. Just like Trump, he had lost his conscience, and he simply did not care who he hurt.

Ironically, in the beginning when I started working with Donald Trump, the man who owned this Resort & Casino had said, "Why are you working with Trump? He's a terrible businessman and he loses everything he buys."

Several of my promoters heard him say this and remembered it later on, when they called to tell me they saw this man sitting with Donald Trump at his Miss Universe contest. They also heard that he and Trump were partners and friends, and they could not believe what a hypocrite this man was, telling me I should stay away from Trump because he loses everything he touches, unlike the man who started with $500 and made billions on his own with no help from Daddy.

I have withheld using this man's real name for three reasons. First, because I remember the years when he was an honest, ethical and really wonderful person—someone everyone liked, including my mother, who was very strict when it came to the wealthy, thinking they have no feelings or emotions, but she really adored this man. She only saw the person we all knew in the beginning. I never told her how he had screwed me out of my show and the MGM deal because she thought so much of him that she would have been devastated, and I would rather her remember him when he was a very special, warm and caring person.

Secondly, I did not use his name because when my mother died he personally hand-wrote a letter that was extremely touching, and I felt the man I had known in the beginning, the one who had a heart and soul far above the billions of dollars that eventually overpowered him—that man had emerged, if only when writing that letter.

Finally, when it comes to this person, it's heartbreaking to see someone who was once a fun, loving and caring friend become a multibillionaire and see all those good traits disappear, buried by the money that overpowers so many.

It always amazes me when someone has the kind of money this man has. He could do so much good with it, especially for the people who care about him and helped him along the way.

As for Trump, he was never like this man was in the beginning because he was born into extreme wealth, never having to worry or work like this man and most of us do. Never having to be afraid of losing his home or always having to earn a living, Trump has never known, nor *will* he ever know, what We the People have to go through in life. This is why he can never be someone that can truly help the American people, because as I'll prove in this book once and for all, Donald Trump is a man without a conscience.

The Hawaiian Tropic
Wedding Challenge

One mutual friend Donald Trump and I had was Ron Rice from Hawaiian Tropic. Ron and I had originally met in the late 1970s when he came to one of my events in Las Vegas. At the time, he was starting a Miss Hawaiian Tropic contest, and since we had already been running events for years, he had come to check out how we ran them. He introduced himself as someone from Hawaiian Tropic, but never told me exactly who he was at that company. We got along well, and he invited me to come see Hawaiian Tropic's headquarters next time I was in the area.

Hawaiian Tropic was only an hour or so from Disneyworld. We loved it at Disney, and because it was just two and a half hours from our home in Palm Beach, we got annual passes every year, allowing us to go as many times as we wanted for one price. Since it was only an hour from Hawaiian Tropic's headquarters, we decided on the next trip to take Ron up on his invitation and stop by to see his company's headquarters.

We entered the building and asked if we could see Ron Rice. They asked if we had an appointment, and we said no. They said, "Then I'm afraid he has a full schedule today, I suggest you make an appointment for a future date." I said, "But he had invited us to stop by sometime." With that, they called his office and told him we were there, and he told them to let us in. You can imagine our surprise when we got to his office and it said "Ron Rice—Founder and Owner—Hawaiian Tropic." I told him, "You son of a gun, you never told me you *owned* this place, much less that you're the founder!" He started laughing, and said, "I never told you I owned it?" I said, "No, we thought that maybe you were an executive helping to start their contest!" He continued laughing, and we started laughing too—it was a pretty funny situation.

Over the years, Ron and I became close friends. He came to my wedding, and I went to his. We had a running joke about who would have the biggest wedding. I told him he was crazy, since I didn't have his kind of money.

He did have a massive wedding at his home in Daytona, Florida. It was so big that not everyone could fit inside the church. Since it was kind of a small place to accommodate everyone, he rented a hall to put other people, where they watched it on closed-circuit video. The reception was in a great hall, and he and his new bride Darcy came in on a beautiful horse-drawn carriage, with a wedding cake so high you needed a ladder to get to the top.

Some people really thought that Ron and I had actually made a bet on who would have the biggest wedding. They came up to me and told me how I'd never top this. I said first, I never really made such a challenge. Second, if I had, after seeing this I'd have to sell my house to top this wedding, it's that unbelievable. They said, "We know you, George, and now that you've seen Ron's wedding, even though you don't have this kind of money, you'll try and top it anyway!" These were some of my best friends who knew me well, so I said, "You're right!" We all laughed.

Then came the time for my wedding. I knew there was no way I could do what he did—it would cost a fortune. I knew I couldn't afford all of that, but just as I had flown in private jets and stayed in hundred-million dollar mansions without owning them, I thought, why not use someone else's place for our wedding?

You see, Disneyworld had a place where you could get married. They had a beautiful little chapel on the water at Epcot Center, which was really special and cost a fortune, but we could rent it to get married there. Having produced shows my whole life, I decided why not go even further, and rent the Disney Dream chapel and have a fantastic wedding there? In meeting with the Chapel wedding planners, I asked if could rent one of their pavilions for the reception. They said yes, and they actually offered us the American Pavilion, a beautiful multimillion-dollar building at Epcot Center featuring the history of America. With my events and my company being called American Dream, what better place to have a reception than the historical American Pavilion!

Then taking it even further, every night Epcot has a $100,000 fireworks display, so I rented a small private island that overlooked the entire Epcot Lake where all our guests were escorted after the reception. With fine wine to help the celebration, they had the best seats at Epcot to watch some spectacular fireworks, the kind only

Disney could afford. At the end of the fireworks display, my friends told me, "You and Ron had two totally different types of weddings, but only you could think of using the million-dollar Epcot Center and Disneyworld to host your wedding. We've been to dozens of weddings, but nothing can compare to the night we just had, it was spectacular!" Of course, renting the pavilion there was extremely expensive, so obviously we only invited our closest friends. Fortunately, we had many friends, but unfortunately it made the loan quite large!

My friends continued, "Of course, George, this was a totally unfair challenge!" We all laughed about it, including Ron and his guest. Ron had missed the Chapel ceremony, but we were just glad he came at all. However, one thing did disappoint us. When we were invited to Ron's wedding, we had looked for months for a gift for him and his new wife—after all, he was a multi-millionaire. What could we possibly buy for them? But after months of looking whenever we went around the country on business trips, we finally found a beautiful handmade framed castle etched out of copper and other metals. It was kind of pricey for us, but I had to get it for our friend Ron because I knew he liked castles and it was the theme for his wedding. They'd gotten a tremendous number of wedding gifts, but his wife Darcy sent us a "Thank You" note telling us how much she liked the castle, which she said stood out because it was their wedding's theme.

When it came to our wedding, our disappointment was that we never did get a gift from Ron, which I'm sure was merely an oversight, but we would have loved to have had something from him because of our relationship with him over the previous twenty years. The cost would not have mattered—we just would have liked to have had something from Ron to put in our home, just to show people we were friends.

We liked Ron and constantly went out of our way for him. When he came to our events we would meet him personally when he arrived with his credentials to judge our events, yet when we went to his events his people always gave us a hard time, making us wait a long time for our judging credentials, etc. And for as much as we spent finding him such a special wedding gift, we never got one from him. These are examples of how having so much money can change even the nicest people like Ron.

Now, don't get me wrong—Ron Rice is *nothing* like Donald Trump, which shows that even though he's wealthy, Ron was still a great guy who remembered his roots and was a down-to-earth person in many ways. At times he would get caught up in having so much money and having so many people wanting to be around him because of his fame and fortune, but I saw through all of that, and I realized what a truly nice person he was. As disappointed as I was about not getting a wedding gift from him, and for also being treated badly by his staff at his events, I still know that Ron is a terrific person, who at times gets caught up in just having to be Ron Rice, founder and owner of Hawaiian Tropic, but I'll always remember him as a good guy and a great friend with whom I've had some great times. He's someone I'm truly honored to have known and to have had in my life.

It really was ironic, how despite the fact that I had nowhere near the monetary worth of Donald Trump, Ron Rice and others like them, I still moved in their circles, which gave me the ability and the experience to write this book in order to show that money really does change people, and more often than not, the more money a person has, the worse they get. However, like everything in life there are exceptions, and Ron Rice is certainly one of them.

The Real Donald Trump

People from Altoona, Pennsylvania, don't really like to lean on their horns. Altoids, as people from Altoona are known, are hardworking, God-fearing and humble individuals who mind their own business while they live and let live. But there comes a time when even an Altoid like myself, spending most of my adult life in New York City (the toughest city in the world), must jump on a soapbox and rail against the waves of deceit, hypocrisy and abuse of power that are now crashing down on the landscape of America's democracy.

This book will prove once and for all the following three things about Donald Trump:

1. He is not as good a businessman as many people think.

2. He is a pathological liar.

3. He has no conscience.

This is a true story. Everything described here happened just as I have written it. Working with Donald Trump, my hero at that time, was a once-in-a-lifetime opportunity. I didn't want to make any mistakes, so I kept a daily log from the day we met until the end of our professional relationship. Therefore, what is written here is 100 percent true and accurate, and I have not elaborated, exaggerated or changed the facts in any manner.

Most of what is written here is even documented from hundreds of witnesses who can corroborate what I am about to disclose. Of course, as is Trump's way, he will lie about it, despite the fact there are hundreds of witnesses to verify what I will say, and the fact there is so much evidence to prove what is written here. Donald Trump thinks anything that comes out of his mouth is the law, Trump's Law, and every one of his followers will also lie and completely disregard the facts. However, none of that can change the truth. Based on the facts you are about to read, you must be the judge as to whether or not the three points I have set forth above are true.

MEETING DONALD TRUMP

I must admit right from the start that no one admired Donald Trump more than I did. As a New Yorker, I grew up with him everywhere. To me he was always very impressive, and as far back as the early '80s I felt that he should run for president someday. I even discussed it with him when we were working together on the Donald Trump American Dream events.

I even used to have dreams about meeting with Trump and starting an empire that would make him even wealthier, and also allow me to make millions and travel around the world. I thought I would have the money and the clout to fulfill my lifelong dream of partnering with the Walt Disney Company to create a new way to entertain children, while educating them in a revolutionary way never before possible.

It took over thirty years, but the day I started to think would never come finally did. I was given a private meeting with Donald Trump himself. Arranged by someone who at the time I had thought was a good friend. I couldn't believe it—I was actually going to have a one-on-one meeting with Donald Trump himself! Despite the fact that I was nervous, and I don't normally get nervous, I felt I only needed one meeting to show him the potential he and I had together.

The day finally came, and of all the days in a year, the day they gave me for the meeting was December 11, my birthday. Of course, Trump didn't know it was my birthday, it was just another day to him. Living in Palm Beach, Florida, at the time, I flew into New York with my wife Jill, who worked by my side 24/7 for thirteen years, and who had become a very sharp businessperson. Hopefully, this was going to be the meeting of a lifetime for us both.

As we checked into the hotel, it started to snow. I had hoped it would not turn into a snowstorm, as the last thing I wanted was to see this meeting cancelled. We awoke the next day to exactly that—a snowstorm, and all we kept thinking was whether or not he would cancel our meeting. That day was extremely nerve-wracking for both myself and my wife. Then the phone rang—it was Donald Trump's secretary. We thought, that's it, he's going to cancel the meeting. I picked up the phone and his secretary said, "Are you still planning on coming to the meeting or are you stuck in Florida?" Of course, I replied, "Yes, we will be there, we came in a day early in case of bad weather." She replied, "That was very smart of you. Since you're here now, could you come in a little earlier? Several of his meetings were cancelled because of the weather."

Thrilled to hear that because I might possibly have a little extra time with him, I immediately told her, "Sure, I can be there whenever you want." She gave us a new time, and we were excited to get ready for what I believed would be the meeting of a lifetime.

Because of the snowstorm it was hard getting a taxi, but we finally found one. We arrived at Trump Tower, and to say we were excited would be a definite understatement. His secretary showed us into Mr. Trump's office. He got up from his desk to welcome us, but rather than come to me first, which he should have, he went directly to my wife, Jill, shook her hand and said, "My God, you are beautiful."

I was, of course, taken aback by this, but I said, "Hello Mr. Trump. I'm George Houraney, CEO of American Dream." Although he reached out to shake my hand, his eyes never left my wife.

We sat down and he immediately said, "I understand you have a program that can make my casinos a lot of money." I replied, "Yes I do, Mr. Trump, and this is not just an idea. I have been successfully running these events in Las Vegas since the late 1970s." Trump replied, "That's a long time. What is it, about fifteen years?" I said, "About that." Then he asked, "So, what was the first casino you worked with?" I replied, "I worked with the Howard Hughes Company, which owned several casinos in Vegas."

He said, "That's impressive ... no wait, did your event

do okay?" I replied, "After the first event they wanted a three-year deal. I remained producing events for them for ten years until they sold all of their casinos. I guess we must have done something right because I was told that ten years of putting on sellout events was a record."

Trump said, "Yes, that's great, but what happened after that? Were you able to get any other casinos to sponsor your events?"

Actually, the mayor of Los Angeles had convinced us to move our events there to the Shrine Auditorium, which was home to the Academy Awards and a beautiful venue. However, our events really worked best at casinos, and after two years in LA we were convinced to move back to Las Vegas by the Boyd Group, which owned many major casinos in Vegas. They put us up at their Stardust Resort and Casino, which at the time was one of the top casinos in Vegas. I explained all of this to Mr. Trump.

Trump then asked, "So, after leaving Vegas, going to L.A. and coming back, did it still work?" I replied, "We've had to turn away crowds since our first event there."

He continued pressing me for more details. "Well if you're doing that good, why do you want to do an event at my casino?" "Because we've grown as big as we can get in Vegas. We need big corporate sponsors, which we know you can tie us into."

His response was, "You're right about that, I know the head of Revlon and many other major companies."

We discussed some other areas concerning the events at his casinos, but for the entire interview he continued looking at my wife, even though I was the one doing most of the talking. Eventually it got to the point where he said, "You've been doing this for quite a while in Vegas and it's been very successful, and you covered the points I was interested in, so even though I have to run it by my people at the casino, let's do it. Draw up an agreement and get it to me by next week."

I almost couldn't believe it. With just a single meeting, he had agreed to my proposal!

Then he asked me where we were staying. I told him we were at the Marriott Marquis. He said, "No, no, I have a much better place for you to stay. What do you think about the Plaza?"

The Plaza! "Of course, I love the Plaza, it's one of the finest hotels in the world, but it's very expensive, and just like with your events, I always watch how much money I spend so the profit margin is bigger. It's also Christmas month—an impossible time to get a reservation there." He then called his secretary. He told her, "I want you to get George and his beautiful wife a suite at the Plaza starting tonight, and make it a comp." That's hospitality jargon for complimentary, meaning free of charge! "Mr. Trump, I believe the Plaza is completely booked up. As you know, December is the busiest month of the entire year, so I don't know if we can get a suite."

"When you call, just tell them Mr. Trump wants a suite for the Houraneys starting tonight." "Okay." his secretary replied.

This was the very first time I saw that Donald Trump does not take "no" for an answer, no matter what the circumstances.

As we got up to leave, Trump said, "Why don't you get some of your contestants and winners from your Model Search and join me for dinner tomorrow night at the Oak Room at the Plaza?" I told him it would be an honor to join him, but with the snowstorm and such short notice, I didn't know how many people we could get to attend. "You run the event, right?" I quickly got the message he didn't want a "no" answer.

"Okay, Mr. Trump, what time would you like us to meet you there?" "I have several meetings that may run late, so let's do it around 8." I agreed, thanked him again for this very special invitation and told him we looked forward to seeing him again the following evening.

My wife and I left his office, and on the way back to our hotel we worried about being able to get enough contestants and winners together to impress Mr. Trump. We got back to the hotel, packed and went immediately to the Plaza. We walked up to the main desk and gave them our names, and explained that Mr. Trump had told us to come there.

Before we knew it, there were two bellhops taking our bags. The person behind the desk handed us the keys, saying, "Please enjoy your stay at the Plaza, and if you need anything, here is my extension. Just call me."

When we got to our suite, we were absolutely blown away. It was so big and so beautiful it was like walking into a movie scene, especially looking out the window with a view of Central Park with the snow falling. It was hard to believe that we were in a suite at the Plaza at Christmastime!

As impressed and excited as we were, it didn't take

long before reality set in. We had to get on the phone and start calling some of our contestants and winners. We spent hours doing this, but we finally lined up a few who could make it there the next night.

With all that had happened that day, it was almost like we had dreamed it. It was hard to sleep that night, especially since all I kept thinking was that we had just met with Donald Trump, and with just one meeting we had a deal, and we were on our way to creating one of the biggest casino events of its kind in the country with Donald Trump himself behind it.

It took a while but we both finally fell asleep, and upon waking the next morning, we looked out of the window at Central Park, with the snow and the horse carriages and streets buzzing with people, and once again it felt surreal—like being in a movie.

OUR NIGHT OUT ON THE TOWN

There is something very special about Christmastime in the Big Apple, especially when you have a complimentary suite at the Plaza Hotel! The cold heart of the big city seems to melt into a peaceful calm under a flood of red and blue holiday lights. It was also my birthday, and as I peered out the window, a flurry of snow raced across the frozen brown landscape of Central Park.

Once we finally got to sleep, Jill and I both slept soundly on our first night at this hallowed landmark, but upon awakening, we were hungry, so we showered, dressed and jumped into an elevator that dropped us at the mezzanine's dining room. We chose a table

overlooking the main lobby as a waiter in a spiffy tux-
edo handed us menus thicker than a small book.

A workingman can blow his whole paycheck having
breakfast at the Plaza, but this one was going on The
Donald's dime, so for once we didn't have to worry about
how much money we were spending.

Since dinner with Mr. Trump wasn't until 8 o'clock
that evening, we took to the New York sidewalks and
tasted the crisp morning air. Jill was a native New Yorker
and I was a naturalized one, so we had no trouble finding
our way to Rockefeller Center with its gigantic Christmas
tree overlooking the most famous ice skating rink on the
planet. The Center has a toney little restaurant, so over
lunch we plotted out a game plan for what was most
likely going to be the biggest night of our young lives.
By mid-afternoon, everything had turned surreal again. I
could not believe that I was really going to have dinner
with the great Donald Trump. I had to pinch myself! I
was on edge like a football player in his first Super Bowl.
I imagined all kinds of scary scenarios that might torpedo
this big chance.

However, I had not come all this way by being lucky.
What sustained me over the years was keeping in mind I
was not working for just any billionaire ... I was working
with Donald Trump! Suddenly I began to relax. Jill took
a nap while I worked on what I would say to Trump that
evening. I gradually began to feel as if everything was
going to be okay.

One of the events we were planning for the Trump
Castle casino was an International Model Search judged
by the high rollers we would import to his casino. Some

of the contestants would be joining us for dinner with Trump, so we arranged a limousine to chauffeur them to the Plaza.

The Oak Room in the Plaza is the most gilded eatery in the world. The walls are festooned with portraits of its most famous dinner guests such as Theodore Roosevelt, Franklin Roosevelt, General Douglas MacArthur and William Randolph Hearst. Mr. Trump had reserved the George M. Cohan booth for us. What an honor that was!

The maître d' had obviously been well briefed. "Good evening, Mr. and Mrs. Houraney. Right this way." Accompanied by our lovely fashion models, we approached Mr. Trump's table, and he rose to meet us. "Who are all these gorgeous girls?" he asked. Trump gestured for me to sit at the far end of the table as he seated Jill next to himself. "I hope you don't mind, George," he said. "I'd like to discuss some things about the Model Search with Jill during dinner." "That will be fine, Mr. Trump," I replied.

"Don't call me 'Mister,'" he shot back. "If we're going to be partners, there's no sense in being formal." Now I was beginning to think The Donald actually liked me! Little did I know how off the mark that thought was.

Dinner had been preordered—surf and turf with a vegetable medley and Caesar salad. A luscious tangerine sorbet was served for dessert. Trump and I nursed lemon water while the models sipped a rare French Chardonnay. After dinner, they smothered me with hugs and kisses for giving them the most exciting evening of their young lives.

Trump then extended an invitation to go clubbing. How good could it get! We had dreamed of a thirty-minute audience with the King of Gotham, and here I was having dinner and now going clubbing with him. It was almost too good to be true!

We went outside and up drove a limousine. Trump sat relaxed, looking regal as he welcomed us aboard. "Let's have some fun tonight," he said. And we were off!

We went to one of the hottest clubs in NYC at the time, and the queue of souls fighting off the cold waiting to get in was proof of that. Trump's bodyguard led us to the front entrance, where a doorman ushered us right in. No waiting in line for Trump! The noise and the music was ear-popping. "Good to see you again, Mr. Trump," the doorman said. "Follow me."

It was sardine city, with revelers packed into every nook and cranny. I wondered where we were going to sit, when a quartet of waiters appeared out of nowhere with two large tables. They carved out a space near the main stage and soon returned with a dozen chairs. Wow! They called that the "Trump Effect."

The eyes of everyone zeroed in on us like a piercing laser. Everyone took a moment to notice Donald Trump and the members of his party. Once again, we were beginning to feel important.

Jill and I had never been ones to revel in the clamor of nightclubs and bars, and after a while it became overwhelming. "Donald, let's get out of here," I said. "I can't stand the noise." Surprisingly, he concurred. Within two minutes we were back in the limo and bound for the Plaza.

That is when it happened—my first experience with the REAL DONALD TRUMP. Trump leaned against my shoulder and began talking about my wife, Jill. "George, she is beautiful," he said. "She reminds me of Bo Derek. I would love to sleep with her. She must be fantastic in bed."

It was like getting cold-cocked by an Ali uppercut. Was he joking, or was he was serious? Had Donald Trump, my idol and new business partner, suddenly morphed into some kind of crazed stud muffin? Did he actually want to crawl between the sheets with my wife?

Then I thought no, he's a businessman, we can make his casino a lot of money, and besides he has all the gorgeous women he wants at his disposal. Yes, my Jill was drop-dead beautiful, but why would he want someone else's wife when he could have some of the most stunning models in the world? So I dismissed it, telling myself he must have been joking or possibly testing me to see how I handled myself under difficult situations.

I told Trump we had an early morning flight back to Florida. He told us he also had a full schedule in the morning. The limo dropped us back at the Plaza, but not before Trump assured me that we had a deal, and he told us to get started on the agreement and the events. I thanked him again and told him I would be in touch.\

Back in our suite, Jill seemed agitated and upset. "Am I glad we didn't hit another club," she gasped. "What do you mean?" I asked. "Never mind," she said. "We'll talk about it in the morning."

We were in bed before midnight but neither one of us slept very well. I was still in shock from Trump's apparent naked desire for Jill, and I could also tell that something was gnawing at her. As I would later find out, what Trump says is not nearly as scary as what he actually does.

We were up before dawn and took Trump's limo to LaGuardia Airport. It had been a great three days, but we were looking forward to the sun and warmth of our home in Boca Raton, Florida. We sure had plenty of work to do. The Trump event could launch us into that lofty layer of major league resort and casino promotion and entertainment. It was our big chance, and we absolutely did not want to blow it.

We were planning to pull out all the stops for Trump's events. As big as our events had been in the past (selling out top casinos in Las Vegas is a major accomplishment all by itself), I would use everything I had to make Trump's events even bigger. I would call on every contact I had developed, which had taken me a lifetime. It was going to be the hardest work of our lives, but to impress someone like Donald Trump, it would be well worth it.

The Donald Trump American Dream Events and the Shocking Surprise of His Sexual Escapades

After many months of working nonstop, the time had finally come. Although we had been producing events since the late 1970s, by far this was going to be the biggest of them all. We had placed Donald Trump's name on the events, and if we didn't live up to his expectations, there would be no future events with him. Of course, we were nervous—after all we were producing a multimillion-dollar event on a shoestring budget for a man like Donald Trump. We were working with people from over thirty countries around the world, and every major promoter I had ever worked with had joined us for this spectacular series of events.

I spoke to Trump a few days before heading to Atlantic City, and he asked me if we were ready, and if was this going to be the big event we had promised him it would be. I told him that I thought he'd be pleasantly surprised. I explained that we'd put everything we had into this show, and despite the fact we really had no budget, we believed it would be one of the largest events of the year at his casino. His reply was, "I certainly hope so."

CHECK-IN DAY

We arrived in Atlantic City a week ahead of the events to get things prepared. When checking in, we were surprised to learn that they had a suite for myself and a separate one for my wife. I told them at the check-in desk that my wife and I stay in the same suite because we work together, and she is one of our directors. They said they had orders from Mr. Trump to give each of us our own suite. I asked Jill if she would like her own, and she said maybe it would be better because I had meetings late at night with my automotive people and others, which kept her awake. I could also get more sleep, which I would really need for this event. So I told them it was fine, and we each took the suite assigned to us. Upon being given our keys, we discovered we were staying on different floors. We told the receptionist we really wanted to be on the same floor, and if possible next to each other. They said those were the rooms Mr. Trump had assigned us, and that we should discuss it with him because they had to follow orders. Little did either of us know that he had an ulterior motive for doing this.

We both checked into our suites and met later for dinner. I asked my wife about her suite. She said it was quite beautiful, but *it was right next to Trump's*. She said she really didn't want to be next to him and she had tried to move to another suite, but they had told her there were no more available. I knew this was not true because we were there one week before the event and there was no way they had completely booked the hotel already, since most of the guests would be registering on the day the event started.

I had known Trump was attracted to my wife, and I was concerned about the way he acted around her, but I figured this was his big event and he would probably be concentrating on making it successful, not trying to work on my wife like he had several times throughout the year. I didn't want to think the worst, and I thought that perhaps Trump wanted to be close to her to keep up with the Model Search portion of the events for which Jill was in charge.

We got to work the very next morning and started registering contestants as they arrived. Besides the models, another really time-consuming part of the event was the Automotive Design Challenge. We had over thirty one-of-a-kind cars being towed in from all over the country, and with rain, sleet and snow throughout the Midwest, we were concerned that some of the World Finals entrants may not make it there in time. This weighed heavily on us throughout the week. We were also going to put on a major stage production so, as the models registered, we started rehearsals for their part of the event, one that would be a major part of the two-hour stage production in the main showroom.

THE PRESS CONFERENCE

One of the most important things we had to do was hold a press conference in New York City. It's about a two-hour drive from Atlantic City, so we had to arrange bus transportation for the contestants. We would hold the press conference at the Plaza—this was when Donald Trump still owned it.

The press conference was held on Thursday. The bus ride was a lot of fun for all the models, as many of them had never been to New York City before. Additionally, this would be the first time they would meet Donald Trump in person, although we didn't tell them they were going to meet him—we wanted to surprise them.

When we arrived at the Plaza, we figured we would surprise Trump as well, so we lined up all the contestants from the Donald Trump American Dream Calendar Girl Model Search on a beautiful staircase. Seventy of the most beautiful women from around the world filled those stairs from top to bottom. It was then when we told them they were going to meet Donald Trump, and they all cheered and were very excited.

I met Trump at the entrance to the Plaza, and told him I would take him to the room where the press conference was being held, and there at the end of the hallway as we rounded the corner, the girls shouted, "Hi Donald!" He was completely surprised, and couldn't help commenting about how many beautiful women there were. We asked him to take a photo for the media, and of course he jumped right in the middle of all of them. From there Trump and all the girls headed to the press room. There we allowed the media to take photos of Trump and the girls and also gave them a rundown of the Donald Trump American Dream Events.

The press conference was a complete success, with both TV and newspapers giving us excellent coverage plus priceless exposure for Trump's casino. We headed back to the casino after it was over, and the girls talked all the way back about how exciting the day had been for them.

THE CARS

On the following morning, the automobiles and their owners started to roll in. Many of them said the roads were terrible—there was a lot of snow and rain that made driving conditions very hazardous, but thankfully everyone made it. They were just as excited as everyone to be part of this Donald Trump American Dream Event. Due to my twenty-five plus years of working with show car producers throughout the world, I was able to put together thirty one-of-a-kind cars that were all truly magnificent. Their competition would be in the ballroom of Trump Castle, which unfortunately was on the third floor, so the cars had to take the freight elevators to get there.

Here is where we faced our first major problem. Although I had asked several times for the exact measurements of the elevators, the figures they gave me turned out to be wrong, and most of the cars would not fit! This was truly a nightmare because the Automotive Design Challenge needed all of the cars on display for an excited public ready to vote on the champion. Most of the car owners were men who had built their cars with the help of friends and family, and they had their families with them, so there was no way on Earth they were going to miss participating in this spectacular event with Donald Trump's name attached to it.

For many of the cars, they ended up having to take pieces off them to make them fit in the elevator, and then put them together again once they got to the ballroom. We were awake for twenty-two hours straight getting all the cars into the showroom on time, and it was truly one of the hardest days of my life. On top of getting the cars into the elevator and into the ballroom, we still had to deal with the rehearsal for the contestants in the Model Search, rehearsals for the Music and Comedy Challenges, plus all of the VIPs and judges coming in from around the world. Needless to say, we had our hands full, and sleep was not an option!

THE UNVEILING

I always like to make a great show out of everything I can, and these cars were so magnificent that I wanted to present them in a way no one ever had ever seen before. We had each car covered up, and with music from Star Wars and Superman playing, we would announce the name of the car builder and the type of car as they were unveiled. The rehearsal went better than expected—all of the automotive people were spot on, and it really was a wondrous sight as the music played to see the spotlights hit each car as the builder and family proudly stood next to it.

When the rehearsals were done, Trump came in accompanied by Marla Maples, and he asked what was going on. I told him what we were planning, and he said it sounded fantastic and that he couldn't wait to see it. While we were talking, Tony, the master of ceremonies walked up (he's the one who got me the meeting with Trump to begin with). Tony had also emceed our events for many years.

I asked him to give me the cards that had all the information about the cars on them. Tony said that he would take care of them, and bring them down when we unveiled the cars that night. I told him NO! I was the show's producer, and I wanted to make sure I had everything in line and that all the cars were in order, so I told him I'd better take them with me. Trump and Tony were friends, and Trump said that Tony knew how to do this and to let him keep the cards, to which I replied that this was not like the beauty pageants Tony was used to doing. I explained that no one had ever done this type of automotive presentation before. Besides, I was the pro-ducer—I was the one responsible for everything, and if it went wrong then the buck would stop with me. I really needed to take the cards with me, but Trump said not to worry about it—Tony's a professional, he'd do fine, and so he let Tony take the cards. I wasn't at all happy about this, especially since Trump should not have interfered with my producing the show because he *knew nothing* about what I was doing, and, with his name all over everything, I wanted to make sure things were as pro-fessional as possible for him. Yet he *had to get his way*, despite the fact that I had forty years of producing such events and he had *zero*. Sound at all familiar?

Opening night at the Trump Palace was set. Jill had slaved all week to tweak our Music Contests, the Com-edy and Vocal Challenges, and of course the Interna-tional Calendar Girl Model contest. That was Jill's area of expertise, and she had everything fine-tuned. When she knew that everything was in place, she was usually perky and chatty, but a pall seemed to hang over her all day. I knew something was definitely eating her up inside.

I had my own concerns that night—my baby was the Automotive Design Challenge. That was our showstopper! Some of those cars were valued at over a million bucks! They had a diamond sheen that glistened across the showroom floor and pulled in car fanatics from all over, and they all wanted their pictures taken next to those beauties.

Pairing them up with a couple of leggy fashion models in skimpy bikinis was a siren call no macho American male could resist. The ballroom was packed with people waiting to see the unveiling of the cars, but soon everything began to unravel like a ball of yarn.

The little spat during rehearsal with Tony the emcee and Trump over the flash cards had left a bad taste in my mouth. I always introduced the car owners and their families, and even though it was not a big deal, it was something you expected to come off without a hitch. But as gorgeous models began sweeping away the taffeta silks, Tony started calling out cars and families *in the wrong order*. When the spotlight would land on one man and his family, Tony would announce them as someone else with a completely different car.

Everyone in the audience could tell So-and-So's "Model T" was not a Cadillac. There were thirty car owners and Tony misidentified *every single one* of them. It was a complete disaster!

By the end, the car owners were understandably seething with rage. Their horror seemed to drip off their faces like melting skin. They were always used to me doing a flawless job of announcing the introductions, but here was Tony flubbing them all like a bumbling buffoon. I felt terrible for the spouses and the kids. They had to stand there slack-jawed and mortified while Tony botched the whole car show. I should have taken the flash cards from him when I had the chance. It was a dreadful start to the biggest night of my life, all because Trump had to have his way. This is a perfect example of how Trump can turn a dream into a nightmare. Of course, as bad as it was, this disaster is nowhere near the damage Trump could cause as president.

The MC later admitted that he had dropped the cards in his room following the previous day's rehearsal, and he had forgotten to put them back in order. At that point, I had lost all faith in Tony, and I was also starting to wonder about Trump. Knowing nothing about what we were doing, knowing that I had decades of experience when he had none, Trump still completely disregarded my decision without any concern about what the outcome might be. Because of this, a year of hard work had just gone down the drain, and all of the time, money and trouble the car builders and their families had gone through, instead of bringing them great joy and happiness, had left them with extreme sorrow, and also so angry that the Trump name was now one they despised!

Despite everything, the show must go on, so we turned on the main lights and allowed the public to walk through the ballroom as the cars were being judged. We still had the other events to put on, plus a two-hour stage production coming up that could add a lot of excitement to the event.

There was still fury on the car owners' faces and

smoke coming out of their ears. They put on a happy face for the crowd but deep in their guts they could not fathom how a Donald Trump event could turn into such a fiasco, especially since the rehearsal had been perfect. People were so angry that a certain few of them wanted to do harm to Trump. The man they had once idolized they now *hated*!

The toothpaste was already out of the tube, but I still ripped into Trump. "You should have never let Tony keep the flash cards!" I could tell Trump was not used to being talked to that way, but I was extremely upset that he had just ruined an entire year's worth of hard work.

"Don't worry about it George," he countered. "It was actually kind of funny the way it turned out. I got a kick out of it."

I winced. Funny? What was so funny? A small legion of families and their one-of-a-kind cars had come great distances through adverse weather at their own expense in order to puff up his casino, and when Tony completely screwed it up, it all turned out to be a joke—one my car owners didn't get!

This man really has a warped sense of humor, I thought to myself. The man standing in front of me was my idol. For the first time, I realized that Donald Trump, this man I had so admired for so long, had *no feelings for those who adored him*. I asked myself, does this man even have a conscience?

The one-of-a-kind car owners were not only angry, they had lost faith in me. It was a daunting task but I had to try winning them back. They were the lynchpin for my entire American Dream Event.

THE FINAL EVENT

The final performance of the event was scheduled for the Castle's large showroom the following night. I thought that if I could bring the car owners up onstage and introduce them, it might ease their pain. It was certainly worth a try.

Before I did this event for Trump, I had been in the business of hyping casinos for twenty-five years. Weeks earlier I had told the Trump Castle showroom's manager that it would be a good idea to sell advance tickets to our final night's event. That way the casino could make a little extra money while controlling the seating at the same time.

If the seats did not sell out, the ticket holders would have the best seats, and those getting in free would fill up the rest of showroom. It was a no-brainer! But Donald Trump was headstrong and would not listen. He told his manager to just let everyone in on a first-come first-served basis for free! This kind of seating can lead to a disaster if you have more people wanting to come in than you have seats available.

It was cold and snowy the night of our World Finals, and the Trump Castle showroom filled up fast. The manager alerted Trump that there were still people outside in the cold waiting to get in. Trump glanced across the floor and eyed the block of seats I had reserved for the one-of-a-kind car families.

"What about those seats over there?" he asked his maître d'. "Mr. Houraney has reserved them for the automotive people," came the reply.

Trump glared at me with a cold eye. "George, they don't need to have seats. They were part of the event."

I tried my best to explain. "Donald, I promised them seats for spending their own time and money for bringing you their one-of-a-kind cars, something they normally get paid for. You had millions of dollars' worth of cars fill your ballroom for free. Plus, we really owe them to make up for the way Tony mangled the introductions last night. I want to bring them onstage to be recognized. These people are one of the reasons why your casino has been sold out all week."

"You can always have them stand outside the showroom, and when the time comes bring them onstage," was Trump's reply.

My patience was starting to wither. "Donald, the show is two hours long," I pleaded. "It would be an insult to them if they had to stand and wait that long. Besides, these families used their own money to come here, and many used their savings to bring their cars here in the rain, sleet and snow. What did the people standing outside the showroom do for you? They're just looking for something for free. I promised my people seats, and I'm going to deliver."

"No, you're not," came Trump's terse reply. Again, it was obvious he didn't like my talking back to him. He turned to his maître d'. "Open that section up to the people outside," he commanded.

The rope line that had cordoned off the seats for my automotive friends and their families was removed, and within two minutes they were all filled up with freeloaders. My peace offering to the one-of-a-kind car gang had just gone *poof*. Now I was furious.

Somehow I had to explain it all to them, but they were not listening. One man had brought his family and his 1957 Corvette all the way from California. He was a good friend who was always zesty and energetic, and we had always had good conversations—but not this night.

"I will never do another event for you again!" he raged in my face. "It cost me a lot of loot to bring my car and my family here, and we were treated like dirt. I am very disappointed in you, George. As for Trump, he's the scum of the earth treating people this way. The American Dream is more like Trump's American Nightmare. Someone should rid the world of such scum!"

Another owner was furious too, but his anger was tinged with a bit of sympathy. He had come into the showroom to find out when they were going to be seated, and had overheard my argument with Trump. He said, "I know you tried, George, but this event was a train wreck. I'm loading up my car and leaving right now. Trump is a no-good son of a bitch, and he can take his casino and ram it right up his big fat ass. He's made a lot of enemies for life tonight."

A New Yorker car builder approached me, and in front of everyone yelled out, "I have a good mind to make sure Trump does not screw anyone ever again!" I knew this man well. He was from a very tough mob family that the police had been after for years because certain people had disappeared. I don't know how his car got into the show, as I never would have invited him knowing his family's background. He most likely took another person's invitation who couldn't make it. That really didn't matter now. I could see how angry he was. He would not care that it was Trump—if he wanted someone to disappear, he could arrange it. As much as I was starting to change my opinion of Trump, realizing that he couldn't care less about anyone but himself, I didn't want my events to be responsible for his disappearance. To calm the man down, I told him I would feature his car in my next calendar with one of the Model Search winners. This was something many car builders wanted, since my calendar went all over the world and only twelve cars could be featured. This calmed him down quite a bit, although now I'm not sure if I shouldn't have just let him do what he wanted. If he had, there would have been no Donald Trump president and America would have been far better off in 2017.

It was devastating. It had taken me twenty-five years to build a bond with my car guys, and now that had all been shattered. These people were my main event—the concrete and steel that anchored my entire operation. Now it all lay in a pile of rubble. Yet, that's not what bothered me the most. These car builders had sacrificed so much for Trump, risked their one-of-a-kind cars in the worst winter weather, spent their own money—some even money they had saved for years. However, in the end Trump was the only one to benefit, having an auto show of one-of-a-kind cars that would have normally cost him a small fortune but didn't cost him at all.

I thought about Trump. I had idolized the man, but now I was beginning to despise him. He was born into wealth and was used to getting his own way, but how could he be so cold and callous toward these people who had sacrificed so much for him, how could he hurt so many American families? No one with any feelings of any kind could do such a terrible thing. Yet, it didn't faze him at all that after all they had done to tow their price-less cars through winter storms FOR HIM, he gave up their seats to people just looking for a free show who had not done a thing for him. Yet, hundreds of family members—husbands, wives and their children had worked for a year for him and he cared so little about them that he gave away the one last thing that could have at least eased their pain a little, he gave away their seats to total strangers. My blood was boiling!

It was hard to soldier on, but Jill and I had a show to finish, and finish we did. The seventy international beauty queens were titillating and spiced up the night like an exotic perfume. Trump's tongue was wagging and his eyes lit up like flashes of lightning. He loved it.

The Model Search went swimmingly, and the audience loved the Comedy and Voice Challenges. The competing bands were rocking' the socks off the music lovers.

Everyone working at the Castle was ecstatic. They had never seen that level of excitement during the winter season. Everywhere we went after the Finals, people stopped Jill and I to shake our hands. "This has been a complete sellout," said the head of the food and beverage dept. "No one has ever done what you just did."

There was a gray afterglow the next morning in my suite. We held a meeting with promoters and winners and casino officials. Two automotive people showed up, but their body language told me they were not there to revel in the wake of what had ended up being a disaster for them. I was searching for the words to console them when the door swung open, and in marched Donald Trump flanked by his chrome-domed bodyguards.

Trump immediately started talking. "I want to congratulate everyone on a tremendous event," he began. "It exceeded my expectations. Next year we are going to bring it to the Taj Mahal and make it bigger and better. Everyone will be invited back and the prizes and awards will be increased."

I was still bitter, but Trump's words were like a salve to an open wound. There was still an ember of hope that I could patch things up with the automotive crowd, and next time there would be no hiccups.

Before leaving, Trump offered everyone a ride back to Manhattan for anyone who needed it. I know he was hoping some of the Model Search winners would take him up on it, but none of them did.

Except for the one-of-a-kind car wreck, it had been a pretty good week. I was used to relaying to my promoters what Trump told me, but here they were, all gathered in one suite and getting it right from the horse's mouth.

Jill and I were thoroughly exhausted. On the way to the airport neither one of us said very much. I think we were both trying to put a label on Trump—at least I was. If he was true to his word and I could make peace with the car crew, there could be a lot of fat paydays down the road. The warm sun and balmy breezes of Palm Beach would be the perfect place to try and figure it all out.

Later that week we received a letter from Trump on embossed gold stationery. Basically, he put in the letter what had been spoken in my suite right before we left for Florida. I was both skeptical and optimistic at the same time. There was still a bitter taste in my mouth after the way he had torpedoed my people.

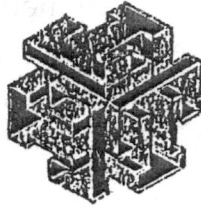

December 2, 1993

Mr. George Houraney
Chairman of Operations
American Dream Festival
P.O. Box 273527
Boca Raton, Florida 33427

Dear George:

My·congratulations to you, Jill and all your staff for
successfully planning, promoting and producing a fantastic
event. The American Dream Festival surpassed all my
expectations, and I am confident it will be bigger and
better each year.

Bravo for a job well done!

Sincerely,

Donald J. Trump

THE AFTERMATH

Jill and I cooled our heels for a few weeks and then called New York. It takes about a year to plan out a Great American Dream Event, so we wanted to set a date with Trump and then give our promoters a heads-up. But for some reason Trump kept avoiding our calls. I asked his secretary to please get a note to him because we needed to lock up a date for next year.

I remember it like I remember the first time I spotted Jill. It was a Monday, and when the phone rang I picked it up and it was Trump's secretary on the line. "Mr. Trump has decided to cancel the event," she breathed into the receiver. What? "But Mr. Trump assured me both ver-bally *and in writing* that we would do another event!" I shouted into the phone. "He gave me his word!" It felt like I had just been kicked in the stomach.

My whole body was numb. The great Donald Trump had milked my American Dream Company dry. Here was someone revered as a shrewd businessman, one with a gold-plated reputation for honesty and loyalty whose word was his bond, who was suddenly reneging on a promised deal.

I had already spoken with the head of Trump's casino and found out that our event at the Castle had netted Trump a hefty profit, in the dead of winter, and it had not cost him a single dollar. Yet now he was tossing us away like worthless chattel.

I soon got the news out to my promoters. They were as shocked as I was. They had been there in my suite when Trump had announced that the next year would be "bigger and better" and had assured everyone that the next event would be at the Taj Mahal. A year of our lives spent working for *free* and making him all that money, and our reward was "YOU'RE FIRED." We were all confused and very depressed.

There was only one way I could try to save my reputation—*I had to sue the all-powerful Donald Trump*. But before I did, there was one backdoor move I wanted to try.

I called an executive at Trump Castle, someone I had gotten along with during the year of planning the events. It took a while but I finally got him on the phone. During our conversation I kept at him, trying to get a straight answer. Eventually I asked him point-blank, "Why? WHY is Trump breaking our agreement?"

He finally got frustrated and blurted out, "Damn it, George, you really don't get it. He couldn't care less about the events, he just wanted to screw your wife. Trump is one callous son of a bitch, now you know. I have to hand it to your wife—she never caved in, but since she never slept with him, you won't be doing any more events with him. But you should also know that doesn't necessarily mean he gave up. He doesn't give up if he really wants something."

I hung up the phone and just sat there frozen in my chair. I am not a drinking man, but at that moment I could have thrown a double scotch down the hatch a few times, it was so hard to believe. I know the super-wealthy are used to always getting everything they want, and Trump does not like the word *no* I knew that he especially liked a challenge, but sponsoring a series of worldwide events, events that affected the lives of thousands, just to try and sleep with my wife? At that point, it appeared that now I had no choice—I had to sue him.

During the litigation, I eventually found out that Trump was after her, and although she said it wasn't a problem and that she could handle him, it turned out that he was relentless from the very start.

I found out that it had all started during our dinner in the Oak Room at the Plaza Hotel in New York City, the day after our very first meeting. I remembered him sitting next to Jill so he could discuss details about the Model Search, but that was not the real reason he sat her next to him. It turns out the first thing he asked her was "if she wore panties." Then under the table he started inching his way up her leg as she became frozen with fear. Imagine, here we are in one of the finest hotels in New York City, we had just met Trump the day before and I, her husband, was sitting at the same table while Trump sexually assaulted her. Although she stopped him, you can imagine her fear.

This man was once my idol, a man who wore a persona of class and brilliance. But here he was, sexually assaulting my wife only mere feet from where I was sitting in New York's most sumptuous hotel. If anyone but Jill had told me that, I would have never believed them. But this was coming from a woman with whom I had spent over thirteen years. Jill would *never* lie about something as serious as this—especially not to me.

Yet there was much more. I found out when we went clubbing that night that he had tried it again. Then when we went to his home in Florida, he told me he had wanted to take her on a tour of the Mar-a-Lago ninety-four–room mansion, but when they were passing through his daughter's bedroom (Ivanka was just twelve at the time), he really pressured her and tried to get her onto his then-young daughter's bed. Imagine a father wanting to have sex on his twelve-year-old daughter's bed while the woman's husband was in the same home—talk about disgusting. He tried to force himself on her, and although terrified, she was still clever enough to tell him that she was sick and wanted to throw up, and went into Ivanka's bathroom and began to retch. That put an end to his advances that time.

Jill told me that Trump was always calling her and asking her to fly to New York. He would tell her that I was a loser, and that he had the wealth to do a lot of good things for her. However, she never took him up on the offer while we were together.

When I asked her why she let this go on so long, she said, "Because this was our big chance to build the biggest event of its kind in the world. You worked so hard all these years to make it to the big time. I wanted you to succeed. Besides, I thought Trump would eventually stop harassing me. I never dreamed he would carry it so far."

I had heard quite enough. A man who was my idol, who I thought was such a great man and a genius at business, someone who for years I had looked up to, was nothing but a sexual predator. For those who may think we are making this up, I say that you know nothing. You didn't go through what we went through. You didn't go to dinner, clubbing or partying at his home, or spend years being close to him, both personally and in business. No matter how much you think you know Donald Trump, or how much you like him and look up to him, no one admired him more than I did. As such, I would never, nor would Jill, make up anything as terrible as this.

Now I really had no choice—I had to take Trump to court. When I told people that I was suing Donald Trump, they looked at me cross-eyed and told me I was crazy. They said I didn't have the money or the know-how to litigate against a titan like Trump, but I had no choice. Decades of hard work plus my reputation were on the line. I was not going to be destroyed by a dishonest predator like Donald Trump.

I told my attorney to file the briefs. It was time for the truth to come out about Donald J. Trump. Little did I know, someday this terrible excuse for a human being would have the most respected and honored title in the world. It's a grave injustice to the hundreds of millions that have made America such a great country, especially to the millions who have lost their lives and their families whose lives changed forever, that a man like this ever was in the White House.

The Court Case: American Dream vs. Donald J. Trump

The very last thing I ever thought I would be doing when we started working with Donald Trump was taking him to court, but then again, I had thought he was an honest and respectable person, one who cared about people and who was a genius at business. I found out the hard way that none of that applies to Trump in real life.

After we had done everything we told him we would do and more, after we had fulfilled our promises and the agreement a 1000 percent, after he had praised us in writing and made a live announcement in front of dozens of people that he was "moving the event to the Taj Mahal and going to make it bigger and better," he went back on his end of the contract and on his word and cancelled everything.

In my seventy-one years on this Earth, working with some of the wealthiest people in the world, I've found that a man whose word is useless is a useless man, regardless of how much money they have. If he had cared at all about others, if he had a conscience, and if he was really the genius businessman the world thinks he is, Trump could never have done what he did to me, my wife and the hundreds of people who gave so much for an entire year to make the Donald Trump American Dream Events such a record-breaking success.

After so many of had worked so hard for an entire year, with many putting their own time and money into his events, and after pleading with Trump to honor his word and his agreement, he did not even have the decency to meet with us to discuss why he was breaking his word and not honoring his agreement. With so many of our promoters (the lifeline of our business) so upset, Trump left us no choice but to take him to court and defend ourselves, and to show the thousands that had participated in the Donald J. Trump American Dream Events throughout the year that Trump had betrayed them, and that *he* was the one who had not honored the agreement and had gone back on his word, *not* us.

Of course, by taking Donald Trump to court, I had everyone I knew forewarning me about how he would crucify me and put me out of business. I was told he had the best lawyers in the world, and he had all the money he needed to pursue any court action I could throw at him, while I had none. However, as nervous as I was about taking him to court, I also had confidence knowing I was in the right and he was in the wrong, and that this would be a true test of our judicial system.

I could write another entire book about just the two years we fought this out in court, with all the ins and outs, the ups and downs. In fact, it could have made a tremendous courtroom-type movie. The famous, all-powerful billionaire trying to get a beautiful married woman to have sex with him versus the small American businessman and his wife. Yet unexpectedly the famous billionaire is forced into federal court—something he had never thought the husband could do. Yet even with that, the billionaire feels the husband is no match for him, that he will crush the husband in court and ruin his business, then get to bed the woman he had been after for years.

The court battle was without a doubt the most stressful time of our lives. For my wife, combined with Trump's sexual assaults, it was so stressful that it tore her apart both physically and emotionally, making her fear Trump would destroy our lives.

Understandably, I was worried about the case. Who wouldn't be, when going up against someone like Trump, and not having the money and resources he did? My business was just about destroyed by him not honoring the agreement and going back on his word. But Trump underestimated me—and so the movie, so to speak, didn't end as one would think.

Of course, the first thing Trump's attorneys tried to do was to get the case thrown out of court. They put forth many arguments, but I had rebuttals that were evidently stronger because again and again the judge denied their motions and refused to dismiss the case.

When that didn't work, they got to a man who had worked for me for years, a man who I had thought was my friend. Here I was at a disadvantage from the start because despite what Trump had done at the American Dream Events, despite this man having worked for me for years and being friends, he *still* thought Donald Trump was one of the greatest people on Earth. Needless to say, he worshipped Trump.

They wined and dined him and got him to switch sides and testify for Trump, but fortunately I had documentation that could prove everything he said was a lie, so his credibility as a witness for Trump eventually amounted to nothing.

The sad part is that this man was basically a very nice person, but he was obviously blinded by his worship for Trump. In the end, this admiration for Trump destroyed what was once a really nice human being. Knowing he had done wrong, he dropped out of the priesthood he had started studying for, and ended up miserable and dying young of cancer, almost as though he was punished for what he had done—yet another casualty of Trump and his lies.

Trump started out with one, but by now he had three different lawyers arguing his case. That really didn't matter to me, he could have had ten lawyers for all I cared—I knew I was right, and I could prove it.

When it finally came time for Trump's deposition, I wanted to videotape it because I didn't trust him at all, and even though they do take court records, I wanted him on video. Of course, his attorneys protested this. In fact my own attorneys said the judge would never allow us to record the deposition, deeming the court records sufficient.

However, my argument to the judge proved to be stronger than they all thought. In a decision that shocked even my own attorneys, the judge ruled in my favor and granted me permission to professionally videotape Donald Trump's deposition. Boy, was Trump angry when that decision came down.

The big day came the following week. The professional crew I hired came in and set up their video equipment. His attorneys, I and my attorney watched, and I could see Trump was upset about all of this because even though he loves being in front of the camera, this would be quite different. He would be sworn in under oath, so he had to watch every word he said or he could end up being in contempt of court, or even commit perjury.

It was lucky for me that I videotaped his deposition because despite a stenographer typing what was said, in no way would it compare to watching Donald Trump in person. Having a videotape of him answering the questions posed to him is simply priceless. There's no way a court recorder could portray how Trump acted, especially when he *outright lied under oath*.

I don't have the deep pockets Trump has, but luckily, I was able to borrow enough money to professionally videotape his deposition. I knew he was capable of almost anything, but I never even suspected he might defy our judicial system and lie under oath.

Despite the fact that we were in federal court and he was under oath, with a professional filming everything that he said and a court recorder typing everything as well, he lied again and again. Sound familiar?

This is a man who is now our president. A man the whole world listens to and mostly believes because he carries one of the most powerful and prestigious titles in the world, the President of the United States of America. Even as far back as decades ago he was defiant to the very court system he's now sworn to uphold as president.

I have *hours* of videotape of him lying again and again, so much so, that at one point he got fed up with getting caught lying, stood up and stormed out of the room, putting himself in danger of being ruled in contempt of court.

You cannot do this while giving a deposition, so my attorneys gave him five minutes to come back, or we would ask the court to find him in contempt, and of course he came back.

We finally finished the depositions, and I was handed the original tapes, which are locked up safely with my attorney.

Throughout the case, his attorneys did their best to intimidate me, but as hard as it was, I stood my ground because I knew I was right. For the sake of all the people he had screwed over during the events we produced for him, I had to go through with this case.

From day one and for the next two years, there were numerous newspaper and magazine articles about the case. Some even did cartoons of Trump stomping on the American flag and people's "American Dreams." After all, Donald Trump had destroyed the American Dream for thousands. This is a man who is now our president. Ironic, isn't it?

This case went on far longer than Trump, his lawyers or even mine ever thought it would last. Battle after battle, argument after argument, sometimes Trump would win decisions, but many other times (and to the shock of everyone involved) we would win the judge's rulings. Then it finally came time to set a trial date, which no one ever thought would happen.

Right before the trial, my wife was so nervous that I sent her to a spa for the weekend. After all, we wanted her to be at her best. No such luck for me—I had to go over everything with our attorneys.

At 7 a.m. I was packing to get ready for the trip to

New York for the trial when I got a call from the federal mediator in the case. He said he was with Donald Trump and that Trump was willing to settle, something he'd been saying for two years that he would never do. I asked if it was the amount we had agreed on, and he said no, but I should know that anything can happen in court, and I could lose it all. I told him I would call my attorneys and get back to him. He said okay, but this offer would only be good for one hour.

I immediately called my attorneys, and they were amazed. They never thought he would settle. I told them the amount was too low, that I would make just a little over breaking even, and therefore I wanted to go to court. They said they understood my position, but they had worked for two years without getting a dollar. They only took the case as a favor to me, as they thought it would be thrown out after a month or so. They never thought I had much proof or that it would go to trial. They said I had to either take the settlement or come up with a lot of money, as they could not work any longer on contingency.

I understood their position, so I called back the mediator and told him that I would accept Trump's settlement offer. I also told him I was packing for a flight to New York for the trial, so I wanted this guaranteed because I didn't trust Trump. I told him Trump's office was close to my attorney's, so I wanted a check delivered to my attorney's office by 12 o'clock noon that day. He said he didn't know if that was possible, to which I replied, "Then I'm not cancelling my flight and the trial is on."

He said, "I'm here with Mr. Trump. I will get back to you." I called my attorneys again and they were furious. "Are you crazy making a demand like that? If Trump agrees to settle to a federal mediator, he can't change his mind. He's not that stupid." I said, "I remember you telling me Trump would never lie under oath." My attorney said, "Well it's too late now, you gave them an ultimatum, but if they don't do it and we go to trial, you'd better mortgage your home—you're going to need the money."

Once I hung up, I thought if I had to, I'd sell everything I owned. I'd come this far and gotten to a place no one ever thought I would get, so either they'd send that check or I'd take it to trial.

I started looking at the clock when suddenly it occurred to me that I was in a movie, one I loved called *High Noon*, since I had given them until noon, or else. Talk about stress! It was only 9:32 a.m., and I was forced to wait until noon to see what would happen. It was like my own *High Noon* showdown.

Minutes went by like hours—it seemed to take forever. Then it was 12:15 p.m. and there was still no word from my attorneys, so I figured I was going to court. I called my attorneys and said, "Don't worry, I'll get you the money for the trial somehow." They had me on speakerphone, and said, "George, in our combined seventy years of law practice you are the craziest S.O.B. we've ever known." I thought *oh boy, are they ever mad at me*, but then they said, "As crazy as you are, you're smarter than all of us, including Trump! You proved us all wrong! We're holding a check in our hands with Trump's name on it, personally signed by him. It came in at 12 noon exactly, and we were so excited we forgot to call you right away. You did it, George, with all the odds against you, you actually beat Donald Trump. We're going to be talking about this and celebrating for years to come. Not only did you beat one of the most powerful men around, but we got paid! Grab your beautiful wife, get your ass up here and let's celebrate!"

I was speechless. I thought the check had not come, but it was true. They had a check from Trump, and the two years of court hell were finally over. I immediately called my wife and told her that Trump had settled. It's over, we're not going to court. At first, I don't think she believed it. We talked for a while, and she told me she would be home soon so we could go to New York, and this time not for court business but, for the first time in years, to have fun!

We went to New York and met with our attorneys. Over lunch they finally admitted to me they never thought it would last for two years and never thought we would win. We signed all the papers and they gave us a check with one condition. Trump had requested that the amount not be revealed to anyone, especially the media.

It took time to sink in that it was finally over and that we had actually beaten the great Donald Trump.

The following day, the *New York Times* had the headline: "Bad Dream Ends for Donald Trump."

For the next two weeks, we got phone calls from all over the country and from many of my international promoters congratulating us. No one could believe we had actually won.

Of course, as always, Donald Trump put a different spin on it. He said he settled because he didn't want to be bothered with it anymore, and that we really didn't win, and had we gone to court, we would have lost. However, most people know that if you're going to settle to save time and money, then you settle quickly, not two years later. After all, you don't save money and time spending two whole years in court, especially when it's someone like Trump spending so much on it.

But of course, as I said, Trump believes what he wants, and this time we couldn't care less about how he interpreted it, all we knew was that his settlement paid for his lawyers and ours, plus all of our travel expenses, etc., and we didn't pay him a dime.

We thought this experience and the nightmare were finally over. Then came a call from none other than Trump's secretary. "Mr. Trump would like to invite you to his annual Christmas party at his Mar-a-Lago home."

WHAT?!?

We couldn't believe it—after all we went through with Trump, here was an invitation to his Christmas party. Was this real or a joke? I checked on it and it was for real, but now came a big decision—should we actually attend? Would people think we were crazy, that after successfully suing Trump we would go to his Christmas party? Jill and I talked it over, and we decided why not! Let's see *why* he invited us.

When our friends found out, word spread like wildfire. A lot of people called us and asked if we were really going to Trump's Christmas party. Everyone was just as shocked as we were by his invitation but also just as curious.

The day came, and we rested most of the afternoon because we didn't know what to expect that night at Trump's famous Mar-a-Lago Christmas party. We had been there several times before, so we knew his home. We arrived, and walking into it was almost like being in a TV commercial where everyone stops to listen to one person. Although not quite as dramatic as the commercial, everyone knew of our situation with Trump because it was in newspapers, on TV and in magazines for years, so many eyes were on us as we entered. Then came another surprise. From across the room, Trump walked up to us, welcomed us and thanked us for coming. We thanked him for the invitation, but I couldn't resist. I asked him, after all we went through, why did he invite us to his Christmas party?

His answer was, "George, anyone that's not afraid of me and takes me on I'd rather be friends with than enemies." That's something I'd heard from him before, but the problem was that, even though it made sense, it only worked when both parties were sincere about what they were saying.

I could not believe that even though it was now years later, Trump was still after Jill, so there was no more pretense about his wanting to work with us. However, I took advantage of the situation, keeping an eye on my wife so he could not hassle her, and we really did enjoy ourselves. Even though we were not at his billionaire level, we'd had a famous International Model Search for decades attended by many VIPs, so we did know some of the people attending the party.

At evening's end, we went to Trump and thanked

him for the invitation. However, this would not be the last time we would see him. Even though the disaster at Trump's events in Atlantic City had destroyed my relationship with the automotive people so I could not continue running those type of events anymore, I continued my International Model, Music and Comedy Challenge events. So, despite all of the damage Trump had done, the American Dream Events continued. Ironically, they continued with another billionaire who would become one of Trump's friends.

Hillary Clinton Wins!

Donald Trump thinks he received more popular votes than Hillary Clinton, but he has no evidence to back up his claim. Yet he *still* thinks he's right! History will show that Clinton won the presidential election of 2016. Trump got seventy-seven more electoral votes, and Clinton almost 3 million more popular votes.

Then why is Trump the president?

He stated he won in a landslide, and that Democrats are upset over their "biggest election defeat." Seventy-seven more individual people elected him, while almost 3 million more voted for Clinton, and he calls this a landslide. As the saying goes, what planet is he from?

Donald Trump is not the people's president!

I am sick and tired of hearing, "The people have spoken, get over it." On the contrary, it was seventy-seven electoral college votes that put Trump, the outlier, into the White House, not the millions of red-blooded Americans who cast their ballots.

A friend of mine who is an airline captain once told me that federal aviation regulations are still in place from the days of the Wright Flyer, and are not really applicable to the aircraft of the jet age like the Boeing 777 or Airbus 320. This brings us to the electoral college, a superannuated apparatus dating back to 1787.

The electoral college, as we know it today, was spawned by the Twelfth Amendment to the Constitution, ratified in the year 1804. Ostensibly it was a device to ensure that the educated elite of our nation chose the president and not someone who could barely read or write. But the real reason for the electoral college was because of our nation's original sin: slavery!

Thomas Jefferson knew that his slave state of Virginia could not offset the voting power of the mighty industrial north. Slaves could not vote, but the Constitution was jury-rigged to allow every slave to represent three-fifths a person for voting purposes. Thanks to this marvel of political engineering, a white slaveholding Virginian occupied the White House for thirty of our nation's first thirty-six years.

As it turns out, We the People do not really elect the president. That task falls to a few hundred people who cast their votes on the first Monday after the second Wednesday of December. Most of these electoral college voters are unknowns and some even have criminal records, but they are the kingmakers. They decide who will exercise the power of the presidency, *not* We the People.

When my eleven-year-old son found this out, he said, "Daddy, if the millions of people who voted for the president don't count, then why do all those people vote? How do you explain that seventy-seven people we don't even know get to elect the most powerful leader in the world?" He then said, "When I'm old enough, I shouldn't waste my time voting if my vote doesn't count." How many young Americans, when they discover as my son did that their vote does not count, will never even bother to vote?

Every statewide election is decided by the popular vote. But in two of the last four presidential elections, the candidate who won the popular vote did not win the White House. In 2016, Hillary Clinton claimed almost 3 million more votes than Donald Trump, yet Trump was elected president. That is like putting 3 million votes in a bag and tossing it into the garbage.

Electoral college delegates are not required by the Constitution to vote for a particular candidate. But some states and parties require their electors to pledge to vote for a specific candidate. These electors can be replaced or even fined if they do not vote as instructed. It is rare for more than one elector to vote against their party's pledged candidate.

In the 2016 presidential election, three electors in three different states declined to vote for their party's candidate. Two were replaced and one changed their vote. This is proof positive that electors, at times, cannot vote for the candidate *they* want as president.

Not long ago I received a phone call from someone who asked if my ex-wife was the one who had filed a multimillion-dollar sexual harassment lawsuit against Donald Trump, and asked if I was writing a book about the *real* Donald Trump. "Yes, who is this?" I said. "Never mind, just listen," came the response.

The caller explained that he had a friend who was an electoral college voter who did not like Trump but cast his vote for him anyway. "Then why did they vote for Trump?" I asked him. He responded, "You must remember that electoral college voters are people, just people," he said. "Like most people, they like and need money."

I was shocked. "Are you saying they were *paid* to vote for Trump?" I asked. "You heard what I said, right?" he shot back. "How hard is it to figure out?"

I told the caller that his friend had probably violated election law and that he should contact the FBI or the Federal Election Commission. "NO! NO! NO!" he gasped. "There is no way I can get my family involved. They will make me disappear!"

"Who will?" I asked.

"Never mind, I've said enough. I'm calling you because you have a pipeline to the media."

"Then at least give me a name," I begged. "Nobody will believe me. I need a name."

"Just have them look into the matter," he replied. "I'm sure they will find out what is really going on. My conscience is clear. I did what I could." And with that, he hung up.

That phone call was surreal! The fear in the man's voice was palpable. I thought of how there are many electoral college voters out there with the same wants and needs we all have. They are vulnerable, yet they get to choose the president, and we don't.

Imagine the sheer power these people wield. Just a few hundred people, who we don't even know are all American citizens, have more power than the 130 million that pay our Congress and pay to operate this country, yet they do not even get to select who should be their president. There is something terribly wrong with this picture.

Then I thought about the Russians and their involvement in the election. Presidential elections are extremely localized, and county voting machines are not connected to the internet. It would be virtually impossible to tamper with that voting infrastructure. But if I were a Russian trying to influence an American election, it would be far more feasible to concentrate on certain members of the electoral college than the millions of Americans who vote at thousands of locations—electoral voters who may be influenced by money—lots of money. After all, what's a few million dollars to Russia? Imagine you are an electoral voter and you are approached with an offer for a million dollars just to vote for a certain candidate, both of whom are Americans. Convinced it's not like voting for a foreign candidate.

I am like most Americans in this country. I have a wife and a young son I hope to send to college someday. I have a mortgage, I pay taxes and I obey the laws of the land. Citizens like myself and my fellow Americans, the real body politic, should elect the president, not a cabal of special interests signified by the electoral college.

The police would not arrest someone before they knew a crime had been committed, but that is exactly what FBI Director James Comey did to Hillary Clinton and her campaign during the waning days of the 2016 presidential election.

Without having a smoking gun, Mr. Comey dropped a bombshell on the Democrats when he announced that the FBI was looking into a breach of security on the laptop of disgraced congressman Anthony Weiner, husband of Clinton's chief aid Huma Abedin.

Eventually no breach was discovered, but by then the Clinton campaign had been mortally wounded, tremendously helping Trump.

American intelligence agencies have confirmed that the Russians played a major part in the outcome of the 2016 presidential election. It would be easy for the Russians to have planted something in the lap of the FBI that caused a red flag to be raised on Clinton. After all—*they wanted Trump to win.*

Which brings us to the bottom line, the facts that cannot be altered. Donald Trump won 304 electoral votes to Hillary Clinton's 227. This was hardly a landslide as Trump claims. In fact, in the last eight presidential elections there were four winners with greater victory margins than Trump.

THE POPULAR VOTE:

Hillary Clinton............65,746,544

Donald Trump............62,904,682

Hillary Clinton defeated Donald Trump by 2,842,862 votes, but Trump won the election because he collected seventy-seven more electoral college votes than Clinton did, meaning seventy-seven electoral college voters whom most Americans don't even know chose the president of the United States of America, *not* We the People, whose hard-earned tax dollars keep this country running, *not* members of the American military who've lost limbs serving their country and, worst of all, *not* those who lost their lives—men and women who will never grow old, never raise a family or share a life with the one special person in their life whom they love. This is not the America our founders created the Constitution for, and *not* the America our founders wanted for their fellow Americans.

That makes 77 people more important than 2,842,862 Americans. I don't get it! Do you feel this is fair? Is this the way our leader should be elected?

And now look what we have for a president. There is hard evidence from our intelligence agencies that Trump's people were in constant contact with the Russians during the campaign. But Trump rails that the CIA got it wrong in Iraq and that they got this wrong too. He shows no respect for FBI and intelligence workers who guard this country's freedom.

His first order of business was to try and cancel the health insurance of 20 million people enrolled under Obamacare and its 3 million attendant jobs. Additionally, he is taking credit for jobs he did not bring to America. He broke many presidential traditions before even being sworn in.

Before even placing his hand on the bible, he acted like he was already commander-in-chief, totally insulting President Obama. He savaged the press, even taking away the freedom of speech from certain reporters, which is one of our citizens' greatest rights.

This is all because of an obsolete system known as the electoral college. One hundred thirty million Americans took off from work, braved the cold weather and stood in long lines in order to cast their vote and have it counted.

Looking back, it now seems like a grand exercise in futility. For at the end of the day, everything was decided by seventy-seven people most Americans could not pick out of a lineup. Seventy-seven people dashed the hopes and wishes of 130 million voters. That does not sound like a democracy to me!

Therefore, I say this to my fellow Americans—you gave Hillary Clinton 3 million more votes than her opponent Donald Trump. She did not get to become the first woman president. But no matter what you think of her, she would never have assaulted our national freedom the way Trump did in just his first months as president, and I doubt we would have the problems we now face with North Korea, nor would we have a president that has divided the country more than any has since the Civil War.

To the more than 65 million citizens whose vote did not count, I say it's time to speak up! It's well past time to do away with the outdated electoral college system!

We the People elected Hillary Clinton. She should be the president, but due to deceit by the FBI, falsely accusing her with no real evidence, and the Russians interfering and possibly blackmailing or paying off electoral voters, Donald Trump became president—just what Russia wanted. Now look at the mess our country is in since Trump took over as president. For the first time in decades, there is serious unrest throughout the entire world. I would bet the house this would not have happened if Hillary Clinton had been elected president.

However, Russia got what it wanted, and we now have a real estate tycoon and reality TV star as president, and his daughter and son-in-law as White House advisers, while all three of them use taxpayers' dollars to create business contacts and deals for themselves, all while our country faces worldwide unrest. Russia could not have done more damage to our democracy if they had blown up the White House.

If Trump had even an ounce of conscience in him, if he cared even a tiny bit about his country, he would resign and recommend Hillary Clinton become president because only she has the experience America needs now with all the unrest in the world. As to his vice president, he was part of the Russian intervention even if he did not know about it, so he also should not be president.

Unfortunately, as I've said many times Donald Trump is a man without a conscience, who cares only about his power and how many billions he can add to the Trump name. His children unfortunately follow in his footsteps. He will *never* give up his position, no matter how much damage he does to our democracy or to our country.

Unlike President Obama, who had no shame showing tears in his eyes when referring to his love for his country, you will never see such caring from the Trump family. They have already proved through their words and actions that they are bereft of any compassion.

We can only hope our representatives in Washington care about their country enough to stop what is fast becoming the deterioration of the office of the president. We now face serious worldwide issues because Trump is president. If you don't think I'm right, take a good look at what the world thinks of Trump as our president.

Donald Trump thinks he received more popular votes than Hillary Clinton but has no evidence to back up his claim. After Trump upset Hillary Clinton in the 2016 presidential election, a female reporter asked him if there should be a Congressional investigation into his claims that massive voter fraud had prevented him from winning the popular vote. The spray tan on the newly elected president began to pale and his eyes began to roll. He wanted an investigation because he "knew" he had won the popular vote. Remember, he is always right!

A congressional probe into voter fraud would only be an embarrassment to Trump and reveal what most of America, the news media and the Federal Election Commission already know: Trump's claims are as phony as a three-dollar bill. Yet Trump carries on with his charade and insists that there should be an investigation.

The U.S. presidential election is delegated to the states. It is an election process that is not perfect and does have its misdeeds. Those misdeeds may number in the thousands but never the millions, as the statistics show. Trump knew that trying to prove voter fraud would be futile. Yet he wanted to waste more taxpayer dollars by trying to prove a negative, simply because his mind only works one way—*he is right*!

I have worked alongside Trump in private meetings, and have sampled the luxury of his private suites at the Plaza Hotel, as well as private and public parties at Mar-a-Lago. I went dining and clubbing with him and much more while constantly observing him, watching his every move, so I got to know him better than any member of the House or Senate.

Trump is the poor little rich kid who never grew up and is always used to getting his way. In my dealings with Trump, one thing became very apparent: the word *NO* is not in his vocabulary.

Our new president may have won the White House, but he lost the popular vote by a margin of nearly 3 million. Knowing him like I do, that grates upon his Titanic-sized ego. Now he has this crazed notion that an investigation funded by taxpayers will prove his assertions. That is pure lunacy and a waste of taxpayers' dollars!

If Trump wants a real investigation into the presidential election, let him peel back the mystique that shrouds our nation's electoral college. For most Americans that entity is a mystery wrapped inside an enigma. It is a million times easier to investigate that body and the seventy-seven electors that provided him with his margin of victory, yet he would never want to investigate that.

Trump is a savage opponent of the mainstream media, calling it fake news. Senator John McCain said that the first thing a dictator does is to muzzle the press, which is exactly right. Every single fascist dictator in modern history has done the same thing.

In working with Trump over the years, I realized that it was his way or no way, no matter what the consequences. He keeps his worshippers on a short leash as they gobble up all the propaganda and falsehoods that roll off his tongue. Even when he is fleecing contractors, it is still not enough to keep him out of bankruptcy court, where he has appeared more times than all the presidents of the twentieth century *combined*.

I once watched Trump sabotage his own business just so he could be right, but that is his way. He now controls the purse strings of our great nation. But scarier than that is that the fate of our great nation is in his greedy hands. Heaven help the United States of America.

A long time ago I wrote a movie screenplay that I wanted to sell to Disney. The story was about a young man who was a product of wealth and white privilege. A meteor falls near him when he is living in his father's mansion. The meteor encounter is like some type of biblical epiphany. Suddenly the young man morphs into a god-like being with galactic intelligence.

He uses his new powers to enrich himself far beyond his father's wealth. With that wealth comes the adulation of his followers. Eventually he becomes a dictator with a lust for worldwide domination. When police and armies try to stop and arrest him, he fights them off easily. Tanks and bombs do not stop him.

Out of desperation, the powers that be decide to nuke him. When the mushroom cloud has cleared, he is still alive and stronger than before. All the energy used to destroy him only makes him more powerful, just as making Trump the president gave him the power he desires and lives for.

Now, my screenplay was not a precursor for the emergence of Trump, except for one major point—Trump's followers and even his friends think he needs attention and needs to be loved. They are wrong. He needs *power*.

I watched Trump for decades, worked with him for years and fought him in court. Trump can survive without love or even the attention his people feel he needs, but he is obsessed with power. He needs it, and he needs to be in complete control. People must always do as he says. It does not matter if they are right and he is wrong, they must obey Trump and Trump's Law.

Trump is the scion of his father's real estate empire, but he went on to forge his own realm of power and influence. Just like the character in my screenplay, the attacks didn't hurt Trump but gave him the power he lives for. Throughout the years, Americans have shed their blood, sweat and tears to carve out the world's greatest democracy, that shining city on the hill. Unfortunately, now we have a president who does not live to help the people, but only lives for the power he has as president.

Trump now has the combination to the world's largest vault of money and resources: we the People's tax money. He plowed through millions of taxpayers' dollars in just his first two months in office, yet accomplished basically nothing except greatly stressing and disrupting the lives of millions of innocent immigrants. He's used Air Force One not for presidential business, but to take him every weekend to his mansion in Palm Beach, so he could justify charging more for a membership there (he raised the price from $100,000 to $200,000 thanks to the worldwide exposure it got from Air Force One). Most of all he showed us that he knows how to throw his power around.

Trump will of course deny all of this, but you cannot change the truth. Only a recalcitrant Trump supporter would stand in denial of what I present in this book.

The 2016 election has finally brought to the attention of voters that, even if a presidential candidate received 20 million more votes than his opponent, and his opponent received seventy-seven more electoral votes, the candidate with just seventy-seven more individual votes would become president because 20 million American votes would mean nothing, If my eleven-year-old, knowing his vote does not count, is already saying he will not vote for the president when he comes of age, how many more are realizing this and will not vote.

If just seventy-seven individuals' votes are more powerful than 3 million American votes, it's time for We the People to take back our right to elect OUR president from a small, unknown group that decides who will spend our taxpayer dollars, who will oversee our military, who will run OUR COUNTRY.

Trump's Duplicity
and Deception

Even though he lost the popular vote by millions, Donald Trump still managed to become president.

He capriciously told America that former POW Senator John McCain was not a war hero, insulting a man who risked his life for his country and who was a POW, while Trump himself avoided serving his country.

Trump pounded his chest and said that he knew more about ISIS than the generals. If anyone actually believes a person who was a real estate developer his entire life knows more than American generals who risked and dedicated their entire lives to serve their country, they had better start researching the truth—something Trump obviously never does.

He promised to erect a giant wall along the Mexican border, and that it would not cost Americans a nickel because Mexico would pick up the tab. His pomposity is exceeded only by his mendacity.

When he found out he had won, Trump was just as shocked as millions of Americans. Knowing Trump the way I do, I could see it on his face—he too was shocked that he won! At that point, I'm sure he was caught off guard and wondered to himself, what do I do now? It soon became obvious Trump had no idea what to do. Then it must have dawned on him—if it worked during the campaign it would probably work when he was actually president of the United States. Regardless of the facts, "I'll do and say what I want. I'm the president now."

Trump was so overwhelmed by his victory in the election, he tried to start governing even before a photo op at Trump Tower. He shook hands with Japanese SoftBank President Nikesh Arora and took credit for the bank's $50 billion investment in Sprint, one of America's telecommunications giants that was projected to create 50,000 new jobs. Actually, that deal had been planned months earlier under the Obama administration.

Then he got on the line to Seattle and began to browbeat Boeing CEO Dennis Muilenburg about the 4-billion-dollar cost of the new Air Force One. "Our new president is trying to save our tax dollars" would look good for him before even being sworn in as president. However, the fact is the new Air Force One was expected to come in under 2 billion dollars, not 4. To Trump, there is nothing wrong with giving Americans the wrong figures now that he is the president, especially when it would make him look like he's saving the taxpayers billions of dollars. It would have taken him minutes of his valuable time to find out the true figures.

Why bother with the truth when the people believe whatever Trump says? That's the way he's been used to running his businesses. Now that he is president, things should always be *as he wants*. Boy, was he in for a rude awakening—it never dawned on him that there are two other equally powerful branches of government with which he would have to contend.

There are a few choice words and phrases in the

Trump lexicon that drive his demagogic rhetoric: "fantastic, amazing, believe me." But his favorite seems to be the one he uses to describe Obamacare. "It's a disaster," he has said many times.

Obamacare had a troubled rollout but soon built up steam, creating 3 million healthcare jobs and putting 20 million Americans under the healthcare umbrella. The program had flaws, but so did Roosevelt's Social Security and Johnson's Medicare or any major new program. Instead of repairing the healthcare apparatus that hired millions, gave millions more the healthcare they never had before and saved lives, Trump wants to get his own credit for healthcare. He would rather toss Obamacare on the scrap heap and replace it with his plan. This would not only cost we the taxpayers billions, but would also cost 3 million people their jobs, 20 million people their healthcare, and worst of all, it would cost lives. However, none of this matters to him. Trump needs to be *right*. Does this sound familiar?

On the campaign trail, he promised healthcare for everyone, however, once elected president, his plan drew fire from even his own Republican party. More time and money was wasted, because instead of trying to improve or fix Obamacare, Trump's idea was to just throw out years of research, waste billions of dollars spent finding out what works and what doesn't, and try something totally new, as if it would be perfect from the day it was enacted.

According to the politically neutral Congressional Budget Office, under Trump's proposal, 14 million people will lose their health care coverage in 2018, and that number will jump to 52 million people by 2026. And premiums for people buying insurance on their own would jump 15 to 20 percent higher in 2018 and 2019 than the premiums would under the current Obamacare.

During his speech to a joint session of Congress, Trump promised to solve the nation's opioid crisis by extending care to those Americans addicted to drugs. Most of those addicts are treated via Medicaid programs, but the Trump budget will *cut* the Medicaid budget by 17 percent while he spends millions of dollars in taxpayers' money to fly to his Florida home on Air Force One.

Trump said that under his plan, rates will go down and benefits will go up. "It will be a thing of beauty," he said. This is typical Trump, anything of his is fantastic, terrific, wonderful, that is until or unless it does not work. Then he changes direction, avoiding or flat-out contradicting what he had said originally.

Our new president's duplicity is staggering. His slogan "Make America Great Again" is a slogan borrowed from the Ronald Reagan era. His wife Melania's speech at the Republican National Convention in Cleveland was a copycat edition of the one given by Michelle Obama at the Democratic National Convention in Denver in 2008. Melania Trump is a very intelligent woman, but she is caught up in the powerful current of her headstrong husband.

I think his biggest and best con job yet was the folly that he would build a great wall along the Mexican border, compliments of our friends south of the border. His base ate that up. When Mexico said that there was no way they would pay for it, Trump said American taxpayers might have to cough up the $25 billion price tag for the wall, but not to worry—Mexico will reimburse us. Does anyone actually believe that?

If Trump had just once bothered to do the research, he would have known the flow of illegals across our southern border is down substantially, and that the vast amounts of drugs smuggled into America are by boats and other means. Drug smugglers and human traffickers have already built underground tunnels. If needed they could easily make their tunnels deeper and longer if he changes his wall's dimensions. In short, building Trump's wall would be a total waste of billions of dollars in taxpayers' money and would be far better spent on healthcare than on a wall that would accomplish nothing.

Trump's temporary travel ban applied to eight countries that, according to the CATO Institute, had no role whatsoever in terrorist activities in this country for the past several decades. But left off that list was Saudi Arabia, the country where fifteen of the nineteen hijackers that killed three thousand Americans on 9/11 were citizens.

In 1995 Trump sold his New York City landmark Plaza Hotel to Saudi Prince Al-Waleed bin Talal for $325 million. It is suspected that Trump has business dealings in that country, but because he refuses to reveal his tax returns, nothing can be confirmed.

How many people remember Hurricane Katrina and the destruction it caused on the Gulf Coast and in New Orleans in 2005? While George W. Bush did a flyover on Air Force One, it was the grit and guts of the Coast Guard that saved hundreds of lives and brought vital supplies of food and water to innocent victims of the storm. As a thank-you to the Coast Guard, Trump wants to slash their budget while he uses his power as the most inexperienced president in history to continue to waste billions in taxpayers' dollars.

The hypocrisy of the man defies belief. One minute he wants to restore our depleted military, and the next he proposes to gut the vital functions of the Coast Guard, the guardians of our shorelines. For God's sake, Mr. President, it is the Coast Guard that provides perimeter security for you when you make those frequent and lavish excursions to Mar-a-Lago. These machinations are the work of a man without experience, logic or a conscience.

Trump is a fabrication machine that spits out lies the way a cobra spits out venom. He was a "birther" who had to eat crow and stand in front of a microphone and admit that Barack Obama was actually born in the United States.

He dismissed reports from all of our intelligence agencies concluding that Russia had interfered with our presidential election, when his own security adviser, his campaign manager and a foreign policy advisor traveled to Russia and held meetings with Vladimir Putin and other high-ranking members in the Kremlin.

When President Trump claimed that former President Obama had wiretapped Trump Tower before the election, he was accusing the former commander-in-chief of having committed a felony. That is a serious charge! But when the Senate Intelligence Committee asked for the evidence, President Trump could not produce a single shred of it.

Trump has disgraced the prestige and power of what was at one time the most respected office in the world. To the majority of Americans, he is an embarrassment, a mistake of history who came to power in a wave of xenophobia and economic nationalism propagated by his confidante Steve Bannon, the former director of Breitbart and a leader of the "alt-right" who has a *proven* track record of supporting white supremacy and anti-Semitism.

During Trump's campaign for the presidency, about a dozen women came forward and accused him of sexual assault. Trump promised that all of those women would be sued in a court of law. So far Trump's lawyers have not started any litigation and they never will. That would be like hoisting their client with his own petard.

Donald Trump has always claimed that the American electoral system was rigged—until he was elected president. Then, all of a sudden, only the votes for the popular election were rigged.

According to Trump, he won a fair and unrigged electoral college but lost a rigged popular vote. Political pundits are still trying to figure that one out. No one can ever say that our new president does not have a knack for selectively parsing the facts. The truth is, it is virtually impossible to rig the tens of thousands of voter locations, yet very possible, especially for a giant country like Russia, to rig just a hundred or less *electoral* votes.

Hillary Clinton looked like a shoe-in to win the presidential election of 2016. Her odds were better that American Pharaoh winning the Belmont Stakes. But three things got in her way: the electoral college, the FBI and the Russians.

It is more than just coincidence that Russia was the biggest news story in that election. Their fingerprints are all over it. Trump's aides did not go to Russia just to chug the vodka, savor the beluga caviar and take pictures of the Kremlin. Their mission was much more strategic.

There is one big reason why Russia felt compelled to interfere in America's presidential election. They did not want to deal with Hillary Clinton. Putin's bare-chested macho persona could never allow that to happen. They had their Manchurian Candidate in the real estate tycoon from Queens. With Trump in the White House, they could push his buttons while pursuing their own agenda in Europe and Africa and the Middle East.

And then there is the issue of Kompromat. Does Putin have Kompromat hanging over Trump's head like a guillotine? Could it be that the salacious material cited in Christopher Steele's dossier is true? Is Trump in hock to a Russian bank? Is he a possible target of Russian blackmail? Only Putin and his comrades know for sure. However, in my mind it's very evident there is far too much going on here for it not to be true.

I think the long lens of history will show that the Russian factor tilted this last presidential election to the Republican camp. It will also show that President Donald J. Trump, a real estate magnate with no governing experience, is about to squander American taxpayers' dollars on the military industrial complex, something President Dwight Eisenhower warned us about almost sixty years ago.

Trump wants to ratchet up military spending by 10 percent. He has aimed some tough talk at North Korea and Iran. If he is looking to pick a fight, either one of those countries might gladly oblige him.

Two days after his election victory, Donald Trump climbed aboard his 757 and flew to Washington to meet with President Obama. After the meeting Trump was effusive in his praise of the outgoing president, a stark about-face from his birther days and his stinging rhetoric that Obamacare was a disaster.

At that meeting, President Obama warned the president-elect that his very first test on the international stage would come from North Korea and Kim Jong-un, the young and pesky dictator of North Korea. If Trump decides to lock horns with him, the outcome could be catastrophic.

At the very least Trump's behavior is unpredictable and unhinged. Kim Jong-un is just as irrational. Barring a colossal diplomatic endeavor to separate the two, it could end up causing the world's first nuclear exchange. And to borrow a phrase from the Trump lexicon—that would be a disaster.

I feel sorry for the thousands of federal government employees who fell for Trump's copying of Reagan's words: "Make America Great Again." America *is* great, it does not have to become great "again," but it just might have to after the Trump administration is done with it.

Why do I feel sorry for them? Most of these men and women have dedicated their lives to do all they can to help the American people, but then in comes this real estate tycoon who could not even hold onto the Plaza, one of the greatest hotels in the world, as well as three casinos and many other properties. He is a man with virtually no governing experience, and worse yet brings with him his daughter and son-in-law, placing them above all the congresspersons who have a lifetime of experience helping our country. Three people with zero experience are now at the highest level of the executive branch and able to directly affect our government's policies. Luckily the president only serves a four-year term.

It's well past time for both Houses of Congress to look at reducing the powers of their executive. America doesn't need a dictator, it needs a president.

The Truth About Trump and the Media

When we produced the Donald Trump American Dream events for him, we were involved with the media in many ways. First, because we had contestants from around the world just as we had done for decades when we ran American Dream events at other Resorts for Trump's events, we contacted the media in each contestant's city. We would send each contestant's local media press releases about competing in the Donald Trump American Dream events. This generated priceless media exposure for Trump's resorts and casinos throughout the world. Then after the event we did the same for each winner, generating still more media exposure for Trump's name and events. Upon seeing all the positive and priceless media exposure we had generated for Trump's name, he "congratulated" us, after all he was basically receiving millions of dollars in advertising exposure for his businesses without paying for it. This is something every business desires, as it can save millions of dollars in advertising expenses. Why else do you see major companies sponsoring events from motorsports to the Olympics?

We also scheduled a New York press conference at Trump's Plaza Hotel. Here we brought most of the contestants, and Trump himself showed up for the media.

He loved the press conference because afterward he received tremendous positive media exposure from many New York media—from newspapers to television to magazines. Once again, he "congratulated" us for producing all of the free media exposure we had generated for his business in Atlantic City.

Trump loved this media exposure so much he bragged to everyone he could about how *his name* was all over the media. Things were terrific with the media, and when I told Trump I had invited the media to the events in Atlantic City, he said, "That's great, even more exposure for my casinos. Make sure they get good seats and comped drinks." I replied, "Yes, I've already set that up."

Then came the *real* Donald Trump. From the press conference in New York, a few media reported not only about the events but also the Model Search part and his involvement with model Marla Maples. Was he going to marry her, etc. He *hated* that, he was very upset and let me know it. So, despite the millions of dollars of positive and free media exposure I had got him, none of that mattered, and just a few articles that addressed the truth about his personal life was all he was concerned with.

I explained to him, "Donald, I know you don't like what the media is reporting about you and Marla, but after all she's carrying around a wedding dress just about begging you to marry her. There is such a thing as freedom of the press, you're a public person and you can't expect the media to just report on what you want and avoid everything else in your life."

Again, I saw the *real* Trump. It was like what I had just said went in one ear and out the other. He couldn't care less about freedom of speech and the media, it was *his* world, and you did as he said or you were removed from it. Again, do the names Comey and Yates ring a bell? He said, "George, you want to keep doing these events at my resorts, just make sure the media that wrote those articles do *not* get into *my* events." I tried again. "Donald, your name is on these events, but as a sponsor that's it, these are public events like the Olympics and football and basketball, and you can't ban the media from public events." Again, my words, although the truth, fell on deaf ears. "Remember, I don't want to see those names on my media list," Trump commanded.

Although I thought banning certain media was against what this country was all about and what so many people had died for, I had no choice. When I told the two media reporters they could not have media credentials, seating, etc., they were very upset, and I heard just how upset they were. "George, you seem like a reasonable person. You've created and operated these events for decades with success, affording thousands the opportunity to live the American Dream, but I doubt you did so by banning the media." I didn't want them thinking I was against free press, so I told them, "Sorry, but those are Mr. Trump's orders, after all he is the boss." Their reply was, "That figures, it didn't seem right you would ban the media from events you call the American Dream." The next day there was more negative media from the two journalists Trump had me ban. Once again, I'm in trouble. He called me and said, "Did you see what those <expletives> wrote? See I was right, those guys are nothing but trouble." Never one to take blame for something that's NOT my fault, I said, "Mr. Trump, you had me ban them from the events. Ban reporters from covering public events they are entitled to cover, what did you expect?" Again, in one ear, out the other. "Just make damned sure these guys are nowhere near the contestants or events this weekend," (the World Finals was that weekend) and then he hung up. This is just one example of what I call "Trump's World"—do as he says, or be *removed.*

Because the media has been reporting the *truth* about Trump as president, it's very negative. What he's been doing as president is in many ways "negative" and he's doing everything he can to lock out the media, degrade them and stop them from reporting the truth. This "fake news" he keeps talking about is just Trump's way to try to divert Americans from knowing the *truth.*

Here is just one example of how Trump gets upset at the media for telling the truth, and also a good example of how he lies.

He said many times, "I love golf, it's a great sport. I play golf every chance I get, but I am *not* going to have time to play golf the way Obama did. I'm going to be very busy working for you, as your president."

FACT: During his first ninety days as president, Obama played golf once. Trump played golf nineteen times. That's right, nineteen times.

That's 20 percent of Trump's time as president playing golf, not only costing taxpayers money for security costs to and from golf courses and while playing golf, but also 20percent of his time—nineteen days, playing golf instead of working on the healthcare he promised all Americans, including Trump supporters, which is going nowhere after seven months. So, Trump wasted 20 percent of his presidential time playing golf. Just imagine how much could be accomplished for a healthcare bill if Trump had spent this time working on it like he promised all Americans. However, you see Trump never really works on anything, he expects his people to do the real work, then he signs it and takes credit for it. That's why he plays golf so much instead of rolling up his sleeves, sitting in a room with healthcare experts and not going anywhere except back in that room until they have a workable healthcare program. Then again, *that's not Trump.*

The media reported how Trump constantly criticized Obama for playing golf while Obama played golf once to Trump's nineteen times. Is it any wonder why Obama accomplished so much while Trump, after he promised a new and better healthcare system, had no different program seven months after he started his presidency? Any wonder why Trump does not want Americans to believe the media? If it were not for the media uncovering this, we would not know just how much the president lied, wasting important presidential time enjoying himself instead of working to give Americans better healthcare. Then again, as I've said, he couldn't care less about Americans' healthcare, after all he and his family have the best healthcare in the world. If he did care, he would not be playing golf so much while Americans struggle and even die because they do not have the kind of healthcare their tax dollars actually pay for.

Remember this is *just one* example of Trump trying to deceive all Americans by saying the media lies and reports "fake news."

Any American out there who thinks the thousands of reporters we've watched for years or even decades are ALL out to get Trump are obviously Trump worshippers because no one in their right mind would think the entire American and world media is against Trump. From the 1960s, in all my years in working with the media, I've found the majority of the media to be very dedicated to reporting the truth. They are obligated to make sure We the People get facts that are as accurate as possible. There is *no way* the entire media world all of a sudden lost their ethics and now report false/fake information about Trump.

In reality Trump hates what they are reporting because it's the *truth*. So, by the president trying to dismiss the media and make them out to be liars like it's a witch hunt, he's abusing one of America's greatest freedoms, trying to stop them from their professional responsibility—reporting the truth. Imagine, the president of the United States of America abusing freedom of speech and freedom of the press! Then again, it's *Trump's World*, so you *must* believe everything he says, and do as he says, or else.

Instead of using his presidential time working on healthcare and all the other important issues Americans face, he's watching television and attacking the media. Just as bad, the president is showing the children of the world that violence is okay; after all if the president does it, then it's okay. For those of you that have said it's ridiculous that he's encouraging violence, and that no one takes the CNN video seriously, I say quit being so brainwashed—because you are.

Here are just three of the many examples of how President Trump has encouraged violence:

1. The time he told a crowd to "Beat the crap out of them" (those not supporting Trump), and "I'll pay your legal fees."

2. He released a video showing someone that looks like him beating up someone from CNN.

3. He said, "My people are so loyal, even if I killed someone in the middle of Fifth Avenue they would still be with me."

It's bad enough the president encourages beating up others, but killing someone?

Again, to those that think no one takes this seriously, this is the president of the most powerful country in the world saying and doing this and setting an example. Just saying these types of things is bad enough, but there are weak-minded people that will actually take it seriously. Then there are the young children of the world, seeing the person in what was the most respected office on Earth beating up people and talking about how killing people is okay. If you think there is nothing wrong with this, there is no hope for you as a true American. You have become a fully brainwashed Trump "worshipper."

Trump says what he is doing is "making America great again." Only he can twist around something that is clearly wrong. If making America great again means beating up the media and killing someone on one of the busiest streets in the world, then he's not talking about the America millions have died for, he's talking about Trump's version of America. Those that would follow that path are *not* true Americans, but are true Trump worshippers.

If Trump continues to waste taxpayers' money while accomplishing little or nothing except for "We the Trumps" and does not change course, America will have some of its worst times under any president in its history. Luckily there are far truer, more dedicated Americans than those that have been brainwashed by Trump. They will eventually get America back on course.

There are those that say the Democrats will never admit defeat, that they will lie and cheat and do whatever it takes to go against Trump. Some even say the Democrats and media plan to get rid of Trump together. How ridiculous! I should not even be addressing this but I must, so the truth at least gets equal time to such biased statements.

First, in reality the Democrats should be very angry not because they lost, but because they didn't. They should be taking Trump's victory to court, for as I explained in the chapter about Hillary winning, the election was tainted and fixed in favor of Trump. If the situation were reversed, and the FBI had released information that hurt Trump at the eleventh hour, if there was information that Russia was favoring Hillary instead of Trump, etc., and especially if Trump had received almost 3 million more votes than Hillary, then knowing his ego the way I do and seeing how he reacts if he thinks he's been had, Trump would never, and I mean *never*, have acted as classy about losing the way Hillary did, including the way she attended his swearing in as president, saying we should all work together.

Instead, you can bet Trump would have a World War III–type reaction and probably want every electoral voter questioned for days. He would call the electoral system outdated, a thing from the past that should be thrown out, and demand that only the people's votes counted. Knowing him, he would get stacks of mail that looks like the almost 3 million votes cast for him over Hillary, saying, "These people wanted *me* for their president, not Hillary. I should be president."

We know how Hillary and the Democrats have acted after losing. It could be compared to a small water tower breaking apart and flooding a hundred homes. However, if Trump had lost and his party was in Hillary's position, it would be like the Hoover Dam breaking apart and flooding the entire city of Las Vegas.

Yet Trump actually won, and ever since he has not stopped complaining. He is actually trying to convince Americans that almost 3 million votes for Hillary are not valid. He wants all those millions of people's names, addresses, Social Security numbers, etc. He wants those millions recounted, and all this for someone who won and became president?

Additionally, saying the Democrats are out to get Trump, which is why they are not voting in favor of his healthcare programs, banning immigrants from certain countries, etc., is again ridiculous! Even some of Trump's own party are against these bills because they were not good for the country. These are true Americans!

The Democrats are not going to approve bills that are

bad for Americans just so they can't be accused of being upset about losing. Pure and simple—they were bad for Americans, so the Democrats nixed them.

Yes, my fellow Americans, this is the *truth*. Instead of spending time creating a healthcare program for Americans, after saying for years that Obamacare is a disaster, instead of trying to ban millions of innocent men, women and children and cause them terrible stress, health problems and even death, Trump spends 20 percent of his time playing golf, every morning sending out negative tweets, and even more time criticizing an election that made him president. This is the man running our country! This is the president of the greatest country on Earth. This is why seven months after being sworn in as president, Americans have no new, better healthcare program and why, despite his false claims that he's accomplished more than any other president, he has actually wasted millions more dollars during that time frame than any of the past six presidents.

Finally, it's totally ridiculous how Trump is trying to cast the media as unfair, biased, liars and fakes when it was the media that made the Trump name famous in the first place. It was the media that for decades reported on his real estate deals, what a genius businessman he was, how he's a giant in the real estate world, and on and on.

Yes, some media exposure in Trump's past was not so flattering, but it still helped make the Trump name famous, which led to him becoming wealthier.

Without the media, there would be no Trump to begin with. Then again, that's when the media reported what Trump *wanted* to hear. However, now the media is reporting what Trump *does not want to hear*, even though it's the truth!

Which countries have a leader who wants the media to report only what he *says* is the truth? One who wants the truth hidden or destroyed? Does the word *dictatorship* sound familiar?

I'll say it again—far too many have died to make this country the greatest country on Earth. The TRUTH can be bent and twisted but *never changed*. It is extremely and painfully obvious that Donald J. Trump is not qualified or fit to be the president of a country so many paid so dearly for. So many presidents have maintained the dignity, respectability and honor of the office of the president. They dedicated their lives doing all they could to help Americans and striving to give Americans a better life. They worked countless hours to achieve all they could for the country they loved. If you read each page carefully and list how Trump has been as the president of the United States, it will be very obvious he is like no other president in history, but in a negative way. It is obvious he has done all he could for his own self and his own ego. After all, what president flies around in the most expensive jet on Earth at his taxpayers' expense, NOT creating programs to help Americans, but to get away from the cold to go to sunny Florida, to go to rallies where the only thing accomplished is thousands cheering him on and building his ego. What president repays those that had so much faith and hope in him with LIES?

Keeping this in mind, America is extremely lucky to have the media we do. In working with hundreds of media groups or individuals over the past fifty years, I've found the majority (especially those from the major media groups) are dedicated, sincere and honest. They work tirelessly to make sure as much as they possibly can that they report the *facts*. The media reports undeniable facts, statements Trump himself makes and decisions Trump makes, many of which turn out to be bad for Trump because they are detrimental for Americans. Trump calls what the media reports "fake news" and tries to deceive Americans and the world and get them to believe only what he wants them to believe. Fortunately, even his own party, the Republicans, are finally seeing he's hurting the country and all Americans, so even they are starting to protect America against the injustices Trump would do by not agreeing with Trump in certain areas. I only hope they continue in this direction as true Americans, even if it means losing a Republican president. They must do the right thing and along with the Democrats and other government employees protect America and its people against anything that would hurt, damage or cause our country harm.

Trump can apply his usual "twist or bend the truth" tactics all he wants to the facts presented in this book. However, in the end the facts written herein are the truth and nothing but the truth, *so help me God*!

How Trump's Casinos Could Have Been Saved

The Super Bowl. The World Cup. The World Series! These are monster events celebrating the apogee of athletic achievement, and their grandiosity usually exceeds the crowning achievement they were meant to celebrate.

Gambling has been around since the beginning of humanity. The events we did for the Howard Hughes Casinos, Caesar's Palace, MGM and many other casinos (including Trump's) were very successful, so successful that, in fact, we had the longest running casino events in the history of legal gambling. Despite this unparalleled record of success, I spent years developing events that would be to gaming as the Super Bowl was to football.

Combining all that made us successful for decades, and with certain new features we developed, we'd created a series of events that would eclipse any casino events ever run, including our own. This is a series of events that, despite all that the casinos in the world have done trying to draw in guests and gamblers, would be something never attempted before.

Armed with forty years of experience producing hundreds of successful casino events for the Howard Hughes Casinos, Stardust, Imperial Palace, MGM and Caesar's Palace in Las Vegas, events in the Bahamas, New Orleans, Turks and Cacaos and Showboat, the next step was what I offered to Trump after I had proved myself at his Atlantic City casino by selling it out in the middle of winter and breaking all records for such events at that time of the year.

Entitled "The Triple Crown of Gaming," it had taken me years to create what would be the world's first "Super Bowl" of gaming. It would consist of a series of regional events that would boil down to three major events, one every three months. The Grand Finale/World Finals would be held at casinos where the champions of gaming would be crowned.

These events contained all the elements of success that for years allowed us to draw record numbers of guests and gamblers from throughout the world, plus many new features that if combined could have literally saved all three of Trump's casinos from closing down, something that put thousands of people out of work, not to mention dealing a major blow to his own financial empire and reputation.

For the first time in history, the world's most beautiful women, the world's top-rated gamblers and the world's top fashions would converge for the most exciting gala of its kind ever. It would entail a week's worth of gaming competitions, parties, dinner banquets and fun events that climax with the crowning of the "Triple Crown of Gaming" champions. The top prize money would be $1 million cash, determined in the end by twenty-one team finalists turning over their hands of blackjack all at the same time to determine the "Triple Crown World Champion."

Just imagine the suspense! The excitement and thrills of a year of competitions, a week of parties, fun events and team competitions (each team would consist of one top gambler and one Super Fashion contestant), and it all would come down to twenty-one teams and just one second for 1 million dollars. With this unique combination, the "Triple Crown of Gaming" would join the ranks of the world's super competition events. For Donald Trump, it could have literally saved his Atlantic City casinos.

Unfortunately, according to one of his top casino executives, Donald Trump was indifferent to the profits and prosperity that American Dream Entertainment injected into his casinos. "The Donald" was thinking with something other than his brain. "He only did your events so he could chase after your wife," his casino's exec let slip out.

Trump denies this, but in the end the truth floated to the top. I brought record-breaking crowds to his Atlantic City casinos in the dead of winter, but his tunnel vision was locked onto my wife.

What my company did for Donald Trump never cost him a nickel. I used his connections to get sponsors to pay for all of the events. In return, his casinos reaped hundreds of thousands or perhaps millions in profits. But rather than continue the events with the Triple Crown of Gaming series and enriching his casinos like never before possible, he chose to bail out of our contract and instead spent a small fortune on attorneys to defend himself in court.

Imagine, Trump had a series of events at his disposal that would not cost him a dollar, yet easily save thousands of Resort & Casino jobs, help boost the prestige of the Trump empire, and Trump's favorite thing—make him millions of dollars at all three of his Atlantic City casinos. Would this work? Since 1978 we had proved hundreds of times at some of the world's top casinos that our events sold out and produced millions in revenues. The Triple Crown events had ten times the drawing power, as did our American Dream events, so they would have delivered Trump's casinos record-breaking numbers, saving all three of his Atlantic City casinos.

Trump had two choices. As a good businessman, which of the two options below should he have chosen?

OPTION #1. Trump could keep his word, honor his agreement and continue on with the Triple Crown of Gaming events, which would not take any of his time, because American Dream Entertainment produced them 100 percent. Even American Dream's lesser events made resorts millions of dollars.

However, he had the option to hold the Triple Crown of Gaming series of events that would easily save thousands of jobs, help boost the prestige of the Trump empire and make him millions of dollars at all three of his Atlantic City casinos. OR …

OPTION #2. Go to court. Spend years of his valuable time in courtrooms. Pay high-priced attorneys tens of thousands of dollars, even if he prevailed.

Ninety-nine percent of the people we put this question to selected Option #1 (the 1 percent who selected Option #2 were strong Trump supporters). Yet the "genius businessman" Trump selected Option #2. In the end, he paid for all his attorneys' fees, all my attorneys' fees, all my costs, all his costs, plus spent two years going back and forth to court. And he's considered a smart businessman?

In court, he said he didn't want to do our events again because he'd lost money. If you have a large resort and casino, sell out every room, fill all the gambling tables and slot machines with people gambling their money away, fill restaurants to capacity, with even the gift shops doing record-breaking business, and you actually *lose* money, then you would have to be the world's worst businessman.

Does anyone reading this think it's a good business decision to spend years of your time in court and pay expensive lawyers, instead of making hundreds of thousands or millions of dollars with no effort on your part, by continuing events that had already proved themselves?

We gave him events that would not cost him a dollar because we would use his connections to get sponsors to pay for the events. In return, his casinos would reap hundreds of thousands, even millions in profit. However, rather than continue doing this, he spent two years in court spending large sums of money, not to mention wasting his valuable time and reputation, only to have to pay out much more in the end than he originally owed.

Having worked with me for decades creating sellout events throughout the world, all of my worldwide promoters agreed this would be a showstopper, a megawatt event like no other in the history of gaming. It could have easily been the salvation for Donald Trump's ailing casinos. Trump denies this, but in the end the truth came out. I brought record-breaking crowds to his Atlantic City casinos in the dead of winter, but his tunnel vision was locked on my wife.

Imagine, here he had a company with a proven history of decades of successful casino events that sold out his casino *in the dead of winter*, willing to prove to him we could turn his casinos away from all the red ink and into a sea of profits at no cost, but instead he was more interested in my wife than in keeping his three casinos solvent, or the thousands that were going to lose their jobs. This was told to me directly by one of his top executives, and in reality, the facts proved all of this anyway.

There is a moral to this story. Trump fancies himself as a shrewd businessman skilled in the art of the deal. But his obsession with my wife clouded what little business savvy he has. Eventually all his casinos went bankrupt while he wasted untold sums trying to beat me in court. You don't mix business with pleasure. It can be financially lethal, especially for Donald Trump.

By now Americans know that President Trump lies. He lied about President Obama's birth certificate. He lied about the size of the crowd that attended his inauguration. He lied about Trump Tower being wiretapped. Anything that reveals the real Trump must be covered up. But in my lawsuit against him, despite his throwing three of his top attorneys at me, despite corrupting my top employee and getting him to lie under oath, despite how he lied about everything he promised us, the truth was undeniable! So, in the end, the great Donald J. Trump lost.

The conclusion is, as Trump's executive told me, that he only sponsored the events to go after my wife. Of course, Trump denies anything that doesn't look good for him, but by now the country should know he covers up anything that shows the real man he is. In this case, the truth is undeniable. Even though Trump did not take advantage of my events that could've literally saved his casinos, now that this book is finished I plan on finding a resort and casino run by people with a keen business sense, and prove to the world that Donald Trump gave up what could've been one of the single most profitable and successful programs of his life, all because he thought chasing one married woman was more important. Please, always keep in mind—*this man is now running our country*.

Like anything he does that reflects poorly on himself, he will deny this. In Trump's world, there is no such thing as a failure—he's the champion at saying losing a business makes him money, and that bankruptcy is good for him because it allows him to avoid paying his thousands of employees. However, in the end the truth came out. After all, there was no reason on Earth for him not to continue doing our events at his casino. We brought in record-breaking crowds in the dead of winter, at a time of the year when the casino was normally empty, and yet we sold it out, something that had never happened before.

Without a doubt, Trump had nothing within any of his three casinos that could draw resort guests and gamblers in such large numbers and be as cost efficient as our events. Yet in court, he said he didn't want to do our events again because he'd *lost money*. As I mentioned earlier, if you have a large resort and casino, sell out every room you have, fill all the gambling tables and slot machines you have with people gambling their money away, fill restaurants to capacity, with even the gift shops doing record-breaking business and you actually *lose* money, then you would have to be the world's worst businessman. Do you really think Trump would admit that?

Now that my book is complete, I plan to take my "Triple Crown of Gaming" blueprint to a resort and casino that really does have good business sense. I intend to prove to Trump that what he had rejected could have been one of the most successful business endeavors of his life, and much more profitable than chasing women.

The Man Without a Conscience

Every day I thank God that in my very early years I grew up in a culture that nurtured priceless human qualities that neither time nor money could ever compromise.

I was a baby boomer who spent my early years in the railroad town of Altoona, Pennsylvania. It was a hard-working and loving community, a candid snapshot of life in post-WWII America.

We managed to survive without cell phones and computers, printers or fax machines. There were not a lot of fancy lawyers filing briefs in court because some slippery businessman had just stiffed a contractor. Back in Altoona, a man's word was his bond. That's the way I grew up and lived my life, which is why I've had the same business associates and friends for decades. Little did I know that one day I would be face-to-face with Donald Trump in situations few, if any, ever experience.

From Altoona, we moved around a lot but finally settled on Long Island, New York, when I was twelve. After years of being a musician, photographer, race car driver and night club owner, I cut my teeth in the field of marketing and public relations. I founded a company called American Dream Enterprises, and soon discovered I had a flair for doing PR for major companies, puffing up casinos and pulling in the high rollers. Because of this I ended up working with a lot of CEOs and billionaires.

Back in Altoona I learned that you didn't go into

business only to make money. You went into business because you were passionate about what you did. That is why I formed my company. I knew that if casino owners saw the zeal I brought to my work, the money would take care of itself.

Unfortunately, I had to work with some people who didn't have the same core values as I did. When you put certain major CEOs and billionaires under the microscope, you will see a viral strain of obsession and greed that courses through their blood and ignites a fever that only more money can quench. Power and money become their love, their passion and their life. As bad as I've seen power and money affect people, I've never seen anyone as cold as Donald J. Trump. He was not born with a silver spoon in his mouth, he was born with a golden spoon, and gold surrounding him. Since the day he was born he's never known what reality is because he has always gotten what he wanted, has never worried about paying for anything, and no one ever said NO to him, and if they did he would simply rid himself of them.

Working with him, I saw a person without any concern for his fellow man and especially women. He actually believes that unless you are wealthy you are a loser and far below *his* station in life.

At the events I produced for him, the things he did to the dozens of families who towed their priceless cars in a terrible snowstorm to give him a one-of-a-kind event proved he has no soul. Only such a person could treat such warm and caring families as though they should be happy just to be in his company. He used them for his selfish financial gain and then tossed them out like a bag of garbage. Trump would sell his soul if he could double his wealth. In fact, he already has many times. The bond of human trust, friendship and love does not exist in the world of Donald J. Trump. This is why he can never relate to 99 percent of Americans or people of the world, or why he can never be a fighter for We the People. He cannot relate in any manner or form to the hardworking, bill-paying family men or women of this world. I saw this again and again, over and over for years.

Much has been said about just how much of a genius Trump is when it comes to business, especially real estate. Much has also been said about having such a person that would understand the complexity of the greatest country in history. However, many thought his genius for business would somehow make him a good president. As it turns out, that's all wrong. Besides the fact that he's not a man for the people, he's *not* the great businessman he's been made out to be either.

Where I come from, success is measured by keeping a business operating, not by bankrupting it. Trump lost his multimillion-dollar yacht, his commercial airline, three major casinos, his interest in the Grand Hyatt (one of the jewels of his holdings), the New York Plaza Hotel (one of the most famous hotels in the world), many office and condo buildings and who knows what else. Is losing this many major businesses a success? Not where I come from. It's bad enough a real estate businessman is running the country, but he is one who has *lost* many major businesses.

As I said previously, I worked for a man in the Caribbean before he had made his first billion. I truly liked and cared about him. He was one of the nicest, most considerate and caring people I had ever met. He was fun to be around while I worked in an official capacity, and my wife Jill was his "gal Friday." She assisted him in both business and personal matters and tidied up some of the loose ends that come with running a resort and casino. She did it all for free because she considered him a friend, and *she delivered results*. Unfortunately, making billions totally changed him, and it was shocking. As much as he changed for the worse, Trump makes him look like a monk.

I recently ran into one of the car builders from the Atlantic City event I did for Trump. He was one of a few that never held what happened at the event against me because he was standing close to me when he heard Trump *order me* to allow the MC to take the information cards with him, which resulted in the automotive competition disaster. Despite this having happened decades ago, he was still extremely upset at Trump.

He said, "Me and my family always admired Trump, and I was so excited when you invited our family to enter our car in his auto design contest. We even gave up our vacation money, our first in five years, to enter it. But seeing what a cold, calculated and callous son of a bitch he was, we've hated him ever since. We still can't believe he's our president and hope our guys in Washington wise up and get rid of him before he causes a financial disaster, or, worse yet, starts World War III! After all, in a few months he's already caused more problems for us than any president I can remember in the forty-five years I've been following the presidency." Boy, was he still upset; I had no idea he was still so hot at Trump after all those years. This proves just how much it hurt him and his family. This is just one of the dozens of families that Trump hurt, and that's from only the automotive event.

President Trump would have us believe that he really cares about We the People, but that is nothing more than his own brand of snake oil and deception designed to advance his own personal agenda. If he really cared about We the Taxpayers he would not be blowing $26 million in just a matter of weeks out the tailpipes of Air Force One as he cruises down to sunny Florida. He would not have let his so-called wife live in another state, costing We the Taxpayers $140,000 *per day*. That's $140,000 for every day she lived away from her husband, making millions running her own business, while taxpayers paid untold millions while she stayed in New York. I ask every American, what could you do with $140,000? And that's *every day*.

If Trump really cared about We the People, he would not have wasted millions of taxpayers' dollars with unconstitutional travel bans on countries that had nothing to do with terrorism in our country, causing tremendous stress, suffering and grief to millions of immigrant men, women and children, while not even including Saudi Arabia, the country where almost every one of the 9/11 terrorists had citizenship. Saudi Arabia was Trump's first international destination as president, and they gave him a Gold Medal. Perhaps that was because he didn't include them in his travel ban.

Two plus two still equals four. Trump not banning Saudi Arabia = A Gold Medal and future real estate deals.

His assault on Planned Parenthood will prevent millions of women from obtaining badly needed services such as birth control and mammograms.

Many are still trying to figure out Trump. I did it years ago, He's power crazy. He will force his will on everyone he can even if it's bad for them. In just one hundred days he managed to ruin what took other presidents decades to build. America's reputation has suffered more of a setback than at any time in history. Countries are quickly losing what respect they had for America all because of one man, and because he has to have it his way. At the Inaugural Ball, as he danced with his distant wife, they played the song "My Way"—perfect!

Just as with the Paris climate agreement, like most everything else, Trump has not done a single day of research to see if it was in the best interests of America. He has not listened to the very people he put into position to advise him based on their research into the issue.

Even though America produces one-third of Earth's carbon footprint, Trump expects the rest of the world to pay for what we've created. It's no wonder the world continues to lose respect for America and its president. Even though every country on Earth except two support the climate agreement, he removed America from what is essentially the largest agreement of united countries in history.

He ignores the strong opinions of some of America's largest corporations who employ millions, advising him not to drop out. He even completely ignores American mayors pleading with him not to drop out.

By dropping out when 99.9 percent of the world stays

in, he's saying that England, France, Germany, Canada, Australia, Cuba, Mexico, North and South Korea—every country except Syria and Nicaragua—are "stupid" and have been duped. It's truly amazing how Trump, with zero experience, knows more than every other country in the world. If this does not prove what I've been saying all along, that right or wrong, Trump wants it his way no matter what, then I don't know what will.

Despite most of the world (including his own advisers) telling him *not* to drop out of the Paris climate accord, Trump uses nothing but his own personal opinion and pulls out. Knowing him the way I do, no matter who he hurts or whether or not he's wrong, he just does not care. This is the undeniable sign of a *man without a conscience.*

PROOF DONALD TRUMP LIVES IN HIS OWN WORLD

Trump said, "We don't want other countries laughing at us anymore." This proves he lives in his own world and in his own mind. When I was growing up and until now, like many Americans, I looked up to the president as one of the most honorable men in the world. Additionally, until now the president of the United States was the most respected office in the world. However, in just a few months, Trump turned the title of president of the United States of America, a title that took hundreds of years to gain respect throughout the world, into what countries are now calling "The Office of a Clown" and "A Liar," a president that "cannot be trusted" and many other similar such titles I've listed in the book. My fellow

Americans, I don't know about you, but I hate thinking of all those who died for our freedom, and the fact that one man is tarnishing the image of the country for which they gave their lives.

To be clear, these are *not* titles I've put on Trump. They are titles with which the world has branded him. My titles for Trump that I've written throughout this book are titles the world is finally seeing, the ones I saw years ago. As I said previously, I have businessmen and women I've been working with since the 1960s. These are men and women that are highly respected in their own countries. They have reported in their media that Trump is becoming the most disrespected American president in the history of their own countries. This is a fact, not just their opinion, it's a fact that will go down in history. Just one man has disrupted and in many cases destroyed what took hundreds of millions of dedicated, hardworking Americans decades to build. Imagine, just one man literally setting America back a hundred years.

Do we now have a dictator for a President?

In Trump's mind, that is what he is and has been his entire life, as, prior to becoming president, people around him did what he wanted, like it or not, whether they were right and he was wrong or not, his decision was final or he removed you from his world.

However, thank God that even though he has so much power as president, Americans will not just stand by and allow him to destroy what's taken centuries to create. He can no longer rule as he once did in his own world. He's now in a world created by hundreds of millions who gave their all to create this great country, millions who gave their lives so others could live in a free country devoid of those who would impose their will on them, although I am amazed that Americans still don't see right through Trump and call for his impeachment. Many still don't see that he is devoid of any ability to relate to 99.9 percent of the people of this Earth. However, it's only a matter of time before most Americans finally see right through him and finally see the "real" Donald Trump.

How much damage does he have to do to America and its people before he's stopped? Just because he has the title of president does not make Trump a god and does not give him the right to destroy what past presidents took decades to create for all Americans.

When London fell victim to another terrorist attack, Trump, who's supposed to represent the best in America, actually insulted the mayor of London. Imagine how heartless it is to go after the mayor of a city who just had his people murdered? It's like going to a funeral and insulting the family who just lost their children. Imagine if the prime minister of the United Kingdom insulted the mayor of New York City on September 11, 2001. We would have been furious, especially since we are supposed to be allies. Many people found it totally unbelievable that our president could do such a thing. Not me. It's just more undeniable proof, more reason than ever, that this man should *not* be president of the United States. He's ruining it for all Americans, and if you don't think the same, then you are not really looking at the truth about Donald Trump.

Many are saying this is a new country now, run Trump's way, so we may as well get used to it. First, where was the American Congress and Senate? Is this now a dictatorship? Both Houses of Congress need to take another look at the powers the president has. How is it that, with hundreds of millions of people in America, one man can tell an entire nation how it will be ruled?

I may not have the money he has because my father was a hardworking American, who along with my mother raised five children and could not give me millions of dollars and major business contacts like Trump got, but despite that I would not trade a man like my father for a *thousand* Trumps. Furthermore, like most hardworking, dedicated Americans, I never put thousands of people out of work or failed to pay hardworking people who had done work for me, for which they were rightfully owed, by declaring bankruptcy! I never sexually harassed another man's wife, or any woman. I never lied in court after swearing to tell the truth. My wife lives with me, no matter where my business takes me, and she holds my hand wherever we go, every day. Most important of all, she married me for love, not because I was insanely wealthy. These are all the things Donald J. Trump does not have because they are the things that all the money in the world cannot buy.

What an image for the president to have—a wife that did not live with her husband for months when he became president, and many times won't even hold his hand. The president of the United States, someone the world looks up to, did not even *live with his wife for months*. That is one of the worst possible images for our country's children to witness. How many American wives, if their husband became president, would not rush to their husband's side from day one? Then again, most men marry their wives because they *love* them, not just because they're beautiful in a physical way. Let's face it, it's very obvious that if Trump's wife was not physically beautiful, he never would have married her. If Trump was not super-wealthy, she would never have married him. A marriage made of money and physical looks is not a good image for our children.

Finally, on a personal note that does reflect on Trump as the president, like most people I'm not wealthy. Because of this, Trump called me a "loser" to my wife (using it to try and demean me just so he could sleep with her). I hope I'm that kind of "loser" for the rest of my life. There is nothing that can bring happiness more than being loved, but then again that's because I have a conscience. Without one, love does not exist.

Trump's First International Trip (Trump First, America Second)

SAUDI ARABIA

Trump received a Gold Medal from Saudi Arabia, a super-wealthy country that he did not have placed on his banned list, despite the fact that fifteen out of the nineteen terrorists from 9/11 were citizens of that country, while no terrorist from that fateful day—not a single one—came from any of the countries he *did* put on that list. Is it any wonder they gave him a medal?

Why did he make that country his first stop on his very first trip abroad as president? As he once said to me, "Since my time is so valuable I spend it first with those who I can turn into future business."

With hundreds of billions of dollars in business up for grabs in Saudi Arabia, every major businessman in the world would love to have had a personal audience with top Saudi government officials and have them roll out the red carpet like they did for Trump. Furthermore, there was no reason his daughter should have been there except to line things up for future business for the Trump name. This is just one of many trips We the People will pay for as Trump lines up future business for himself and his family.

MORE JOBS AND MONEY FOR AMERICA

Trump said he's responsible for a 100-billion-dollar arms deal with Saudi Arabia. Again, he is taking credit for something *he did not do*. That deal would have happened no matter who went there. Does anyone really believe such a complex deal worth $100 billion was put together in the one day when Trump was there, especially with all the activities planned? I would bet the Saudis took months to put together that deal for 100 billion dollars' worth of complex military equipment, well before Trump even became president.

Part of Trump's deal is that America will be teaching Saudi Arabia how to produce the same equipment that they are now buying from us. How is it a great business deal to show one of your best buyers how to produce what they buy from you, so they no longer have to buy from you again?

The worst part is Trump is giving away American intelligence and knowledge that took us decades to gain at a cost of billions—*for free*! Now do you still think he made us such a great deal? We got a deal we would have gotten anyway, only in a few years they will not need us anymore because they will be producing their own, all thanks to Trump.

NATO

In front of the entire NATO membership and the world, Trump scolded NATO members for not paying what they owe, saying that America pays what it owes while others do not. Here Trump tries to make himself look good and receive credit for bringing it to the attention of the American taxpayers, pointing out that certain countries are not paying their fair share. Of course, he *should* bring to their attention the fact that Americans are paying their end but others are not, but certainly not *in front of the entire world.*

To get along with other countries, one must be diplomatic, not scold them like they're children. How embarrassing it must have been for NATO members, as the United States told them they are not paying their bills. This should have been done in a more diplomatic and discrete way, not one that embarrasses the representatives of countries that are our allies. Here Trump had a chance to show that he can be presidential. Instead he displayed his usual arrogance, scolding other countries he should be getting along with. Despite this, he claimed he "did good" with NATO.

He then returned home, claiming what a great trip it was, and it certainly must have been—for him! He planted the seeds for the Trump family to work with one of the wealthiest countries in the world. Mark my words, in the future you will see Trump's name in Saudi Arabia, all thanks to We the Taxpayers.

The Trump Family Kleptocracy

America is a country whose strength and character are defined by its courage and determination to survive crises. Somehow it gathered up the will to survive a bloody, fratricidal Civil War. Seventy years ago, it led a universal struggle against the spread of Adolph Hitler's ruthless fascist aggression. And when President Richard Nixon abused the power of his office, Americans rose up and tossed him out of the White House.

Today, Americans face a new governmental crisis—one of nepotism and incompetence. Trump was an outlier who, despite the fact he had absolutely no experience at even running a small city much less an entire country, somehow managed to weasel his way into the White House through an extremely outdated voting system, hijacking his own country and turning it into a kleptocracy littered with family members and millionaire cronies. For those who may not know what a kleptocracy is, it's when those high up in the government enrich themselves at the cost of their own people. Trump himself has made sure his daughter and son-in-law benefit from his presidency. In short, using our tax dollars, Trump and his family will use America's powerful status among world leaders to enrich themselves in ways they never could before. After Trump and his family leave the White House they will have created a lifetime of contacts that was only made possible using his office, because without being President of the United States no person on Earth could collect the type of contacts Trump's family will have.

To those that say they don't care if they make contacts, I say We the People should care very much because instead of working for the people, those contacts were made at the taxpayers' expense and will turn into billions of dollars in profit for the Trump family.

The new administration stumbled right out of the gate. President Trump's travel ban was issued twice and shot down twice by federal courts. After seven months, his American healthcare Act still does not exist, leaving Americans with a healthcare plan that Trump calls a "disaster." The Trump administration was labeled "Amateur Hour at the White House" and "The Gang That Couldn't Shoot Straight."

During his presidential campaign, Trump boasted that he likes being unpredictable, but now most Americans see him as being unhinged. He has elevated his daughter Ivanka and son-in-law Jared Kushner to key cabinet positions with responsibilities at the White House despite the fact that they have no experience or skills at all in politics or government.

Imagine how the men and women in Washington feel, those who have dedicated their lives to serve the people, when Trump's two family members take over government jobs. Not having served one day in public office nor having any knowledge about serving We the People, they are immediately elevated higher than all as key advisors to the president. This is the highest form of insult to those who have dedicated their lives to better their country.

President Trump does not like to shoulder the blame for failure. When Navy Seal Ryan Owens was killed in a botched raid in Yemen, Trump tried to shift the blame from himself to his generals. Now when there is a flub, he has the option of shifting the onus to others, including his daughter or son-in-law.

It is a big leap of faith to think that Ivanka Trump, a child of privilege, can transfer her expertise of high heels and wraparound skirts to solve the crucial domestic issues of Chicago gang wars, cyber-crime, and health-care. No one would pardon Bernie Madoff and put him in charge of the Treasury Department. So why is a fashion queen holding the reins that steer critical domestic decisions?

Ivanka's husband, Jared Kushner, emerged from his father-in-law's presidential campaign as America's newest wunderkind. Laboring in the shadows, the New York real estate scion called the shots that produced the greatest presidential election shocker in United States history.

The vexing problem of Israeli-Palestinian relations has been a pebble in the shoe of every administration for the past seventy years. Not even Henry Kissinger could craft a solution. Yet with no international political experience, Kushner became his father-in-law's point man for forging a new policy of peace—a daunting challenge for any experienced person, it's just crazy for a thirty-something rookie still wet behind the ears.

If President Trump wished to seek peace between Israelis and Palestinians he could easily enlist the services of former diplomats like Colin Powell or Condoleezza Rice—not his own inexperienced family.

The logical choice to broker an Israeli-Palestinian peace would be Trump's Secretary of State Rex Tillerson, but America's top diplomat seems to be playing second fiddle to Trump's own son-in-law.

When Secretary Tillerson spoke on the situation in North Korea, he left reporters in a fog about the administration's policy toward that rogue nation. "North Korea launched yet another intermediate range ballistic missile," he stated. "The United States has spoken enough about North Korea. We have no further comment."

If that comment to the press was murky, no one knows how North Korea's President Kim Jong-un might have taken it.

Later, Tillerson left this quote dangling in front of a bewildered media: "I think ... the longer-term status of President Assad will be decided by the Syrian people."

Syria's president may have seen that as a sign of American hands-off policy toward his country. A few days later he launched a sarin gas attack that killed dozens of women and children. Were the careless words of an incompetent American diplomat the basis for that attack? Most likely the answer is yes!

Above all, Jared Kushner and Rex Tillerson are businessmen. The diplomatic contacts they've made will help Kushner sell the Trump brand, and Tillerson is Exxon's inside man at the State Department. Their first obligation is to their sires in the corporate world, *not* to the American people.

There was one item in the Kushner portfolio that must be bouncing around like a ping-pong ball in the mind of America's newest boy wonder. It's the Kushner

Companies' skyscraper at 666 Fifth Avenue in Manhattan, which is draining the Kushner family war chest. Rental income from the building can't keep up with its debt payments, and Kushner Companies have abandoned negotiations for a bailout with Anbang Insurance Group of China.

Kushner sold his interest in the family property when he left for his gig at the White House, but blood is thicker than water. Even a clever Harvard graduate like himself must have had great difficulty trying to divorce himself from the family business's attempts to salvage New York City's most expensive patch of real estate.

Like our intelligence agencies, the United States Department of State is a vital organ of our country's defense posture, yet it seems President Trump feels he and his next-of-kin cabinet, without a single day's experience, can function just as well without it.

Kushner definitely appears to be our new president's full-time consigliore. His first assignment from his father-in-law president was to head up the newly minted Office of American Innovation, a guise for Trump's vendetta to dismantle the federal government.

The United States of America has evolved into such a great country because it is a nation of laws that generate bureaucratic infrastructure. That bureaucratic infrastructure is the steel bar that anchors the strength of a great nation. President Trump thinks he and his cabinet of the top 2 percent can demolish that infrastructure, just like the wrecking ball that demolished Trump's World's Fair Casino in Atlantic City.

Trump wants the country to think his daughter and son-in-law are doing Americans a big favor by working for free. Perhaps the only thing more shocking than Donald Trump's victory in the last presidential election is the naiveté of his base. They seem to think that bringing his daughter Ivanka onboard to work for free is a noble act of selfless patriotism. Nothing could be further from the truth.

Ivanka does not have a lick of experience in the world of government and politics. She would not know a filibuster from a pair of designer high heels. Yet there she is in the White House, formulating domestic policy and who knows what else.

She joins her husband Jared Kushner and a staff of multimillionaires that make up the most well-heeled cabinet in the history of our nation. Ivanka and her husband Jared were weaned in a world of wealth and privilege. Even now as parents they are freed from the angst of making a monthly mortgage payment and providing food and healthcare for their kids.

America's premier power couple are rookies in the high impact world of domestic and international politics. But are they really there to serve the people, or have they come to Washington for some other clandestine reason?

Over the years, I have dealt with more than a few billionaires and learned one very important lesson: In business, it's not what you know but *who you know*!

A job applicant can be extremely qualified and well educated, a superior candidate for the position, but will get nowhere unless he has a direct pipeline to the man at the top. It's all in who you know!

Years ago, I worked for a billionaire who would always bring his young son to important business meetings with his top executives. I asked him why he did it. "I want him to get to know these people and for these people to get to know him," was his response. "Down the road this will lead to more business for my company."

I don't like to lean on my own horn, but over the years I've gotten pretty good at promoting casinos. I know how to entice the high rollers to come to the tables. For years, I courted the favor of a particular casino magnate, but I could never seal the deal because I could never talk to him in person. I was always relegated to dealing with his surrogates.

But fate dealt me a winning hand at last. I had a chance meeting with this man and convinced him that his casinos could do better. He gave me a shot and it paid off in spades. For many happy years, we were both rolling in the chips.

Another wealthy person I worked for once sent his daughter to work for a competing company under her married name. She labored there incognito for over four years and built up a string of contacts that brought added business to his company, one that would someday be hers.

Presiding over her own fashion line or her father's International Hotel in Washington, D.C. is small potatoes when stacked up against the exclusive access Ivanka and her husband will have when world leaders traipse into he White House and Mar-a-Lago.

It is no secret that the Trump Empire includes real estate interests in China. When Chinese President Xi Jinping came calling I don't think he and Ivanka discussed the price of tea.

China is the second largest economy on the planet, and since the government owns all real estate in China, it will be virtually impossible for Ivanka and her father to separate their official government duties from their private business interests.

Even before his father-in-law was elected president, Jared Kushner was entertaining executives from Anbang Insurance Group, a Chinese firm willing to invest billions in Kushner Companies' flagship building at 666 Fifth Avenue in Manhattan.

It is also worth noting that neither Ivanka nor Jared Kushner ever liquidated the assets they have in their companies. Yet Trump somehow convinced his followers that he was the right choice for president and has sold them on the notion that his daughter and her husband are working for free!

Ivanka and Jared might be working pro bono, but you can bet the farm that they are racking up a slew of political and business capital. In financial parlance, you might call it a gilded package of deferred compensation—a portfolio worth billions when the Trump family eventually leaves the White House.

However, as bad as this is for the American people, worse is that the leader of America did not have a single day of experience running any kind of political office prior to becoming president, yet now he's running the most powerful office in the world. Add to this the fact that no one in his family has a single day's experience either, and yet they are the ones advising him. It is truly the blind leading the blind. Now Americans not only have a totally inexperienced president, but a president with inexperienced advisers. It's like an Indy 500 driver and his crew who've never been in a race competing against forty other drivers with many years of experience. Just imagine what a disaster that would be. That's what America now faces.

Do you still feel that Trump should be the president of a country built on the lives of the millions who have died serving their country?

Trump is not the wealthiest man in the world, not even in America, but he sees the White House as a personal force multiplier that could bring in riches never before possible until he became president. He is using the taxpayers as a stepping stone to amass an even bigger fortune for himself and his family.

It makes me cringe when I think how We the Taxpayers are handing to President Donald Trump and his family a Rolodex of the world's most powerful politicians and entrepreneurs. Trump is a man of divided loyalty. Knowing him as I do, he will use the power of his office to promote his own agenda and not the welfare of We the People. He already proved that making connections for his family after being president for seven months is more important than the healthcare he *promised* Americans again and again.

The wealthy businessmen I have known in my life all have an insatiable lust for more money. When one of them told me that he had eclipsed the billion-dollar plateau, I told him he could now relax, that he had it made. "Relax? Are you kidding me?" was his response. "Now it's on to making 2 billion!" After he had passed the 3-billion-dollar milestone, he simply set his sights on 4. Trump is no different, in fact he is far worse, putting his own agenda before his country.

To the super-wealthy, it is almost like a burning fever they can never extinguish. They don't know how much is enough and when to quit. For President Donald Trump, the fever will never cool until he maximizes the leverage of his office for his own personal gain and that of his family.

If anyone out there thinks that Trump is putting his family to work for free, they need to think again. I saw enough of Trump to know that he and his family come first, and he is playing America like a fine violin. He is doing what is good for the Trump name and not what is good for We the People.

Yes, certain other presidents may have put their families to work at the White House, but those were the days when our country was still being built, and they were never in such high positions as those Trump has put his family in. No past president has ever had the tremendous amount of business interests throughout the world as does Trump and his family. When it came to the American people, those who served before actually had a conscience.

What Trump Is Costing
We the Taxpayers

Imagine, even before he was sworn in as president, Donald Trump had cost taxpayers more money than any other president in United States history.

How is that possible? Simple—the security around him at his office and living quarters in New York City costs a ridiculous amount of money per day. We're not talking hundreds of thousands, we're talking *millions* of dollars, and that's before he's even been sworn into office. Even worse, Trump said he planned on "returning often" to his homes in New York and Florida, which he does, wasting millions in taxpayers' money like no other president before him.

Why do you think he would do this, when any other American would consider it the greatest honor of their life to call the White House their home, and live there as much as possible? After all, he could live in his Trump Tower penthouse and Florida mansion all he wants after his term. The answer is simple, and he will deny it all he wants, but he will return home often because that's where his business is, and you can bet he is going to do business that has nothing to do with our country while he is at home. Additionally, the more he stays at his Florida mansion, the more media exposure it gets, the more famous it gets, and the more he can charge for his Mar-a-Largo club memberships. After returning to his Florida mansion in Air Force One every week- end for seven weeks, he received so much publicity he was able to raise the cost of the membership in his club there from $100,000 per person to $200,000 and he sold out memberships, making him millions. The cost to We the Taxpayers—over $26 million, just so Trump could go home every weekend to get away from the cold winter weather.

Besides the fact that it's an insult to the office of the president to not want to stay at the White House the way other presidents have, while in his offices in New York, he will cost We the Taxpayers hundreds of millions of dollars in security, while he conducts personal business that will make him wealthier than he ever could have been without the presidency.

If you were elected president of the United States, would you want to return home often, especially know- ing it would cost the taxpayers hundreds of millions of dollars, besides disrupting the daily life of thousands of Floridians and New Yorkers? Anyone who would do that obviously doesn't really care about how much money hardworking Americans pay in taxes for their security that while in the White House would cost a fraction of what it costs while in their personal home. With that in mind, there's obviously an ulterior motive here. Why would any president waste taxpayers' money with ridic- ulous amounts of security so he can go home, when he has the White House, with its history and the honor that comes with living there? As I said it's obvious, and he will deny it all he wants, but I guarantee you he will be conducting business—personal business—that will make him even more wealthy after he leaves office.

Of course, any president is entitled to return home for holidays, but any president that cares about We the People, who cares how much will be wasted in security that could be saved if he was in the White House, would keep his visits to home at a minimum or travel to destinations on vacation where security will not be prohibitive in cost.

One thing I learned about Donald Trump, which he proved without any doubt, is that he always comes first. What he wants is the most important thing to him, no matter what the consequences are for others. What he did to the thousands of people he hurt during the Donald Trump American Dream events didn't bother him one bit because he had to have it *his way*.

I got together with someone who is excellent at numbers, and we did a rough estimate on the cost of his security in New York, and if he returned home X amount of times more than the past three presidents. Why the past three? Because the value of the dollar during their terms and figuring for inflation gave us a more accurate figure. Here is what we found.

At the end of Trump's term, each American family should have been $75,000 wealthier and individuals $50,000 wealthier than what they normally earn. That is what it will cost We the People in security, while he conducts his personal business, and that is just the cost of additional security, which no previous president has ever had or needed.

The Healthcare Crisis

Vice President Pence has said, "Trump is a man of his word."

If ever there was a lie, this is it. By his saying this, it shows that Trump's followers are part of a cult, not actual politicians.

THE TRUTH ABOUT OBAMACARE

Trump's and Pence's top priority is to repeal the Affordable Care Act, known commonly as Obamacare. Imagine, with ISIS killing innocent people day in and day out, North Korea threatening nuclear warheads that could reach the USA and all of the other serious problems America faces, President Trump's top priority is depriving Americans of their healthcare. He is attempting to take away the only help many people have ever had when it comes to their health, without a better plan to replace it. His attempt at eliminating 3 million jobs in the healthcare sector and taking away the only healthcare available to over 20 million Americans is even more proof that Trump has no conscience.

One of the main things that affects one's life and all those around them is their health. This is something that affects us all, yet many have to suffer needlessly, worry needlessly and even die needlessly because they have little or no healthcare or cannot afford what they really need when it comes to healthcare.

People as wealthy as Trump have no clue what it's like to not have the best healthcare available to them. They can't fathom what it's like wondering how you're going to pay for your medicine, or what it's like to stay sick because you can't afford medication, the right doctor or any doctor at all.

I doubt very much if Trump has ever even read the Affordable Care Act. Most of his comments come from his head or from comments he's heard from others, *not* from facts that any responsible person (most especially the president of the United States) should base his comments on.

A true, good leader of any country would put that which is most important to the people *first*. He or she must prioritize those issues that would affect the people of that country, focusing on what will help the people the most and then proceed, not simply take away the only healthcare that 20 million Americans have.

So far, Trump and his administration have gone back on most of their campaign promises.

Does Obamacare have problems? Yes, of course it does. However, Obama had to create the most complex system that any president had ever attempted. Anything created that is a first of its kind and so complex is bound to have bugs to work out. When NASA built the space shuttle, did it work perfectly from the start? Of course not, in fact, people died to get it running properly.

Obama did what no other president had ever done. He knew it would not be perfect, and that it would take time to find the problems it had and to fix them. Unfortunately, he was not our president long enough to find out what was wrong. However, Trump saying it is a disaster is another of his smoke screens. Now he says he will build a better healthcare system. As usual, he will take credit for something Obama did, because if it were not for Obamacare, Trump and his party would have had no idea what problems they would face. Trump had it easy because, thanks to Obamacare, they know what works and what doesn't. It's far easier to build a better healthcare system than starting from the very beginning.

Imagine if NASA had been able to take over the space shuttle after another organization had built it, flown missions and then had people die from a small yet fatal mistake in an O-ring? Of course, they could have then built a better space shuttle because they would have known what problems to face and been able to fix them for far less money and time than the party that had built the shuttle in the first place. Sound familiar?

Despite the Republican party and President Trump knowing what problems to face (thanks to President Obama getting his healthcare system going), they had over *six years* to work on something better, yet to date they have not presented anything better to replace Obamacare.

Obama has been the only president to give healthcare to Americans that have preexisting conditions. Keep in mind that reaching millions of people in one of the most complex programs in United States history is a major undertaking, so it was bound to have problems out of the gate. However, like starting anything new, especially something as large and complex as Obamacare, there are bound to be problems and issues that must be corrected. I'm sure if President Obama had been around another year or two he would have addressed those problems and corrected them.

Clearly, some parts of Obamacare work, or there wouldn't be people living today that would have died without health insurance. There are also many people that would be far sicker if not for Obamacare. Even my son, who's in sixth grade, said, "Daddy, why is Trump saying Obamacare is bad when it helped so many people?" Even a sixth grader figured it out—it's easier to build something better when you know what went wrong before.

In the end, no matter what Trump does, it will be an extension of Obamacare. No matter what it's called, without Obamacare to begin with there may not have been any national healthcare at all. Donald Trump, with literally no experience in Washington, would have had far more trouble trying to introduce a new national healthcare, which seven previous presidents tried but could not accomplish.

It is obvious Trump and his people never did their homework about Obamacare because if they had, they would have had a backup plan that would work immediately. They already knew what worked and what didn't.

Trump acts like Obama spent a few days throwing together a healthcare program. Obama and his people spent years and countless hours developing it. Maybe it isn't perfect, but anything that big and complex is always hard to implement at first. Whatever Trump does, he will never be able to take away the fact that Obama gave millions of people the relief and support they never had before. Whatever Trump does will just be an extension of Obamacare because Obama was the pioneer of national healthcare in the United States.

As I've said many times, Trump is an egotistical man without a conscience, and except for himself and his family, he does not care in the least about others. This was once again proven by his attack on Obamacare, something that this country has needed for centuries, a program that despite its flaws has helped millions of people, and yet Trump could not care less and is constantly criticizing it.

If Trump was a man with a conscience and possessed any class at all, he would give credit to Obama for creating the country's first national healthcare system and doing what no others before Obama could do. He would admit that Obamacare has helped millions, given millions more jobs and paved the way for whatever comes next.

Throughout his entire life, Trump has lived like a king, a living god, and he hasn't the faintest idea what it's like not to have good healthcare or have to worry about paying for healthcare.

Again, no matter what he does concerning healthcare, he should give credit to Obama and try to improve it, not erase all the good Obamacare has done. However, that's not how Trump's mind works. A Trump trait is taking credit for what *others* have done.

Seven months into his term, there is *still* no new healthcare plan. It was just another lie—one in a long list of broken promises from Donald J. Trump.

SOLVING THE HEALTHCARE CRISIS

All of the time and money being wasted trying to fix the healthcare crisis shows poor leadership. Logically, since money is the main issue, everything must be done to save it when possible.

If you have a home where the roof is leaking, there are electrical problems or other issues, do you spend a small fortune to tear the entire house down? Do you clear the land to build a new one? Not if you're smart, you don't. Logically, you *fix* the problems. How? First, find out from doctors, hospitals and from citizens that have used Obamacare what the main problems are. It's doubtful that whatever isn't working can't be repaired or replaced. Of course, due to Trump's massive ego combined with the fact that he has no conscience, he creates excuses about why Obamacare will not work.

However, logic dictates that unless something is burned to the ground or tainted with radiation, it can be fixed. There could be a solution to fixing Obamacare with doctors, hospitals, insurance companies *and* patients all having a say in what needs fixing and how to go about it, while also saving millions in the process, so the billions the taxpayers already spent on it is not wasted. However, Trump will not stand for a healthcare program with a black president's name on it, and he wants *his* name on it because it fortifies his brand name around the world.

Whether it's healthcare or any other issue Americans face, the main problem is usually having enough money to do what is needed. So where will the money come from? Regarding healthcare, just a few possible logical solutions include:

1. Create a new law limiting the use of Air Force One to only important and necessary business for America. Right there, I guarantee you there will be well over $200 million more for healthcare in just two months. President Trump spent over $26 million in just a few months going to and from his home in Florida on weekends.

2. Don't build a border wall that will be useless. That's another $25 billion out of the Federal budget that could be added to healthcare.

3. Rethink our fiscal priorities. What's more important right now, exploring Mars or providing healthcare to all American families? Add billions more.

4. We already have a very strong military. There is such a thing as overkill. Therefore, add what we absolutely need, but do not overspend like Trump wants to do. That adds billions more to Americans' healthcare.

All the above will not only help fix Obamacare, but give Americans the best healthcare ever by finally insuring them all.

Trump will, of course, say this is ridiculous because it's not *his* plan, and also because he does not want Obama to have his name attached to it. It will forever disturb Trump that he could not get Obama removed as resident by continually stating that Obama was not born in the United States.

The above are just a few examples, but there are many other areas of government spending that could be explored. This is a totally logical approach to solving the healthcare problem, which involves research, not simply throwing away a program that took years and cost billions and then starting all over again. Besides the extra costs involved by starting over, there will be areas that don't work, just like when Obamacare was rolled out, that will waste billions to fix, and in the meantime tens of millions of Americans will once again be without healthcare, leading to more Americans dying.

If Congress would look at this very carefully, they could create the finest healthcare program in American history in a matter of three months. With so much fighting going on between the political parties, this would show the world that the United States remains united! However, this is next to impossible with a president that operates by his opinion rather than through research and facts, and who allows his personal feelings to get in the way of what's best for all Americans. After all, he and his family have the best healthcare in the world and they don't have to worry about the ridiculous cost of medicine. He's in no real hurry, that's why he played golf so many times, went to his Florida mansion so many times, flew to the areas that had the most supporters so many times, so they could cheer him on, all costing taxpayers millions and wasting presidential time that would have been far better spent on fixing Americans' healthcare. Isn't anyone wondering what happened to Trump's promise that "I'm going to work my ass off?" As I said, Trump's in no hurry—he's got better things to do.

YET ANOTHER BROKEN PROMISE

President Trump promised he would help bring down the ultra-high price of prescription medication. So far not a single thing has been done about this. The following is proof of how ridiculous the price of medicine is, something I've experienced firsthand.

I've been fighting injuries from a bad auto accident. When I was stopped at a stop sign, someone talking on their phone hit me hard from behind. If that was not bad enough, I also developed cancer. The cancer pain became so bad that nothing, not morphine or even the strongest oxycodone helped. Only a medicine called Subsys kept me out of the emergency room. It consists not of a new miracle drug, but a sublingual form of Fentanyl, a drug that has been around for decades. A one month's supply costs over $16,000, a year's supply over $190,000. Sound impossible? You read it right—and here is a copy of the prescription to prove it:

Ira's Pharmacy

Pinewood square
6338 Lantana Rd., Ste. 5253
Lake Worth, FL 33463
561-353-1292 • 888-262-3978 • Fax 561-353-1293

TAX RECEIPT

RX # 2006768

06/27/17

HOURANEY, WILLIAM
XXXXX XXXXX XXXXXXXXXXX DRXXX AMOUNT 16246.60
XXXXX XXXXXXX XXXX XXXXXXXXXX YOU PAY   812.33
SUBSYS 600 MCG SPRAY   INS PAYSXXXXXXXX

120 SPR
ORG DT-06/27/17
20482-0006-30

1717835190870 3

Not even my insurance company's representatives had ever heard of a prescription medication that expensive. If one is lucky enough to have insurance, a co-pay alone is over $800 per month, or about $10,000 per year. When you receive just $14,000 from Social Security and one single important medicine costs $10,000, how are you to live?

This is only one of the medications I need, so combined with the others, the cost is so high that I have to do without the Subsys at times because I can't possibly afford it. Without Subsys, the pain gets so extreme that my normally good blood pressure goes into the "danger of heart attack" zone, and my wife has to call an ambulance. This then ties up an ambulance and paramedics, an ER and all the nurses and doctors, all because the price of one medication is completely ridiculous.

Of course, this is just one example, and although most medications are not this costly, they may as well be for those with limited income and little or no insurance. This is one very important area that Trump said he would address, yet, like everything else, he has not done a thing about the crazy high price of prescription medication. Then again, neither Trump nor his family has to worry about this—they have the best healthcare in the world and can easily afford anything it does not cover. This is just more proof that Trump is not helping Americans in the areas where they really need it the most.

WHAT IS TRUMP DOING ABOUT THE BILLIONS BEING WASTED IN AFGHANISTAN?

First, I must be honest. Trump is not the first president wasting billions of our tax dollars fighting a war that will never be won in Afghanistan. In fact this has been the longest war in American history, lasting over sixteen years so far. Sounds terrible doesn't it? Well it's far worse than this.

So far our government, which GETS PAID BY US and LACKS THE BEST HEALTHCARE AND SCHOOLS FOR OUR FAMILIES, ETC., from our tax dollars has spent over 685 BILLION DOLLARS in Afghanistan alone. Here we are trying to get decent healthcare for our families but cannot because there is not enough money to pay for a good healthcare plan while twenty times—got that twenty times—what we need for healthcare for our families has already been spent in Afghanistan, with nothing really accomplished for all these billions We the Taxpayers have paid.

What's amazing is why on Earth are we fighting this war with ground military, which dates back to World War I and II, when we have fighter jets, drones, missiles and rockets that would be far more effective, cost a fraction of what we are spending, plus save lives? Also why after over sixteen years are we even still there?

Trump has talked a lot about America first. Why do our hardworking Husbands, Mothers, and children have to suffer without good medical care and other important things while we spend billions in Afghanistan?

As much as I believe Obama was a good president,

he was not a great one because he allowed this to go on. He allowed his fellow Americans to go without the best healthcare while billions are basically wasted over there.

Now the ball is in Trump's court. With his biggest speech about America first, he has not done one thing about this ridiculous situation. Could you imagine any business in the world spending over 685 billion dollars over sixteen years and basically getting nowhere?

This has to be one of the largest WASTES of taxpayers' money in the history of our country. Just imagine what good this money could do for decent schools for our children, a better healthcare system, improved infrastructure of our roads, etc. It may be different if this was doing us and the world some good, but it's done nothing but injure and kill American soldiers and totally waste our tax dollars.

While on this subject, the Iraq War cost We the Taxpayers over 814 billion dollars, yet the Iraqi people are afraid and even accused us of taking their oil. We lost American lives and spent billions to free them of the tyrant they had. By rights they should have, at the very least, paid us back some of our money—we paid for THEIR FREEDOM.

So between just these two countries, Americans spent over a TRILLION DOLLARS.

Once again, just imagine what this kind of money could have done for our families. After all it's not like this money grows on trees here. It takes Americans not only millions of hours of hard work but, because we must pay our taxes, we deny ourselves and our families many things we rightfully deserve as WE WORKED FOR THEM.

Yet, our government sends all this money overseas. WHY? Why must we save these countries?

There is always this talk of keeping countries from having nukes. Why must America be the chief nuke gatekeeper?

Like North Korea, what are we worried about? If they are crazy enough to start a war, before they kill millions in one day, we could destroy their entire army. That is, if we use air attacks not ground. We hear that Korea may have a missile to reach America. First, that's very doubtful. However, when and if that time comes, we should be able to destroy it before it ever gets here and at same time send missiles enough to blow them away. If we don't have anything to stop their missiles from getting here, then we should be spending money on missiles that will prevent theirs from hitting us, and not only Korea's missiles but any other country that dares to attack us.

The bottom line here is government mismanagement and wasteful spending. After all, why does government care. The people in power live well; they don't worry about healthcare and many other things that We the People don't have.

It's like you have a family of ten children. You have $ 50,000.00. You spend $ 10,000 on YOUR OWN CHIL-DREN, which is not enough to get them dental work, good medical care, etc. Then you send $40,000.00 to countries where you don't even know anyone, and deny your own children what they need most. In short it's time our government starts taking care of its own. Those that earn the money that powers this country.

I'm not saying we should just ignore all other countries; we should definitely not. We should, however, balance things better and take care of our own better.

So now that I've brought this up, let's see if Trump stops this wasteful spending in Afghanistan. Stop a war that's doing nothing but waste money.

Finally, our Congress should also step in and balance this better. Figure a way to stop spending so much overseas. There has to be a better plan than to just keep pouring billions into a country and achieve nothing. If not, then it's time to clean house my fellow Americans and fill OUR Congress and OUR Senate with Americans that care about We the People.

Now a question. Why am I, your basic businessman, pointing this out? Why has not Trump said one word about this? Just a part of a year's cost of this could pay for a terrific healthcare program for Americans.

Mr. Mexico

Just imagine how many Americans could be helped and how many lives could be saved with the billions of dollars Trump wants to spend on a useless wall along our border with Mexico.

Here is proof that Trump's Mexico border wall will not work, and proof that he cares more about his wall than Americans' healthcare.

The Trump wall scenario shows that he is not fit to lead America. I will prove that this wall will do nothing but waste billions of We the Taxpayers' dollars. That is money that could help millions of Americans instead of making a handful of construction people very wealthy.

He is dead now, but when he used to frequent the casino in the Bahamas where we did events for twenty-five years, I met a man known as Mr. Mexico. He was a drug kingpin in Mexico's Gulf Cartel. On a hot summer day in Nogales, Mexico, he escaped a hail of lead from the assault weapons of two assassins from a rival cartel. As they like to say in organized crime, it was strictly business.

I never could remember his real name, but in the gambling world he was known as a whale, a high roller. He would open at blackjack for $50,000 to $100,000 per hand and sometimes more. Naturally my casino pampered him and treated him like he was royalty.

When he came to the casino, it was always with four bodyguards and a suitcase stuffed with a million dollars in cash. He was somewhere between short and tall with a solid build and coal colored eyes. He was probably thirty-something but the gunk he used to slick back his black mane could not mask the streaks of premature gray. His olive skin seemed to glow, and he flashed a row of finely manicured chops that must have made some dentist awfully rich.

The first time he came to our event, he gathered up ten of my Model Search contestants and hustled them off to his suite where a party was brewing. This made me quite upset when I found out. Unless they had written permission from me, our code of conduct did not allow contestants to visit anyone's room except for other contestants', and especially not judges', which this man was.

So, I entered Mr. Mexico's suite and began to round up my girls when I suddenly turned into the bulk of a three-hundred-pound colossus with a cue ball head and a dark Fu Manchu. "We would like you to leave now, and alone," he said in perfect English.

I don't scare easily, but I began to tremble. It was one of those moments when your mind floods with fear knowing that someone could crush you like a grape. "Let me handle this, Manuel," came a soft voice from behind me. It was Mr. Mexico. His bodyguard dropped his sinister glare and slowly walked away.

Mr. Mexico was going to be a judge in our Model Search, so I explained to him that we have rules for our contestants and that it would be improper for him to be entertaining the girls in his suite. "I understand," came his placid reply, which I did not expect, because I thought

I was in for an argument, since people like him usually get their way.

"Señor, would you mind if I brought the girls down-stairs and have them gamble with me?" he asked. "These girls do not have money," I shot back. "Is it okay if I give them some money to play with?" he countered. "As long as there are no strings attached," I said.

Then Mr. Mexico started to talk. "I have all the beautiful women I want in Mexico," he seemed to boast. "You have a first-class event here. The ladies are from all over the world and they are wonderful. I just want to have a good time with them."

I thought it over. This guy was a whale and we needed to coddle him, plus the girls would be out in public on the casino floor. So, I told him it was okay.

When I approached the girls, they nervously told me that someone from the casino had said it was fine for them to attend Mr. Mexico's soirée. They were on edge, so I told them to relax and that I was not going to shave any points off their record. Then I surprised them. "He wants to take you to the casino and have you gamble with him," I told them. "He is even going to give you a few bucks to play with."

The girls were ecstatic! They jumped up and down and screamed like a movie star had just kissed them. Everyone then strolled down to the casino where staff had set up a special table for Mr. Mexico and the contestants. In front of the girls, he thanked me for the privilege of getting to gamble with the contestants and everyone cheered. I wished them a good time and reminded them that they had a 1 a.m. curfew.

It was then that Mr. Mexico's burly bodyguard stepped forward with a tan leather suitcase. When he opened it, everyone began gaping at the million dollars in cold hard cash. It was as scary as it was jaw-dropping. It was in bundles of $5,000, $10,000 and $20,000. To the shock of everyone, Mr. Mexico gave each contestant a $5,000.00 stack of money. Suddenly, it got very quiet. Everyone, including myself, was a little numb.

The girls looked at me with questioning eyes, wondering whether or not to accept it. "If Mr. Mexico wants you to have the money, it's okay with me," I told them. "He can do what he wants. I hope you all win even more." They all cheered. For them, it was like something out of a fairy tale.

It was around curfew time when I drifted back to Mr. Mexico's table. The girls were still reeling with excitement when I reminded them it was time to shut things down and get their beauty rest. "Georgie, please let them stay a little longer ... maybe one more hour," came the softhearted plea from Mr. Mexico.

Just then the casino manager intervened. "George, we don't want to make one of our whales unhappy," he whispered to me. I began to rationalize. The girls were all together in the casino with security everywhere. They were probably safer than in their own homes. "Okay, just one more hour," I told them.

I got a lot of hugs. Mr. Mexico even threw me what looked like a $50 gambling chip for being so accommodating. I told him I could not accept it, to which he replied, "Then buy your beautiful wife a present."

The contestants were all tucked away in their rooms

as I was making my final round through the casino before crashing. "Georgie, come talk with me, amigo," came a voice from a bar room table. It was Mr. Mexico, and he was floating on a mellow high of booze and who knows what else.

Having once owned a nightclub on Long Island, I knew there were two kinds of drunks: those who fall asleep and those who like to talk. Mr. Mexico was a talker. He draped his arm over my shoulder as I caught the cold gaze of this man who wore the image of money and power as well as he wore the diamond rings on both his hands.

"We are good friends," he slurred. "Sit down with me and have a drink." I am not a drinking man, but I did not want to insult the guy. So, I ordered a beer.

During the next ninety minutes Mr. Mexico spun a tale of crime, one that had made him wealthy and powerful, but at the same time made him a huge target in the crosshairs of American justice.

He came from a prominent Mexican crime family with connections to the country's Gulf Cartel that dealt in drugs and human trafficking. "I can get away with just about anything in Mexico," he crowed. "The United States can increase their border patrols, but that does not hurt my operation. It only hurts the little guys who work for peanuts."

Mr. Mexico informed me that, if things got too hot along the southern border, he would just shift his operation to the north. "It's easy to get things into Canada through Alaska," he said. "From Canada, it's a cinch to bring them into your country." He also reminded me that he slipped more drugs into our country through South Florida than he did across the Mexican border. These are the same people Donald Trump claims he can keep out with his wall. I found out they had all kinds of backup plans, so if they could not get in one way, there were always other ways. Little did I know at that time that this information would pertain to Trump and the presidency. Here was one of the very people Trump thinks his wall would keep out telling me how he can go around anything the United States puts in his way. Finally, Mr. Mexico grew tired and I was able to return to my room.

When I got in, I told my wife what had happened. I threw her the chip he had given me, still thinking it was $50, and I told her to keep it as a tip.

Jill looked at the chip and immediately got bug-eyed. "George, this is a $5,000 chip! Where did you get it?" she gasped. After I got over the shock, I told her I had thought it was only $50; I never dreamed he'd given me a $5,000 chip. I told her we'd better give it back to him, and the next day we tried but he refused to take it, saying he appreciated that we were so nice to him.

Mr. Mexico always looked good in his high-class designer clothes. But beneath the fancy wraps lay a dark heart that slithered through the seamy underworld of drugs, death and destruction. The cash he dished out like candy was probably all blood money. You don't achieve that kind of wealth and power without having whacked a few enemies.

Later on, we discovered he was on the FBI's Most Wanted list, so he could never get his kicks in this country for fear of being arrested. Then one day news spread through the casino that he had been gunned down in Nogales.

Now when I think of Mr. Mexico, I also think about President Donald Trump and his harebrained notion that America needs a great wall along its southern border. Nothing could be more absurd. As one drug smuggler was recently quoted: "This is never going to stop either the narcotics trafficking or the illegals. There will be more tunnels. More holes. If it doesn't go over, it will go under."

As usual, Trump never did his homework when he concocted a scheme for his great wall. Mexican crime syndicates who deal in drugs and human trafficking are clever enough to breach any barrier President Trump might erect on the southern border. If they decide they don't want to bother crossing through Mexico anymore, they already have plans to move locations. Trump's own Republican-controlled Congress has understandably refused to appropriate any funding for this proposed wall, since it's by far one of the biggest wastes of time and money on Trump's agenda.

The wall is not so much an issue to be debated as it is an elixir whose passage strokes, soothes and fortifies Trump's ego. Trump's mind is locked and focused on having his way, as it has always been. I found that out the hard way when I watched him destroy decades of work and relationships when he made decisions on matters about which he was completely ignorant. Luckily that can't happen as a matter of course while he occupies the White House—thankfully, our democracy has its checks and balances in place for exactly this reason.

When Donald Trump rolled out his presidential campaign in 2015, he savaged the Mexican community by calling them murderers, rapists and drug dealers. Then he unveiled his plan for a huge and somehow impenetrable wall that would stop the flow of these criminals and their contraband into our country.

That in itself was a huge campaign promise. But then he offered up the kicker: Mexico was going to pay for it! His followers roared their approval for their new messiah. If this billionaire real estate tycoon can build landmark structures all over the globe, getting Mexico to pay for his wall should be a walk in the park ... a walk in the park during a hurricane, that is!

Today, as president of the United States of America, Donald Trump has lifted the tail of the cow and is now staring the situation right in the face. Holding public office is nothing at all like campaigning for it. His Great Wall was not exactly shovel ready. Of course, President Nieto of Mexico has said his country will never pay for the wall.

Perhaps former Mexican President Vincente Fox mirrored the sentiments of his nation better, when he tweeted that his country "would not pay for Trump's f---ing wall." It's just another campaign promise Trump cannot keep.

The Trump base now anxiously awaits the president's newest calculus for cementing the funding for his Great Wall. Recently, President Trump modified his campaign promise by saying American taxpayers might have to pay for the wall and then be reimbursed by Mexico. That is kind of like Bernie Madoff calling a client and telling him the check is in the mail.

Congressional leaders estimated the cost to American taxpayers would be $14 billion, but a report in the *Washington Post* estimated the cost at closer to $25 billion.

One option floated by Trump would be money raised via a 25 percent tariff on Mexican imports, but that would be a disaster because Mexico is America's third largest trading partner. If imposed, Americans would see steep price increases for items like TVs, cell phones and other electronic devices. The price of that happy hour margarita would spike from a levy on your favorite tequila.

When President Trump offered to scrap NAFTA altogether, someone reminded him that it would eliminate 14 million American jobs. He quickly changed his tune.

When the *Washington Post* asked Trump if any of his options were realistic, Trump leaned on his horn as he always does. "It's realistic if you know something about the art of negotiating. If you have a bunch of clowns negotiating, it's not realistic."

Trump also says he wants his wall to be beautiful. How to dress up a concrete structure that burrows five feet underground and rises to a height of fifty-five feet is a task worthy of a Frank Lloyd Wright.

The great Trump Wall also butts heads with a whole slew of important issues. How will it impact the delicate ecosystem of the Rio Grande basin? Will it impede the ability of endangered species to cross the border during mating season? Will the shifting sand on the floor of the southwestern desert be able to support the weight of Trump's "very beautiful" wall?

During the last presidential campaign, Hillary Clinton urged Trump to build relationships, not walls. President

Ronald Reagan had demanded Mikhail Gorbachev tear down the Berlin Wall. And the greatest wall of them all, the Great Wall of China, didn't exactly stop anyone either.

Yet our president is hell-bent on building his wall along our border with Mexico. Such a boondoggle might help reduce the flow of narcotics and other contraband, but the primary purpose of Trump's great wall is to halt the flow of illegal immigrants into our country from Mexico, as if that could ever happen! But I believe there is an easier and much more practical way to do that.

Every now and then I catch a performance of Bill Maher and his show *Real Time*. He once dished out a morsel of truth that hit me right between the eyes. "There would be no illegal immigrants in this country if American businesses didn't hire them," he said. That would certainly hurt our economy far more than most think.

Here is a simple and effective way to solve this problem—*don't build the wall, and use the money for healthcare*. It's easy and it would work. It would save our country a lot of money, a lot of brick and mortar and raise the quality of millions upon millions of Americans' lives.

THE BOTTOM LINE FOR TRUMP'S WALL

FACT: Most illegal drugs and "bad hombres" do not even enter into the United States where Trump wants to build his wall. They come from the southernmost part of the Americas via boats and helicopters.

FACT: No matter how many billions Trump spends on a wall, it will not work! Those who are determined enough already know how to tunnel under, go over or around the wall Trump proposes.

FACT: Centuries of history have proven that no wall ever built can truly prevent people from getting past it somehow.

Here is the most important fact, direct from a Mexican drug lord. As Mr. Mexico once told me, the large majority of smugglers captured by the United States Border Patrol are small-time operators without the money or the means to sidestep the obstacles in their way, including any such wall.

Major Mexican drug cartels have unlimited amounts of cash to go over or under any wall. Cartels also have the option of going around the wall by switching operations. They have the resources and cash to ship drugs to Alaska and bring them in through Canada. I never would have thought our neighbor to the north would be a waypoint on the drug trail that leads to this country. But as Mr. Mexico always said, "We will find a way!"

Racism in Trump's America

I will never forget my first meeting with Sammy Davis Jr.—I felt like I was dreaming. Here I was, on the top floor of a major casino in Las Vegas, in a private meeting with a man who was to me was one of the absolute greatest entertainers of all time.

Mr. Davis said, "It's okay, George, you can call me Sammy." But despite that, I had so much respect for him that it was "Mr. Davis" for quite a while. I told him how I felt he was one of the best all-around entertainers in the history of Hollywood because he could do just about anything. He did terrific impressions, danced like few ever could, sang, was an excellent drummer, and most of all, made people laugh. He was so down to earth in the humblest of ways; he thanked me and said he was not quite *that* good at everything. I begged to differ, saying, "I don't know anyone alive today who's as good as you are at everything." He said, "Stop, George, you're embarrassing me. Enough already!"

I laughed, and we started talking about why I was there. Through a mutual friend, he had agreed to meet with me and hear the ideas I wanted to propose to him. Sammy said, "Whatever this is, it must be big and important. I've known our mutual friend Karen for twenty years, and not once has she ever asked me to meet anyone, which is why I have so much respect for her." After that speech, I was a little worried. So, I asked him, "Mr. Davis, hearing that, I hope I was not imposing on your twenty years of friendship with her. I'll leave now—I know you have a show to do tonight." He laughed and said, "No! No! Don't worry, this is just fine. So, exactly what do you have that you'd like me to be involved with?"

I explained that I had two programs that I felt would be terrific for us both. First, I told him how I felt the younger generation was not hearing the great music created in the 1940s and 1950s. I told him, "You, Frank Sinatra, Bing Crosby, etc., sang so well, I would like to create the 'Sammy Davis Jr. Music Challenge' with a TV show that would have today's generation sing your type of music." I went on to explain exactly how it would work. I kept looking at my watch, since I had been told by Sammy's manager that I had only forty minutes because Sammy had to rest for his show that night. He noticed this and said, "George, do you have to go somewhere?" I immediately said, "No! I was just told I only had forty minutes with you, and I shouldn't run over." He laughed again, saying, "Don't you worry, I'll tell you when I have to go."

I could not believe how nice this superstar was. I had finished telling him this first idea and said, "Mr. Davis will you do this?" He said, "No!" I had thought for sure that he had liked it, but then he said, "No, but then added, not unless it's a 'Frank Sinatra & Sammy Davis Jr. Music Challenge.'" I was in shock! Not only was he interested, but he wanted Frank Sinatra in it too! I said, "Of course, that would be the powerhouse of all time, but I don't know if I can even get to talk to Mr. Sinatra, much less convince him." Again, he laughed, and then said, "Don't worry, I think I can reach him." Of course, he could. They were good friends, and at the time they were touring together with Liza Minelli. He got Sinatra on the phone in a minute. He had me explain the idea to him, then Sinatra said, "I love it. Let's do it, but it's got to be the Sammy Davis Jr. Frank Sinatra Music Challenge. George came to you for the contest to have your name. Why are you putting mine first?" They joked about this for a few minutes, then Sinatra had to go so he left it to figure out later.

Sammy then asked, "What's next?" I explained my idea for a new kind of children's program that included a major movie, books and a TV show that would create a whole new way to educate kids using a new kind of Disney style. After another twenty-five minutes he said, "I really love it. I want to create something special for kids and that's the best idea I've ever heard. I'm in."

By now it had been over an hour and I felt like he and I had known each other for long time, not just an hour. He was so easy going, such a nice person. I don't know how it started, but we ended up talking about his early years in show business. I was shocked when he told me how he would headline a show in Vegas, yet he not only had to stay at a motel out of town, but he had to enter through the kitchen every night to do a show. It was almost impossible to comprehend that one of the biggest names in show business could not even stay at the hotel where he was performing and making them millions. Even worse, he had to eat in the kitchen, as he was not allowed into the dining rooms. I really could not believe it. I was hearing just how bad racism still was in America. So, with all that being said, what does it have to do with Donald Trump?

When discussing the contestants for the American Dream events with Trump, he asked me, "Do we have any blacks in our Model Search?" That really caught me off guard. I wondered in the back of my mind if he actually didn't *want* any blacks in the Model event. I told him, "Some years we've had up to eight or more, and other years just one or two." He then said, "Can we make this go away?" Now, does that sound all too familiar?

I could not believe what I was hearing. Did Donald Trump *truly* want no black contestants in his event? I told him, "We have events around the world, including places like the Bahamas and Jamaica, which if they send a winner, they would most likely be black." He said, "Okay, just see what you can do."

That night I was so upset that I couldn't sleep. Of course, like most people, throughout my life I knew racism existed, but I just can't believe that even today it still exists. In fact, I don't know why it exists at all. Growing up and even today, I have great friends who are black, and I still don't understand why some people insist on discriminating. Now, I can understand why I would see racism in some, those whom I call "lowlifes" who believe white people should be the only race in the United States, but that's explained simply because their brains don't function normally. However, when I hear about racism by the owners of major hotels, even though it was back in the sixties and someone I really looked up to like Trump, I still just cannot understand it. After all, there are famous black people in every field, and it's ridiculous to blame an entire race simply because a few of them cause trouble.

I know, like most other things I've written about in this book, President Trump will not like these facts being revealed, and so he will categorically deny them. However, as I said, this is a book of *facts* and of *the truth*. Even if Trump denies it that doesn't automatically mean it's not true, especially he can't remember things from a day ago, much less years later. Another time I started to see that Trump was not the hero I thought he was, and he was by far *not* the great person whom I thought could do so much good for the world. Of course, these events were in "his world," so he was used to calling the shots. However, despite this I had spent my life creating these events, and not even Donald Trump was going to tell me what to do if I thought it was wrong. I'm sure this attitude also had something to do with him not wanting to work with us again. Even though he never realized it, my saying "NO!" was good for him because if I did say no, it was to make things better, and certainly not to defy him. Unfortunately, Trump never sees it that way. He only sees things "his way" and doesn't care in the least if he's wrong.

Now as president, Trump is completely out of his element. Although he's trying, he can no longer force his "wrong" decisions on those around him, which is one major reason why, for the first time in decades, *nothing* is getting done in Washington.

If ever there was a person who's his own worst enemy, it's Donald J. Trump, which is too bad because he had incredible potential. Unfortunately, he's been so spoiled his entire life that he only knows his own way of doing things and no other.

Our Sexist-in-Chief

What Donald Trump put my ex-wife through sexually was as bad as it gets, yet he got away with it, just as he's getting away with hurting America, all Americans and the country itself.

My first meeting with Trump (a meeting I had waited for my whole life) was about as awkward as you can get. Once we sat down, and throughout the entire meeting, Trump could not take his eyes off my wife. I couldn't blame him—after all she is a beautiful woman. However, it was a business meeting, and it was the first time we had all been together, and to barely look at me, the one giving the presentation, was extremely rude and unprofessional. It was not a good start, but as I've stated, Trump became very nice to us, inviting us out to dinner, so I just let it go.

Unfortunately, not knowing him personally at that point, I had no idea he had an ulterior motive. I did not realize it at the time, nor would I ever have believed it if anyone had warned me to watch out for my wife around the great Donald Trump. That is until my wife finally told me that at the dinner table that night at the Plaza, he had actually moved his hand up her leg. I was shocked to learn this and, with just about anyone else, would never have believed it. However, I was with my wife at that time 24/7 for over thirteen years. If there was anyone in the world I trusted, it was my wife, Jill. I was basically in shock that my idol for years would do such a thing. I knew some, and I want to stress *some*, billionaires would do such a thing. I decided to wait and see what he did.

At a private party he threw for some of our contestants at Mar-a-Largo, while taking my wife for a tour of his ninety-four-room home, he cornered her in his then twelve-year-old daughter's bedroom, and she had to resort to pretending she was getting ill in order to stop him from sexually assaulting her.

Because she didn't want to ruin our business deal with Trump, and because she thought she could handle him and never thought he would continue to be so sexually aggressive, she never told me about these additional sexual assaults when they happened. This all came to a head after we had completed producing his casino events, when he left us no choice but to take him to court for breaking his agreement with us. Then, with no more risk of ruining our business deal with him, she filed a multimillion-dollar sexual harassment law suit against him. Despite this, Trump never gave up chasing after her.

When Trump first saw my wife, she was young, happily married and drop-dead gorgeous. Wherever we went, she turned heads. Even at our events with seventy of the most beautiful women in the world competing against one another, she stood out and had all types of men chasing her. This made Trump attracted to her, plus despite his advances, she said NO! Then there was the fact she had been with just one man, me, for thirteen years, and had never slept around like some do. I can testify that it was obvious Trump really was infatuated with her.

Some women got millions from media powerhouse Bill O'Reilly when they sued for sexual harassment, yet my ex didn't get a dime from what she went through with Trump. After listening to what these women went through, although terrible, I can say without hesitation that what my ex endured with Trump were far greater sexual attacks and far more stressful situations.

Everything with Trump had taken a toll on our marriage. Unfortunately, certain people who were envious of her lifestyle and pretended to be her friend, plus Trump himself, still communicated with her. She was still saying no to him, but together they all eventually convinced her that she should get a divorce.

Losing the man with whom she had now spent eighteen years, being constantly harassed by the media, the stress from working for so many years, and now being alone in New York (she moved back because that's where her parents were and Trump convinced her he could get her a better job there), naturally she became emotionally weak.

Because Trump has no conscience, his only goal was to break her down with no concern about what he was doing emotionally and mentally to this young woman. His constant attention to her for years, plus financial problems we were having due to Trump all but destroying our years of building American Dream events, eventually convinced her to leave me because he said that I was a loser. He got her away from me and out on her own. Once alone, it was far easier for Trump to work on her; before she always had me and "our true friends" to lean on. After being together, traveling the world and enjoying many beautiful experiences that our business gave us, all of a sudden, she was totally alone in one of the largest cities in the world, having just gone through a terrible divorce. Then after her brother (whom she dearly loved) died at a young age, she grew even more emotionally weakened.

After chasing her for years, Trump finally had her just where he wanted her—alone and with no one to turn to. With him promising her a job and with her now feeling desperate, she went to him. You ask, was she crazy? After what he did to her, why would she go to him? Remember, after the lawsuit was over, he invited us to his Christmas party. There he put on the "Trump Charm," saying to just forget the past and look ahead. We saw him again and again as we judged the Miss Hawaiian Tropic beauty contests. My wife, the good-natured person she was, always thought people who were negative or caused problems, etc., could change for the better, which is true at times, but unfortunately for her Trump was Trump, and he would never change—which she found out too late. Just look at how Trump is president, how he has deceived and lied to hundreds of millions of Americans. Look at how he is destroying many people's careers. My ex doing what she did was really not such a stretch.

He could have easily helped her, he could have given her a job, especially since he saw how hard she worked and how smart she was at the events we did for him. With just one phone call, not only would he have kept his promise to her to help her get a good job, but he would have had one of his hardest workers and most faithful employees. However, once he got her to bed, once he had completed his own personal "challenge," she could barely get him on the phone.

It had taken him years, but Trump had finally accomplished what he had been determined to do, what he had said he would do right to my face one day, even using his casino and pretending he was interested in my American Dream events, which in the end destroyed the dreams of thousands of people. I've seen this before with others—when you have the wealth and power like Trump has, when everyone says YES to you for your entire life, when a beautiful woman you desire says NO! it becomes not just about having sex. It becomes a "challenge" to get that person to say YES! no matter how much time or money it takes because nobody says NO! to Donald Trump! Just look what he's been doing at the White House. He's fired some of the best talent America has for lame excuses. The TRUTH, they would not agree with him; they did what their years of experience told them was the right thing to do for America and all Americans. By trying to do the right thing in saying NO! to Trump, they were unjustifiably fired, costing America a loss of very experienced and dedicated people. So if Trump does this using his presidential powers, it's certainly believable what he did to Jill.

Because of what Trump had done to her, she was never the same. He had changed a woman who was always full of laughter, who loved people and treated everyone with respect, who was a caring, considerate and faithful wife who took good care of her husband and who was always willing to help those who were less fortunate. In fact, he had changed her so much that I was shocked when she told me she was living in an abusive relationship with me. I don't drink or smoke and never went out with the boys because she liked doing things together. Although we never made big money during the casino events, we always stayed in suites that were fully comped, so we could charge just about anything to our room, including eating at the best restaurants at the resort. We flew first class many times, and I bought her the most beautiful gowns to wear because she always dressed up for the events. I bought her beautiful jewelry, and on every birthday, any money I ever had I spent on her. She did many things most can only dream about. I trusted her to fly alone to Chicago to do a test shoot for Playboy's fortieth anniversary. No possessive husband would ever let his wife do that. I *never* hit her or barked orders or screamed at her—in fact, just the opposite. When we were having problems, she yelled at me so loudly the neighbors called the police, who after seeing the situation made *her* leave the house and stay in a hotel until she calmed down. In short, she lived a great life with a husband who never abused her in any way. Yet, playing on her weaknesses Trump moved in convincing her of things she NEVER would have believed before.

Her statement was so shocking that I talked with a professional, who after hearing everything and especially after reading the birthday cards, Christmas cards, letters, etc., that she had given me over the years, said, "What she wrote in these cards, notes and letters over eighteen years clearly shows she had a wonderful life, and loved you dearly. There is no way an abused woman could write so many words of love and happiness as she did. Her saying that she was in an abusive relationship is her way of convincing herself she did the right thing by leaving you. She obviously has never since had the life or love she had with you, or she would have been happily married for years by now. Therefore, to live with it she had to convince herself there was something bad in your relationship. To do this, Trump must have really emotionally voided her, and caused real emotional damage to her. This must be a really 'terrible person' to do such damage to another, one who obviously trusted him. He really must be devoid of any feelings for others. It's too bad you two had a run-in with such a person." This from an expert at such things.

Now it finally made sense why she said what she did. Unfortunately, once again it proved just what kind of damage Trump did because he just does not care how his actions may affect others.

A truly beautiful woman inside and out, Jill was an exceptional woman. She was the type that would always give 110 percent, was as loyal as you can get and as faithful as one can be. I can safely say that after meeting over 100,000 women in my life due to operating the International Model Search for forty years, Jill was one in a million. Unfortunately she was damaged forever by Trump, all because he has no conscience; so much so he could not even give her the job he had promised her that, in the end, would have benefitted him far more than her because she was such a smart, strong, dedicated, hard worker and faithful woman,

What Donald Trump put my ex-wife through sexually,

every word of this I swear is true. I saw how it affected her, I saw how it changed her, I lived through it as did she. I saw a man who I once thought was the smartest and greatest man ever, someone I had prayed to some day meet and do business with turn into the most selfish and uncaring person I had ever known. Trump was someone who truly had no conscience.

To the women who stand by him, I guarantee you that, if he had done to you what he did to my wife, not only would you no longer want to be with him, but you would want to sue or kill him. You might say that I'm crazy, you would never feel that way. It's easy to say that when you NEVER went through what Trump put Jill through. Just remember, you can never tell a woman who's been abused that you know what it's like. Don't ever think you can know what Jill went through.

THIS MAN IS RUNNING OUR COUNTRY!

THIS MAN HOLDS ONE OF THE MOST POWERFUL POSITIONS IN THE WORLD.

THIS MAN IS SOMEONE OUR CHILDREN LOOK UP TO.

A Message
to Trump's Supporters

Reports say that the majority of Trump's supporters still stand behind him, but before you stand behind him or anyone else in public office, you should make sure you know the facts. Make sure you know the truth!

His supporters are making the same mistake that I and hundreds of hardworking Americans did years ago. With Trump standing before me and my people, he made us a promise. He said we had kept our word and delivered results, in fact more results than he ever expected. His exact words were, "You exceeded my expectations." He promised to keep up his end of our agreement and went into detail about what he would do next. We believed everything he told us. We soon found out, despite his standing before us in person and giving us his word, that it did not mean a thing. In a court of law that would be considered a binding agreement, making him legally responsible for his actions.

Now, by supporting him despite his constant lying, you are giving the president of the United States permission to lie without restraint.

What does this mean? It means that as the person in charge of the most powerful military in the world, you would give him permission to send your sons, daughters, fathers and mothers into war even if there was no reason to go, except that Trump wants to show the world he has control of America. Sound ridiculous? Just one year ago, if anyone had said it was okay for the president of the United States to lie, We the People would have told them that's ridiculous—lies from our president could put us into a recession, or even worse, a war!

Do you really think that all of the trouble we are now facing with North Korea, Russia and others is just coincidence? After more than a decade of fighting terrorists, all of a sudden, we have to face the prospect of a nuclear war? If you think all of this has nothing to do with Trump, then you have a big problem. The world sees that America has a president who caused more unrest in his first one hundred days in office than any others before him. The world sees that America has a president that tells outright lies, and yet there are people who still support him. I could go on and on, but most know that America has not seen this much unrest in decades, and that it's clearly because we have a real estate tycoon as our president.

You might say he's new at this, and to give him a chance. So, while Trump learns how to be president, while world unrest is at an all-time high, while Washington argues about healthcare, while Trump has time to use Air Force One and costs We the Taxpayers millions of dollars so he can play golf, we should *give him a chance?*

To Trump's supporters, I say that if you had gone through what my promoters and I had to suffer, if you had used *your* savings to fulfill your end of an agreement with Trump and had expected him to live up to his end, if you had heard him promise and give in detail what he would do to live up to his end of the agreement but then not even take your phone calls, I guarantee that you would no longer support him.

How can you ever trust someone that stands before you and lies directly to your face, someone that spends more time and money trying to build a wall that history has proven will never work, instead of providing healthcare for all Americans that need it so very badly?

What kind of president alienates his allies? If there was ever a president who has put America in a position to start a war, it's Donald Trump. It's becoming more and more obvious that he is so busy setting himself and his family up to make *billions* once he leaves the White House that nothing constructive will ever get done.

The first and main requirement for anyone to be a good president and serve his country is that they must have a conscience because only someone with a conscience will care about We the People and put them first. In Trump's mind, it is very clear that we come last.

Trump stated, "If I shot and killed someone on Fifth Avenue my people would still be with me."

It's bad enough Trump said "this is fun" and "I didn't know it would be this much fun" when commenting about running our country, with war threatening us and still no better healthcare plan as he promised. Now the President feels he can actually murder someone, and his followers will still support him. Knowing him the way I do, I can tell you that he meant every word he said.

For the president of the United States of America to utter these words to the world is beyond egregious, and it clearly demonstrates that he should not be the president of a country for which so many have died defending.

For those who still believe in him, it's only because you have never seen the *real* Donald Trump as I have. You should open your mind and see how clear it is that he *always puts himself and his family first*, even before his own country.

I am also getting sick and tired of my fellow Americans being lied to and misled about who made Donald Trump the president.

Here are just a few samples of statements made that are misleading:

"Americans in all fifty States elected Donald Trump."

"Americans in fifty states elected Donald Trump as our president."

"Donald Trump was elected president by the people of this country."

None of these statements or any others like them are accurate. The following pages state the truth about just who made Donald J. Trump the president. It was not Americans in all fifty states—at least not the majority of them.

IT'S TIME THE TRUTH COMES OUT AND STAYS OUT!

Those of you who are misleading Americans should go back to school and get it right. Just seventy-seven people made Trump president in 2016, *not* We the People.

My fellow Americans, please read the following pages, and once and for all understand the truth about who is really responsible for electing the president of your country. Although Trump supporters may bend the truth, they cannot change it.

Ask yourself the following:

- Who pays the president's salary?

- Who pays so that the president and his family can live in the White House?

- Who pays all expenses so that the president and his family can travel in the safest and most expensive aircraft ever built?

- Who makes it possible for the president to have a budget in the hundreds of billions of dollars?

- Who pays for and makes sure the president and his family have the best healthcare in the world?

- Whose children get protected better than any children in the world?

- Who pays for and makes sure the president's children have the best education in the world?

The answer to the above has always been those who have faced stress, hard work and dedication to America for their entire lives—We the People. How many Americans would like any of the items listed above for their own family?

So why don't *we* get to elect our president? Why do a few hundred people we don't even know have more power than all Americans *combined*?

It's time for We the People to take back the rights that are ours.

Trump is someone who, since the day he was born, has never had to worry about the things We the People have to deal with every day of our lives. Therefore, he can never relate to that which he has never personally experienced himself. All of this, plus the fact he has absolutely no concern for others, makes him exactly the wrong person to be president of a country founded by people who care, people who have struggled and who know what real work is all about. This is why he will go down in history as the absolute worst president in the history of the United States.

The First Lady

I have never met Trump's new wife (his third), but that doesn't matter. What I feel does matter is that so far, she has expressed little, if any, regard for American traditions and the American taxpayers' money.

From just about the day a president is sworn in, he and his wife, now America's new first lady, and their family move into the White House, but after her husband's inauguration Mrs. Trump went back to New York. This is just one of the many American presidential traditions that have been broken by the Trumps.

I believe most of us have always looked up to the first lady of the United States, seeing her as someone who is classy and who truly cares about our country. As an immigrant, Melania Trump, of all people, should have felt excited and privileged to live in the White House and to be the first lady. It became apparent very quickly that she couldn't care less about moving in right away, saying she'd rather have her young son stay in the school he attends now. To the many people I've spoken to about this, they thought that was a very lame excuse. In my case, my dad had five kids, and we moved three times to different states just so he could pay the bills and support us. We did not have the honor and privilege of living in the White House. So, for Mrs. Trump to say she wants her son to stay in New York to go to school is really a selfish excuse with no regard for America's position as first lady.

Apart from breaking with American tradition, what's really wrong here is the cost and trouble needed to protect her and her son, with no regard for how much it costs the American taxpayers. Also, I doubt the thousands whose daily life was affected in New York City thought what she did was just fine with them. Putting those issues aside, let's now address a serious and important reason why she has proven that she is not concerned with what her decisions cost American taxpayers.

For the extra security for her to stay in New York, We the Taxpayers paid $140,000 per day, or $6,000 *per hour*. Imagine $6,000 an hour of your money being spent just so her son does not have to change schools, even though he had to eventually. How many Americans have had to move and take their kids out of school? Many thousands, I'll bet.

However, the Trumps feel they are *not* like most Americans; they feel they are privileged, and despite the fact that it cost Americans millions of dollars, they deserve to do *whatever they want*. So, their son staying in the same school for the last half of the school year ended up costing the American taxpayers over *20 million dollars*. Imagine how many Americans could have health-care coverage with that much money. Yet Trump's son gets to stay in his school while We the Taxpayers shell out a ludicrous amount of money. If Trump and his wife were true Americans and it had meant that much to them that their son not move in the middle of the school year, then *they* would have paid for it, not put the burden on the American taxpayers.

Another thing that's upsetting to many people to

whom I've spoken is that she was an immigrant who came to this country as a model, not someone who could contribute to the welfare of the country. Despite being first lady, she already had privileges that 99.999 percent of all American women never have, and yet she abuses that great honor.

Additionally, many were upset when she made a speech that was, in one section, exactly word for word what Michelle Obama, a true first lady, had said in a previous speech. For those of you that missed it, believe me, it was upsetting to hear the words of Mrs. Obama, a real first lady, being spoken verbatim by Trump's wife. Then again, she's now a Trump, so obviously he's taught her to take credit for what others have done.

So why did Trump's wife do all this? Because she is really not in love with this country. It's obvious by the fact that she did not even move into the White House after her husband was sworn in as president, as did other first ladies before her. After all, she's married to a wealthy man, she gets all she wants, and he's the president, one of the most powerful people in the world. Just like her husband, she feels she is far above all of us, that she's far better than us, so she will do what *she* wants, regardless of tradition or what is expected of any first lady of the United States.

If you think I'm overstating this, it's because you have not seen firsthand like I have how certain rich and powerful people really are. Believe me, certain ones, and I want to stress that it's only *certain* ones, believe that they are far better than us because they have money—*lots* of money. In fact, Trump continuously told my wife

I was a loser because I wasn't rich. I've also seen this in other very wealthy people's attitude. They feel they are far superior simply because they have massive wealth, despite the fact that some of them, like Trump, inherited their money and didn't earn it themselves. Who among us wouldn't want to start out their life with millions of dollars, even if it was a loan? Who wouldn't want to have had a father who was so powerful and so wealthy that they could have just about anything they could ever wish for?

Every woman I spoke to about this basically said, "I would feel so honored to be called the first lady of this country. Even if I had a dozen children, I would take them all out of school and move into the White House so fast my husband would not even know I had left." It's very evident Trump's wife doesn't feel that way.

The person I really feel sorry for is their eleven-year-old son. His mother refers to him as a "mini-Trump." He has, at this tender age, actually fired his housekeepers. Just imagine what a terrible person he will be when he grows up if he's already depriving people of their livelihood at such a young age and is allowed to do that by his parents, and is even commended for it, rather than his parents teaching him why he should care about and be considerate of all hardworking people, and to have respect for the working Americans of this country. Then again, it's no wonder when you understand who he has for a father.

Once again, I'll refer to the Donald Trump American Dream events, where he couldn't have cared less about the thousands of people he had hurt. Just as bad were the thousands he put out of work in all those businesses he bankrupted, a demonstration of his complete lack of regard for the hardworking people in his employ.

Trump has talked very negatively about immigrants, and yet he married one. Of course, if she wasn't beautiful, then there's no way he would have married her, and no way she would be living this charmed existence that is unlike the lives of almost everyone else in the world.

Previous first ladies of the United States have been first-class women and true lovers of their country. Most have contributed tremendously to the betterment of all its citizens. What will someone like Melania Trump ever contribute? Only time will tell.

I will give Mrs. Trump the benefit of the doubt, and give her time to see if she can do any good the way our past first ladies have. However, she was not off to a very good start, wasting over $20 million of the taxpayers' money just so her son didn't have to move schools, which when he's older won't mean a thing. If that amount had been spent on healthcare, it could have helped thousands upon thousands of Americans and even saved lives.

Let's face it—no woman who loved this country and its people would have stayed in New York for months knowing it was causing thousands of New Yorkers and their businesses so much trouble on a daily basis. Nor would she have stayed in New York knowing it was costing hardworking Americans $6,000 an hour, when just one hour would have paid for two to three families' and their children's healthcare for a year.

Dealing with Our Enemies

Whether it is North Korea or any other country threatening to become a nuclear power, I think America should do something that no other country has ever done; something that will show the world just how powerful America really is.

This may sound a little crazy to you at first, but if you think about it, I mean *really* think about it, you will see the potential this idea has. Also, keep in mind I've been in marketing and public relations since the 1960s. For major companies, I was able to reach millions of people and affect their buying decisions through many unique programs. I've applied these decades of successful programs to the following idea that I believe is far more powerful than simply talking because images can portray that which mere words never can. The saying "a picture is worth a thousand words" is very true. Keeping that thought in mind, the following is an old but revised approach to getting a certain point across in the most powerful way possible.

Hire the best there is from Hollywood, like Spielberg or Disney, and create a short film with a simple message. In the beginning, show a composite of thousands of American jet fighters, bombers, submarines, helicopters, supersonic planes, aircraft carriers, destroyers, drones and other such military equipment in action with a voice-over that says something like:

"America has the most powerful military in the world; so much power that if anyone ever attacks us, we will not hesitate to use the entire American military force to strike back, totally destroying those that would start any such hostile action."

Using mock cities and people, it would show them at first peaceful, with beautiful skylines, fountains, etc., and then all of a sudden, from out of the sky would come the entire American military.

As this massive military starts to fly over their city, the people would look to the sky and start watching their TVs, tablets and smartphones, worried and terrified, but then the camera would cut to onboard an aircraft carrier showing the two sides signing a *peace treaty*, with word going out that the peace treaty was signed and the military would fly over each city, then drop leaflets saying America and your country are at peace. It's time to celebrate.

Then comes a voice saying, "America shall only use the most powerful military force ever gathered if another country strikes first."

The purpose of this film would be to try to *prevent* a war. With the power of America's military shown in the film, no one would attack.

America has shown the world small clips of our might before, but *never* all of our military strength together in a full-blown Hollywood production.

Just imagine how compelling this film would be if created by the best talent in Hollywood. The way in which a movie studio could produce such a film would scare even the craziest of dictators, or at the very least get them talking about peace.

Unlike the way North Korea shows its hordes of soldiers as though they are robots, this film would be a thousand times more powerful, showing everything from battleships and submarines firing rockets underwater to the fastest fighter jets in the world, etc. It would show the billions of dollars' worth of the most powerful fighting machines ever created, but made in the style of a blockbuster Hollywood action movie.

Many people have said I come up with the best marketing and PR they have ever seen. Well, I have no doubt that what I've described here, if released by the United States Department of Defense, would be so powerful and so terrifying that even the North Koreans would have to take notice.

Of course, this film would have professional writers and voiceover artists, and the best directors shooting the military's fighters, ships, planes, etc., with the best editors cutting the footage. It could easily be the most powerful military film ever produced, one that would show the entire world, including our enemies, once and for all the full military power of the United States of America.

Let's face it—how many of us have seen a movie that emotionally affected us? Now, just imagine the best in Hollywood using America's mightiest military and weapons to make this film.

Of course, this is just a very rough draft. With A-list producers and studios putting this together, it could be the strongest and most powerful marketing film ever produced, and would easily get the message across to countries such as North Korea, Iran or any others that consider attacking us.

The message would be simple, yet crystal clear: Do *not* mess with the United States of America. Peace between us is *always* the best choice.

The Challenges Facing President Trump

When history is written about this era, it will be proven that during Donald Trump's presidency, more negative incidents (both nationally and internationally) occurred than during the terms of all of the presidents in recent memory *combined*.

Despite saying he wanted to know whether or not Russia intervened in the presidential election, Trump did everything he could to undermine the investigation. This includes doing what no president in history has ever done—firing the director of the FBI. There was not even so much as a hint that Trump was going to fire James Comey. In fact, he said, "I have faith in Comey." However, once Comey revealed that he was closing in on the Russia/election connection, Trump fired the man out of nowhere with no warning. This is still more proof that Trump has no conscience because instead of getting Comey on the phone and telling him that he had to let Comey go, before the media and others found out, Trump just fired the man, telling the world before telling Comey. Without a doubt, this was the wrong way to have handled this situation, unless you do not care about another's feelings, unless you have no respect for the office of the top official of the FBI, and unless you really don't care whether or not it's the wrong way to go about it. Trump does what he wants! Sound familiar?

James Comey is a man who has dedicated his life to serving his country (unlike Trump who never served before). He is a man who was appointed to one of the most prestigious positions in our government, one that only a handful ever achieve, and yet while speaking at a conference in California, he had to see the news flash across the screen that the president had fired him.

Imagine how this man felt, finding out that he just lost his life's work without warning *on television*. Imagine his realization that the president of the United States did not even have the decency to pick up the phone to tell him before he told the world, but instead sent his personal bodyguard to the FBI offices like a common messenger. For the president to fire him in this manner is, to say at the very least, disgraceful, and it shows Trump has no respect for the office of the president. It plainly shows that without proper cause or reason, if Trump gets upset he just fires top government officials as if the United States government was one of his corporations. In this case, Trump clearly fired Comey because Comey was closing in on the Russian situation, regardless of Trump's comments as to why he fired him.

TRUMP'S FORM OF DAMAGE CONTROL

I experienced this myself, firsthand. After producing the most successful series of events ever seen during the dead of winter at Trump casinos, after praise upon praise about how we had done such an incredible job, out of nowhere Trump was telling people we had lost him a lot of money, we were a disaster and that he was not going to do it again, despite the fact that in a room filled with promoters, contestants, family members and staff he had announced, "Next year I'm moving this event to my Taj Mahal and it's going to be the biggest ever." This is how he turns things around when things don't go his way. One minute you're great, and the next *you're fired*.

Imagine you owned a resort and casino and you sell out every room you have during the dead of winter when you are usually lucky to have people at all. You also have a record number of gamblers in attendance. You receive millions of dollars in free media exposure that saves you from spending large amounts to promote your event. Imagine you have people coming to your casino from all over the world and going back home saying how wonderful your resort is, priceless word of mouth advertising for future business. If this is a disaster, what is a success? Yet Trump *lied under oath*, trying to turn my success into failure. This man is running our country.

Trump was not prepared for the firestorm that occurred when he let Comey go. To cover up his "mistake" he acted like he had this planned all along, but I can guarantee you he didn't. This is just the way he tries to do damage control. He is so used to getting his way and so used to people believing every word he says that he really believes he can say and do anything and get away with it just like he did with his own business empire. However, he is no longer the ultimate boss he once was. He now has many people to answer to, and they are finally catching on to the games he plays, the lies he produces and the

THE CHALLENGES FACING PRESIDENT TRUMP   217

contradictions that are part of the way he operates. Trump can no longer simply do anything he wants.

Trump called Comey a "showboat" and a "grandstander." He is so oblivious to the truth that he doesn't understand that he was totally describing *himself*. In my entire life, despite the hundreds of Hollywood celebrities I've worked with, despite the presidents and CEOs of major companies I've known and worked with, despite the billionaires I've worked with, not a single one of them can come near to the showboating and grandstanding that I saw in the years I was working with Trump, or come near the way he has been acting since he started to campaign for president.

He can deny it all he wants, but there is no doubt Trump is extremely worried that the government is closing in on the truth about Russia affecting our presidential election. He is worried because he knows that people in his campaign did in fact conduct business with certain Russians. At one time, I told him he needed to be very careful about certain top people within his casinos because with all the cash they go through it's easy for them to get money out without his knowing it, to which he replied, "I always know what my key people are doing so they can't hide anything from me." If he was that smart and careful as the owner of casinos, as president it's obvious he would want to know what all of his top people are doing because *he could potentially be responsible for their actions*. Those loyal to Trump will lie for him. I saw it in person in federal court. Anyone at the top with him would rather take the blame than have Trump involved.

Furthermore, despite the pleas of many (including those that backed him), Trump refuses to release his tax returns because he must have certain ties with others that would greatly affect his presidency. By his own words, a person must have something to hide if they refuse to be questioned. Trump could have very easily put to rest any doubt there is about this, and regain the faith that many that believed in him have since lost, simply by releasing his tax returns. By not releasing them, it points to the fact that he is hiding something.

I predict history will write that Russia did affect the election for the president of the United States of America by helping Donald Trump win! Wanting to undermine democracy, they knew that having a totally inexperienced real estate broker as president, a man who is used to having total control over everyone around him, a man who you never say "no" to would accomplish their goal, which Trump obviously has done with America.

However, what Russia did not count on was the power of We the People.

Donald Trump is a man with no government experience, one who is used to getting whatever he wants, a man who has never had to answer to anyone. Despite these facts, he has not been able to disrupt our democracy the way Russia had hoped he would by firing Sally Yates because she would not do what he wanted—in other words, for doing her job. He was blocked from carrying out what would have been unconstitutionally banning immigrants from certain countries from entering the United States. The president, however powerful his office may be, is still held accountable for his actions.

Despite having no military experience, Donald Trump said he knew more about ISIS than all of the army generals. I can honestly say that with the experiences I did have with Trump, I know more about him than the United States Congress and all the generals put together.

I once worked closely with Donald Trump. We conferred together and planned his events together. I went clubbing with him. We dined together in New York and had private parties at his private club in Mar-a-Lago. I shared the podium with him at press conferences. And unbeknownst to me at the time, he had sexually assaulted my wife. Yes, America, I really do know Donald Trump!

Although everything he did eventually shocked me, nothing was so scary as when America elected him president. Up until that moment the American presidency was the most honored and respected office on the planet. But in only one hundred days, Trump desecrated and disgraced one of the most distinguished, honorable and powerful political offices in the world.

Since I began working with him twenty-five years ago, Donald Trump has not changed at all. In fact, now with the power of the presidency he's far worse. When things go his way, he tosses out compliments like they are baseballs. However, when things are not the way he wants them, Trump goes into "savage mode." "That is all fake news," he counters. "That is disgusting, terrible, the worst I've ever seen." Like Rumpelstiltskin, he has a flair for spinning cold hard facts into gold-plated lies. That is the Donald Trump I know.

Trump's journey to the White House was a scorched earth event. Along the way he hurt a lot of people. Trump operates in a twisted state of mind. It is a mind without logic, common sense or compassion. It is a mind too warped for the job of world leadership. His unhinged temperament and galloping paranoia could provoke worldwide financial issues and, even worse, a war.

In spite of the bombast and bluster, in his first one hundred days Trump cost We the People millions of dollars! The following will outline just some of the reckless spending and outrageous claims of an inexperienced and insensitive president.

His unconstitutional travel bans have heaped extreme emotional stress on millions of innocent families worldwide. The cost to American taxpayers is still growing and soon will be hundreds of millions of dollars.

He fired Sally Yates because she did her job based on her decades of experience, a job with which Trump once again had zero experience. But as I said, even one of the most dedicated and experienced attorneys general in our country's history should never have said "NO" to Trump.

Despite their lack of experience, Trump has installed family members in key White House positions where they will make large personal financial gains while We the Taxpayers pay for their staff and travel costs.

He has used Air Force One to gain priceless media exposure for his private club at Mar-a-Lago, making it justifiable for him to raise membership fees from $100,000 to $200,000 per person. The weekend flights on Air Force One to Florida cost We the Taxpayers *26 million dollars in just two months*, while he raked in millions in profits.

At a cost of $200,000 per hour, President Trump is

using Air Force One to puff up his ego as he cruises across America thanking his base for voting for him. A friend of mine who voted for Trump said it best: "This is an insult to the office of the president and downright disgusting. This guy has no respect for us. We are just his pawns. To think, I voted for him." Using Air Force One to boost his ego and promote his club in Florida is a total waste of our money. Remember, *we are paying for this*.

Now that America knows that Mexico will not pay for his wall, Trump wants to build it anyway. History shows that walls do not work. No one in our government even wants the wall. Right now, in Congress, there is feeble support for this monstrosity. It could cost Americans 25 billion dollars, money that would be better spent on healthcare. For Trump, the wall would be a personal Mount Rushmore, something to stoke his elephant-sized ego.

Trump is claiming that he has signed more bills in his first one hundred days than any other president. In order to make himself look good, he applies what I call "deceptive facts." None of these bills came from Trump—they were started during the Obama administration. This is just another lie, and more of taking credit for what others did—something which is finally catching up to Trump.

It's also insulting to our country that for the first time, the woman who is supposed to be the first lady of the USA did not even live in the White House for months. She is a wealthy and spoiled immigrant, who of all women should have been overjoyed to be able to live in the White House and should have wanted to move in immediately. However, she is just like her husband in that she comes first, not America or We the People. She did not move into the White House to live with her husband, the president. What a terrible image for American families. Making this even worse, and showing that she also has no conscience like her husband when it comes to We the People, it cost taxpayers $140,000 per day for her to live in New York. Do you realize how much money that is? It cost this country $140,000 *every single day* just so she could live in her penthouse, with no regard for the millions of dollars the citizens of this country must pay just so she gets her way. Her excuse of not wanting to take her son out of school is a joke. My father moved the five of us many times just so he could make a few dollars more at a better paying job. Here she had the honor of living in the White House being America's first lady, yet she opted to stay in New York, costing We the People millions of dollars. I don't know about you, but I could never do that to the people of this country if I were in that position. I could never cost taxpayers $140,000 every single day, nor would I refuse the honor of living in the White House.

THE MOST IMPORTANT CHALLENGE OF TRUMP'S LIFE

At his present rate of spending, four years of President Donald Trump will end up costing We the People of the United States of America billions in wasted tax dollars, far outweighing any good he may do in that time.

To any red-blooded American with a lick of common sense, it is painfully obvious that Donald Trump is totally unqualified to be president of the United States, a country that so many died to create. Trump does not drink or smoke but he has one deadly vice that is costing our country dearly, he lies and lies and lies!

He makes big promises but never delivers. He talks about how terrible things are and that they must change. Then, without skipping a beat, what was terrible becomes terrific.

One day he calls President Obama ignorant and the next day he has great respect for him. One day he wants to lock up Hillary Clinton, but after becoming president he gives her a "Get Out of Jail Free" card. One day he vows to sue the women who accuse him of sexual harassment, but after being elected he never files the briefs.

Trump has fooled his base into thinking Mexico would pay for his "Great Wall" along the southern border. But that is Trump's dream and *no one else's*.

By now it should be apparent to most Americans that for President Trump, his family comes first and We the Taxpayers come last. His trips to Mar-a-Lago represent the reckless and wasteful spending that he vowed to eliminate. Every time he visits his private club in Florida it is a universal plug for his brand.

After being elected, President-elect Trump said that he would have no problem running the country at the same time that he was taking care of his business empire, and that is exactly what he is doing. He is taking care of the family business first while running our country *into the ground*.

Looking back at the last presidential election, I think I can say that the majority of Americans got it right. Almost three million more of them voted for Hillary Clinton than

Trump. Clinton was not as pure as the driven snow, but she came with a wealth of domestic and international experience critical to manning the helm of the world's peacekeeper.

President Trump might know how to close a real estate deal but mostly cannot hold on to that deal, and when stacked up against the diplomatic savvy of Mrs. Clinton his grade is "F." Our relationships with countries like Russia and North Korea are bewildering to an amateur like Trump, but they play right into the wheelhouse of a skilled stateswoman like Hillary Clinton. I would much rather see the refined skill of a serious diplomat like her handle the touchy issues of North Korea and Russia rather than a trigger-happy novice with his pudgy little index finger on the nuclear trigger.

An example of Trump's incompetence came not long ago when he said, "I thought it would be easy. I didn't know it was this much work. I miss my old life." The president of the United States is responsible for the greatest country in history and the most powerful military force that comes with it. What kind of mind would ever think that would be *easy*?

Running the country and being a commander-in-chief is a staggering commitment. How many times must a steel beam smack his worshippers on the head before they see that the real Donald Trump is not equipped to run our country?

Only someone who knows what real work is like, who knows what it means to work in order to pay bills, and only someone with a conscience can run the most complex country in the world.

CHARTING A COURSE TOWARD PREMATURE DEATH

I predict the presidency will bring about a premature death for Donald Trump.

There is one thing everyone experiences in different degrees, and it's one of the most life-threatening medical conditions we as human beings must try to avoid. It's called stress—a condition that can take years off one's life. Trump should take a look at how past presidents have aged during their terms. Even though they were far better suited for the position of president of a world superpower, stress and rapid aging got to them all.

For Trump, performing the job of president means being exposed to extreme stress. At seventy years of age his life on this Earth is already very limited, as time seems to pass faster than ever. Now that Trump has had a dose of presidential reality and knows he cannot always have it his way, the stress builds.

At his present rate of spending, he will cost the people of the United States of America hundreds of billions in wasted tax dollars, outweighing any good he may do.

A great leader unites a country—a poor leader divides it. Donald Trump's presidency has caused a major rift in our country.

Trump's actions have proved he is the person I remembered from years ago. Not only has he not changed, but unfortunately, he has become far worse. As president people are finally seeing the *real* Donald Trump. He is a man who is self-serving, constantly lies, has no conscience and puts himself before all others, and even his country.

What the World Thinks
of America with Donald Trump
as Its President

My American Dream Entertainment Company is fifty years old, and during that time I have had the opportunity to work with many wonderful people who helped promote our events. These promoters ran competitions in segments like our American Dream Automotive Design Challenge, American Dream Music Challenge, American Dream International Model Search, Comedy Challenge and more, sending their winning contestants to our Regional, State and World Finals. Over time these promoters became more than just my business associates—they became very good friends.

These promoters are scattered all over the world, so when I decided to write a book about Donald Trump, I called and emailed as many as I could in order to get some feedback about "The Trump Effect" in their countries, and here is what they had to say.

Most of the feedback came with a common caveat: "George, don't get mad at me for what I have to say," wrote a woman from Germany. "But there are a lot of disturbing reports in our media about President Trump."

A couple from England fretted that the partnership between our two nations as allies and peacekeepers was now fractured. "Nigel and I have watched trouble flare throughout the globe," wrote my friend Beatrice. "We feel it is because Donald Trump is your president. He is not a traditional American leader. Most of us do not feel he is a leader at all."

My promoter from Spain could not believe America had pinned their future on a real estate tycoon. "His lack of experience and the baggage he comes with make him a very weak leader," he said. "He is not feared and respected like other American presidents. That is why I feel like there is so much trouble brewing with countries like North Korea."

The common complaint from my promoters is that President Trump plays fast and loose with taxpayers' dollars. They feel his weekend jaunts to the "Winter White House" at Mar-a-Lago are ostentatious displays of his life of privilege, and he is chewing up tax dollars that would be better spent on healthcare for lower- and middle-class Americans.

"He needs to spend more time at the White House," said my friend from Norway. "He's not running a casino anymore. He needs to park Air Force One and roll up his sleeves."

One of my promoters from France wonders how women could vote for a man with a track record of assaulting them. "That is a terrible image for your children to grow up with," he said. "We all know this is true because of what your wife Jill went through when you were working with Trump."

Another current running through the consensus of my promoters is that our new commander-in-chief is often referred to as the American "Liar-in-Chief." "He has lied so many times you don't know when he is telling the truth," said a promoter from Columbia.

Some of my promoter friends called my attention to American media reports about President Trump that had been broadcast in their countries. I decided to check up on them.

FACT: On the campaign trail, Trump promised to spend most of his time in the White House. But in the first eighty-four days he spent $21.6 million flying Air Force One to his estate in Florida. That is more than all of the presidents of the twentieth century spent traveling to their homes during their first eighty-four days in office.

FACT: If you count the $140,000 per day it cost to guard his family in New York, no other President in our history will have spent this much money on travel and security during the same time frame.

FACT: To "save money" Trump proposes budget cuts for government agencies including the IRS and EPA. This will put thousands of Americans out of work, not create jobs as he constantly promises.

All of these government workers will lose their jobs, while President Trump cruises on the world's most expensive jet to Mar-a-Lago where he promotes his club and plays golf. All this from the candidate who said he would cut waste and add jobs.

No wonder the world thinks Americans are stupid! Billionaire President Donald Trump is living better than he ever did in the private sector at the expense of *We the Taxpayers*.

First Lady Melania Trump refused to honor the sacred

tradition of first ladies when she eschewed the White House in favor of her New York penthouse. That decision cost taxpayers an additional $140,000 per day in security costs.

FACT: On the campaign trail Trump promised that if elected, "I will spend all my time in the White House working my ass off." That was just another Trump lie! He had accused President Obama of playing too much golf, yet in the first eighty-four days in office, he played more golf at his mansion in Florida than President Obama did in six months. During his first three months in office, he flew to Florida almost every weekend, abandoning the White House and the frosty temperatures in Washington.

FACT: He promised to prosecute Hillary Clinton and throw her in jail. When supporters asked President-elect Trump when he would go after Hillary, he replied: "We don't need to do that anymore."

FACT: He promised to build a Great Wall along our southern border, and that Mexico would pay for it. That promise is now on the back burner, but one thing is for sure—Mexico will never pay for it. If it is ever built, We the Taxpayers will pay for it.

FACT: During the campaign, Trump said that the North American Treaty Organization was obsolete and a waste of tax dollars. Then at a recent White House meeting with NATO chief Jens Stoltenberg, President Trump stood right next to him and expressed his strong support for an organization he had called obsolete.

FACT: He promised to repeal and replace Obamacare with a plan that would cover all Americans at a very low cost. However, the truth is he never had a plan, and when he tried to rush a half-baked concoction through the House, there was initially no support from Republicans and his bill was dead on arrival, and now it's died in the Senate.

FACT: He promised to cut government waste, but the money he saves by pink-slipping thousands of government employees is wasted on *multimillion-dollar* excursions to Mar-a-Lago.

FACT: When four women came forward with civil rights attorney Gloria Allred and accused him of sexual harassment, Trump vowed to sue them, but so far, he has not filed any briefs. There is a reason for that—he's probably guilty!

FACT: Trump is the Flip-Flopper-in-Chief. First, he said China is a currency manipulator, but when Chinese President Xi Jinping came to Mar-a-Lago, he changed his mind and said that they are no longer currency manipulators.

He once called President Obama ignorant, yet after a White House visit following his victory, he said he had great respect for the man.

If I was asked to sum up Trump's presidency, I could do it in three words: LIES AND HYPOCRISY. If we cannot trust what the president of the United States of America promises, if he outright lies about serious issues that affect hundreds of millions of Americans, how can we ever expect the world to admire and respect us and to be our allies?

The True Bottom Line
for Donald Trump

As I said in the beginning, what you will read here is based on the truth, on true life experiences with Trump. As I also stated, no others have had the type of experiences with Trump that I have had, nor do they have the type of knowledge I possess.

By producing worldwide events for his Taj Mahal and Trump Plaza casinos, having dinners with him, going clubbing, spending two years fighting him in court, having him sexually abuse my wife, the numerous phone calls, press conferences, and on and on, I can say that no one has had to travail the Donald Trump maze in as many ways as I did. Accordingly, no one saw what I did nor could they write about him the way I have.

Although just about everything he did eventually shocked me and my associates, nothing was more shocking than him becoming president. History will write that up until the Trump era, the presidency of the United States was the most honored and respected office in the world. It will show that no president, not even Richard Nixon, abused and demeaned the presidency as much as Trump did.

Since I worked and spent time with him over twenty years ago, he has not changed one bit. Back then the things he liked, he praised—they were fantastic, wonderful, the best, none better, best in the world and on and on. It did not matter if what he "rated" them was true, if Trump liked them, then they were fantastic.

On the other hand, those things he did not like are things he rated fake! Disgusting, just terrible, the worst and on and on. It did not matter what the truth was, if Trump said it, then that became the truth no matter how obvious, it was a Trump Law.

As bad as it was, as many people as he hurt because he operated in a twisted state of mind, where logic, common sense, doing the right thing, and caring were words that did not exist in Trump's world, as president of a world superpower, to operate in that "exact same frame of mind," which he clearly is, affects billions of people and could lead to serious worldwide financial issues and, worse yet, war!

By everything written in this book and by his actions as president so far, it's extremely clear in his first one hundred days that Trump cost America hundreds of millions of wasted dollars.

The following is just a partial listing of how an inexperienced, uncaring president cost America hundreds of millions of taxpayers' dollars in his first one hundred days:

1. With travel bans that would not work, causing extreme emotional distress for innocent families worldwide, the cost to American taxpayers is still growing and will soon be in the hundreds of millions of dollars.

2. Despite having zero experience, Trump put members of his family in important White House positions where

they will make large personal financial gains while costing the taxpayers millions for their staff, travel costs,
etc.

3. He has used Air Force One to gain priceless promotion for his Florida mansion, making it possible for him
to raise membership fees from $100,000 to $200,000 per
person, and costing taxpayers $26 million in just the
first two months of his presidency.

4. At an operational cost of $200,000 per hour (figures
released by the government), he uses Air Force One to
fly around to thank those who voted for him, making
the same speeches and promises he made during his
campaign. Millions of dollars and presidential time is
wasted just so Trump can boost his own ego. One person I spoke with said it best: "This is an insult to the
office of the president, downright disgusting that our
so-called president can command the costliest jet in the
sky, a jet paid for by us that is supposed to transport
him safely so he can conduct business for America, yet
Trump throws it in our faces that he uses it as he pleases
so he can keep the people brainwashed and hear them
cheer for him. What a total waste of our money. This
man has no respect for us—we are just his pawns. To
think I voted for him."

5. Regarding the wall between the USA and Mexico,
thousands of years of history has proven that walls do
not work, and in fact no one in our government even
wants this wall built. Despite the fact that it could end
up costing us billions of dollars, Trump still wants it,

proving he cares not about his fellow Americans or the country's needs, only his own. It's just more presidential time and money wasted that could have been spent helping those in need and not feeding Trump's ego.

6. Trump claimed he signed more bills than any other president in his first one hundred days. As usual, to make him look good, here is where Trump applies what I call Trump's "deceptive facts." First, not one of these bills came from Trump, they were started during Obama's administration. Second, most of those bills are not important. More lies. More taking credit for what others did. Someday this will catch up to him.

7. Regarding shutting down the government: Trump once said he "wants to shut down the government to fix it." What this really means is he's the spoiled rich kid without a conscience who is not getting what he wants. I've said it again and again, Trump is so used to getting what he wants that he will do whatever it takes to get his own way.

Trump never wanted Obama as our president, and he didn't hide it. Why? He never really knew the man, so why such bitterness? Why spend so much time on someone that obviously Americans wanted as their president? He classifies those that are not wealthy as losers, and puts those whose skin color is not white even below that. Now he insists there will *never* be an Obamacare health program during his presidency, even though with the billions already spent on Obamacare it would make far more sense to fix the parts that don't work rather than throw out a program that clearly has certain parts that do work. This equation is simple—Trump will deny it all he wants, and will now more than ever, because he's in the White House, but the color of Obama's skin has everything to do with his opinion of him. Think of it, why else go after someone you never really knew? Here again we have millions of dollars being wasted as the reform in healthcare that is badly needed by Americans goes around and around while people are dying, and after more than half a year, this legislation has gone exactly nowhere.

When he runs his own companies, he does whatever he wants because he has no one to answer to. However, now he is responsible for America. Being responsible doesn't mean shutting down the entire government because the people in Washington are doing their jobs and watching out for We the People. It's clear that Trump's programs are not good for Americans, yet he wants them anyway and threatens to use his power to do just the opposite of that which he has sworn to do.

If he would sit down with the right experts and one by one go over the healthcare program, maybe they could come up with something that would work. However, that would take long hours, days and nights. Trump is so used to just telling people what to do that he has no idea how to actually create a program.

America needs a president that will gather up the best in their field, get them all in a room, roll up his sleeves and say, "Let's get to work." The biggest obstacle is the fact that Trump has never worked in his life.

There is one thing everyone gets, just in different degrees, that's been proven to be one of the most life-threatening medical conditions there is. Therefore, to live longer we must avoid it as much as we can. If you haven't guessed it by now, it's stress—a condition that can easily take years off one's life. Trump should look at photos showing how much past presidents aged during their terms. That even though they were far better suited for the position of president of a world superpower, stress got to them all and led to their rapid aging. For Trump, it will clearly be extreme stress. In his seventies, Trump's life on this Earth is already very limited, as time passes faster than ever before as you age. For Donald Trump, he's now had a dose of reality; he cannot do whatever he wants, and for the first time in his life he knows what hard work really is and faces extreme stress. Four years of what he is now going through will, without any doubt, shorten his years on this Earth because even he, the great Donald Trump, cannot escape the great equalizers of us all—time and stress. Is his ego more important than living longer? We shall soon see.

At his present rate, although it may become a little better overall, four years with Donald Trump will end up costing the people of the United States of America hundreds of billions in wasted tax dollars, far outweighing any good he may do, and that's assuming he can accomplish anything of importance for We the People. It will also take *years* off his life.

Some of his worshippers keep saying, "Give him a chance, quit getting on his case." To that I say, why should the country's taxpayers spend their money so Trump can *learn* to be president? He, his daughter, his son-in-law and certain other people around him making serious decisions for our country are the blind leading the blind.

It's very obvious Trump is not equipped or fit to lead a country that so many died to create. Although he speaks of "wonderful, terrific things," he, unfortunately, has the worst habit of any president in history—he lies, again and again and again. He promises great things but never delivers. The thousands in our American Dream programs saw this better than anyone. He talks about how terrible certain things are, that they must go, and then without skipping a beat, all of a sudden what was terrible is now terrific!

It cannot be made any clearer, that to him, Trump and his family come first and We the People come last. No matter what is said about Hillary Clinton, if she were president (which she should be because We the People voted for her), then by now many good things would have been accomplished or be in the works, without wasting months of presidential time and taxpayers' dollars. Furthermore, it is very doubtful there would be all the worries we now face surrounding North Korea and Russia.

As written in this book and by his own words, the bottom line for Trump is "I didn't know it was this much work, I miss my old life." It's clear that he should not be president because he will do far more damage and cost far more money than he will ever save We the People and We the Taxpayers.

One of his comments that best demonstrates his ineptness is "I thought it would be easy." He thought running the most powerful country in the world, being commander-in-chief of the most powerful military in history, being responsible for hundreds of millions of people's lives would be *easy*? What kind of person would ever think it would be easy?

My eleven-year-old son said, "Easy? Daddy, not running our entire country, maybe a small country, but America?" Imagine an eleven-year-old hearing the news I was watching and questioning Trump's thinking that it would be easy. Imagine an eleven-year-old saying, "Maybe he could run a small country but not a big country like America." Yet Trump, our president, actually thought it would be easy. This person is running our country? This person is in charge of our military? How many times does a steel beam have to hit his worshippers on the head before they see that the real Donald Trump is not equipped to run our country? When will they finally realize that only someone who knows what real work is like, only someone who knows what it's like to pay bills, only someone with a *conscience* can run the most complex country in the world.

37 Lies and Counting

Are lies important? Most of the time when someone lies it only affects themselves and certain people around them. Of course, some lies mean very little, like "Sorry I have a headache, I can't go with you today." Although a lie because the person saying it really feels fine and just does not want to do what the other person wants to do that day, it basically hurts no one. Then there is the lie, "I'm going to play golf today" by the husband, or, "I'm going to have lunch with the girls" by the wife, when they are really meeting someone for an affair. Of course, this hurts not only their marriage but many people around them. Then we get to the lie that hurts thousands of people, like the one Trump told to me and my people, which is serious because it hurt so many. Finally, we get to the ultimate lie, the kind that hurts millions or hundreds of millions. This type of lie can *only* come from someone with extreme power, the leader of a country, like the president of the United States, whose lies affect the very lives of hundreds of millions of people throughout the world.

There is much concern, and there should be, about the indisputable fact that President Donald Trump is a habitual liar. This is not speculation, it is a *fact*.

How many remember these words by Trump, judged by a score of 0 being complete falsehood and 10 being something he actually accomplished?

- "I can bring everyone together—I alone can do it." SCORE: 0

- "I'll build a wall along our southern border. Mexico will pay for it." SCORE: 0

- "I'll get rid of Obamacare." SCORE: 0

- "I will rebuild our country's infrastructure." SCORE: 0

- "I will save Medicare, Medicaid and Social Security." SCORE: 0

- "I will prosecute Hillary Clinton." SCORE: 0

- "I will never take a vacation." SCORE: 0

- "I will work my ass off." SCORE: 0

- "I will stop spending money on space exploration." SCORE: 0

- "I will bring back waterboarding." SCORE: 0

- "I will be the greatest jobs president that God ever created." SCORE: 0

- "Rather than throw China's president a steak dinner, I will buy him McDonalds and say let's get down to business." SCORE: 0

I could go on and on about the promises / lies Trump made while campaigning for president. Of course, these turned out to be lies *before* he even became president.

So why does he lie so very much? If you know Trump the way I do, have seen him operate and lie the way I have seen, the answers are clear. Trump lies to *achieve a goal*, to cover up the truth he does not want to have to face or that gets in his way of what *he wants*. By misrepresenting the truth, he can bend it to fit his needs. Being closely involved with him in a worldwide project, I saw firsthand how his lies hurt so many people.

Unfortunately, now he is president of one of the most powerful countries on Earth, and his lies have already hurt hundreds of millions by promising Americans a new, much better healthcare bill, and after seven months there was still none.

Speaking from fifty years of personal experience, and having witnessed for myself the scale at which he lies, I tried counting how many times Trump spoke false-hoods—saying outright lies starting from his first day as president. Even when only counting those lies concerning major domestic and foreign policy issues, *I stopped counting at thirty-seven.*

Long before he campaigned for the presidency, I, along with hundreds of others from across America and in over thirty countries, experienced firsthand the scale at which he lies—in ways that devastated us all. Because of these terrible experiences at the hands of Donald J. Trump, I wanted to see if he would continue lying even as president of our great country. Would he lie to the millions of Americans whose hard-earned money allows the president and his family to live like a king, have the best healthcare in the world, travel in the safest jet in the world, have the best security in the world and be set for life? So, I started counting his lies from his very first day as president. Even when counting just the lies concerning major American and foreign policy issues that would affect both Americans and the entire world, I stopped counting at thirty-seven, feeling that was more than enough from the office once considered among the most honest and ethical on Earth.

Donald J. Trump, as the leader of the most powerful country in history, LIED to the American people and to the world a minimum of thirty-seven times within just his first one hundred days in office, with each lie being about issues that concern every American. So why should he be trusted without making absolutely sure what he says is indeed the truth?

I based this book on years of personal experiences with Donald Trump that involved him lying to me, my wife and my staff, as well as to my promoters from around the world and to the public. These were lies that hurt many people who trusted him, costing much pain and money for many who believed in him. He had created a hateful situation so extreme that some actually wanted him dead, and had I not intervened they may have made their wishes come true, but his lies continued even into federal court.

Although not near the scope of America's present issues, the principal here is the same, yet the end results for the country are far worse. Presidential lies can lead to the most serious of problems for America and the entire world. At this point, anyone who continues to support Donald Trump is blinding themselves to the truth. I personally saw what happens when someone in a position of great power does not speak the truth. I saw the pain and destruction it caused, and I saw how those lies can turn normally calm people violent.

If just one year ago you would have told me that the president of the United States of America, the man holding the single most powerful and respected position in the world, had lied thirty-seven times about important issues that affect America and the world, I would have said you were crazy.

The world looks to America's president for knowledge, respectability and honesty, yet we have a president who constantly lies and can irreparably tarnish the entire country's reputation. Congress must not allow this to happen! If America underestimates the power of lies, it could well lead to situations far worse than those of September 11.

The events I produced for Donald Trump involved people from over thirty countries. It was like a small United Nations gathering. The speech he made to us then was so impressive and so powerful I can still see and hear Trump standing before all of my promoters from around the world, the winners of his events, my staff and top VIPs, telling them how great they all were. I can still recall him announcing that the next year he would be moving these events to his largest casino, with much higher awards, more activities and more events.

Everything he said was like music to our ears. We had all sacrificed so much time and money for an entire year, this was exactly what everyone wanted to hear. Hearing it directly from Trump himself was more than we had ever expected, and it was one of the greatest moments of our lives. Returning home with Trump's words still ringing, we continued to celebrate, gaining media exposure and admiration from our home cities and countries for weeks. Then all of a sudden came the news that every word Trump had said to us was a lie.

There would be no top casino representatives, no big awards, no exciting competitions, and no more Donald Trump American Dream events. We were all devastated, and many lives were turned upside down. We had given our all to Trump, and many had spent thousands of dollars of their own savings for him. For all we had done for Trump, he had repaid us with nothing but lies.

This is just one example of how lies can affect honest and hardworking people's lives in the most tragic ways.

His attempt to ban people from certain countries from legally entering the United States, although shot down by our judicial system, caused those people tremendous pain and suffering and American taxpayers millions of dollars.

There is an untold amount of video footage showing our president making statements that are outright and undeniable LIES. I had stopped counting at thirty-seven, but it's easy to believe there have been far more since that time.

If the leader of the most powerful military in the world consistently lies to the entire world, it could easily lead to war.

Trump said he is "100 percent willing" to testify under oath about the situation with FBI Director James Comey. When Trump testified during my own court action against him in a sworn deposition that took hours, Trump was professionally videotaped by us through special permission from the judge in that case. He was so very convincing that even my attorneys were worried that he would be believed, rather than me. After all, it was the great Donald Trump who was speaking. However, as convincing as he was (if I hadn't known better, even I would have thought he was telling the truth), I knew for a fact he was lying. I was always one step ahead of him and could prove he was lying, and I did. To the shock of even my own attorneys I gave them the proof, which when presented to him, catching him in lie after lie after lie, Trump got so upset he stormed out of the room, something you just can't do or usually see during a federal deposition.

My attorneys told his to either get Trump back, or we'd ask that he be cited for contempt of court. They got him to come back, and the deposition continued for hours with even more lies spoken under oath.

In the end, as I wrote previously, Trump settled and paid us.

The moral of this story is simple—it's much easier to tell the truth. The stakes in my lawsuit were small to him, all Trump had to do was pay us what he owed, which was a drop in the bucket for someone like him. However, despite this he spent two years of his life going to court, even though he had always said his time was worth a lot of money, and he ended up having to pay a settlement, his attorneys' fees for two years (for some of the most expensive attorneys in the country), plus my own attorneys' fees and costs. So, Trump spent two years of his life having to deal with depositions, sworn statements, witnesses and many other court actions, *plus* spent many times what he'd originally owed me. Does that sound like a smart businessman to you?

More important, he constantly lied under oath when he could have easily settled the case in a matter of minutes before it ever got to that point, while I consistently told the truth—something which the federal mediator, my lawyers and even his lawyers saw.

If Trump ever testifies, with his job as president at stake, does anyone really think he will tell the truth about anything that could possibly get him in trouble? James Comey has nothing to lose since Trump already took care of that by firing him, and those that have known Comey for years have stated what an honest and ethical man he is. But Trump has constantly lied to the American people and to the world, both before and after becoming president. Trump has everything to lose, and since lying is part of his nature, it's nothing to him, whether under oath or not. I witnessed firsthand how he lies so much and so easily, and that at times he actually believes what he says because he cannot separate the truth from falsehood. This is not speculation—I've seen it happen right before my eyes many times.

The good thing is that Comey was smart about this. Even though Trump is the president, Comey was concerned that Trump would lie. He probably never suspected he would be fired, but he was still cautious and documented what Trump said to him as much as he could, which shows how professional he truly is.

For forty-one days, Trump led the world to believe he might have tapes of his conversations with Comey, when he knew he didn't. How totally ridiculous is it for the president to play a game with such an important issue? Leading the world to believe he may have recordings when he really doesn't is not presidential behavior. Then again, most things Trump does demean the office of the president.

If Trump ever testifies about anything, the entire world will be listening. I guarantee you when it comes to anything negative, he will LIE. If he lied so many times in our years in court, he will surely lie about anything that might make him look bad while he's president. The most important thing to him is to look good.

Trump has tried to limit free speech by going after the media because he doesn't like what they say because it's the truth about him, and not a witch hunt like he keeps saying. He routinely ignores or cuts off questions he doesn't like. If that's not a direct attack on free speech, then what is? Furthermore, not allowing cameras during a press conference, a tradition for decades, is still further proof that Trump is trying to control the media. This is the behavior of a despot, not a president.

What's most ironic is when he says how upset he is with the media for "not reporting the truth." Talk about a hypocritical statement—no one misleads the American public more than Donald Trump. Also, you'd be hard-pressed to find the legitimate media like ABC, CBS, NBC, FOX, CNN telling outright lies like Trump has. For example, as soon as the Supreme Court announced their amended position on his travel ban, immediately from Trump's White House came an announcement that it was a "9-0 decision in favor of Trump." I heard and saw this myself on several news stations. However, not long after came the actual truth. Only very specific parts of the ban favored Trump's position, far from the "9-0 decision" the White House had announced. If it wasn't for the media reporting the truth, Americans and the world would have been misled and fed LIES.

The White House belongs to We the People, Not Trump. The media room is equipped with cameras and lighting to allow Americans to see what's going on in their country. Denying Americans their right to see a media conference is something a dictator would do, not the president of the United States.

On top of everything else, when the U.S. college student unjustly imprisoned in North Korea died, Trump stressed, "He should have been brought home sooner, much sooner," basically pointing a finger at Obama. Yet there are three other Americans still there and he's done nothing to bring them home.

It is amazing that Trump has had the CIA, FBI, NSA and the Department of Defense *all* telling him Russia did indeed affect our elections, yet he dismisses it, even though he has zero experience in this area. Just imagine if our intelligence agencies tell him something that could lead to a disaster like 9-11, and like the Russian situation, he doesn't believe it. Thousands or even millions of Americans could die. It's quite unbelievable that the president of the United States does not take his own intelligence community seriously. Does that not constitute a treasonous act, since it could potentially lead to terrible disasters for America and its citizens? Who reading this, if they were president and found out our country had been attacked, would dismiss it the way Trump has? Who would think they know more than the entire American intelligence community? This alone should be an impeachable offense—for what is more anti-American than not paying attention to our intelligence community?

Since Trump became president he has accomplished nothing of real significance, his statements that he has signed more bills, etc., than any other president is basically false, as most were already in the works before he assumed office, or the bills were something others did that he just signed. Consider all the time he has spent flying to his Florida mansion, flying around the country to make what were basically speeches praising himself, instead of doing something that would help Americans. All the time he spends criticizing Democrats. All the time he spends defending the Russia situation and more. All this time, and We the Taxpayers' money, wasted.

It's an incredible waste of presidential time, instead of working on a better healthcare law and scores of other programs to help We the People, the president of the United States watches hours of television just about every day. Is this what America really wants? Instead of getting important information from all the government agencies, with thousands of staff that are experts in their respective fields, so he may better serve, America's president gets his information from television.

Then there is all the time he spent criticizing Obamacare as a disaster, yet after half a year he still has no healthcare plan in effect. Aside from bills, etc., created by others that he just signed, one would be hard-pressed to come up with any real accomplishments of President Trump. One thing he has accomplished that every American should be very upset about is that, since he became president, certain of his personal businesses have increased in revenues. Think about that while you struggle to support your family.

If all that's been said in this book doesn't prove to you that Donald Trump should not be president because he's not for We the People, he's for himself, then this fact should. In office as president for only twenty-four weeks, he spent a minimum of sixteen weeks at his own properties. Isn't the White House supposed to be the home of the president? It's no wonder nothing is getting done when the president is never in the White House!

While the country he promised "to make great again" is in the worst shape it has been in years, with division within the country and serious issues throughout the world, he personally is becoming richer and richer from contacts he's made as president. He will, of course, deny this, as he does for anything that is basically negative about him, despite being the truth.

He can deny it all he wants, but there is just too much evidence about these statements. While he has accomplished nothing major for America, except taking credit for what others have done, Trump personally is becoming wealthier than he's ever been thanks to using the presidency to accomplish this. This is exactly what I've predicted because as I've constantly said Trump is about Trump first, everything else including America is second. After all, what can one expect from a president that lies to those he swore to serve?

I only hope that the people who feel he's a good man and a good president end up questioning Trump, eventually see right through him, bring justice to the country and don't allow someone who clearly puts himself and his family before everything, even America, to get the upper hand.

To those who still support Trump, it's time to wake up! He is ruining America and the reputation of the president of The United States.

No president in American history has ever started his term in such a negative way, and no president has caused so much division within the country since the Civil War. Then again, no president has ever lied at least thirty-seven times to We the People in his first few months in office.

Is this the kind of president that Americans really want? I very much doubt it.

Finally, certain media and politicians keep saying how we must improve our election system so that voters have knowledge of what's going on to allow them to make a better judgment about who to vote for. Are these people brain-dead? The American voting system is a scam. As I've clearly stated, Americans who vote are just wasting their time because their vote has nothing to do with electing the president of the United States. Once again, the president of the United States is NOT elected by the American voters. A few hundred people from the Electoral College vote to determine who will be America's next president. It doesn't matter that hundreds of millions of Americans vote, since just seventy-seven people elected Trump as president. The millions of Americans who voted may as well have stayed home because their vote meant nothing.

That's right, folks. The hundreds of millions of Americans that pay taxes to run this country, pay the salaries of Congresspersons, finance the military and the millions of military men and women who risk and give their lives for America—their votes are worthless because they do not get to determine their president, only a handful of unknown people do. This is by far the biggest deception ever perpetrated on the American people in our history, the fiction that all Americans actually get to elect their president.

Now there is proof the Russians did affect the election. They hurt Clinton and helped Trump, combined with the FBI leak that made Clinton look guilty without even a trial.

Everyone keeps saying Trump won, why doesn't he just leave it alone and move forward? Why is he always defending his winning? It's amazing no one gets it but Trump. He knows he did not win the presidency, he knows the Russians caused Hillary to lose the electoral vote, that Hillary won the popular vote, because even the Russians could not affect the hundreds of millions of Americans that went to the poles and voted for her.

Forty-four out of fifty states plus the District of Columbia have refused to provide certain types of voter information to the Trump administration's "election integrity commission," with the rest citing that the information is *already public*. Yet Trump suggests through his favorite mouthpiece, his smartphone, that the states have something "to hide."

From wanting to be president so badly because of the invaluable business contacts he can gather to make himself wealthier than he ever could be without being president, not caring what he is costing America or what he has done to the office of president, and being an unethical man without a conscience, he will do all he can to remain president despite knowing that Hillary Clinton is the rightful president of the United States.

Millions of men and women lost limbs, and far worse—their lives—from serving in the American military. Millions of wives and children have to go through their lives without their husbands and fathers because they fought for their country, fought so they and others have the right to live in a free country. They gave their lives so they and their fellow Americans would have the right to vote for the person who would be their commander-in-chief, their president. Yet here we are: Americans' votes don't count. We the People DO NOT ELECT THE PRESIDENT.

The American people are getting sick and tired of Congress accomplishing little or nothing. Look at how many disturbances there have been. In speaking to people around the country, it's clear things are going to get worse, far worse. In fact, many have told me that unless every Congressperson starts doing their duty to serve and protect Americans, and to make things right before Trump does even more damage to the greatest country in history, they want ALL the legislators replaced. In my seven decades on this Earth, I have never heard such dissatisfaction with our government, and Americans mean it—they have had enough. If this was a trial in an American court, with all the deception, meddling by Russia, etc., it would be declared a mistrial.

Accordingly, the legislators should overturn America's first "tainted election," no matter what it takes, and make Hillary Clinton the winner, the first female president of the United States of America because Americans deserve justice. They deserve the president *they* voted for, not one for whom seventy-seven unknown people voted. Yes, sounds crazy, but even worse is what *is* going on in Washington, what a mess the White House has been, the fact that more time and money is being wasted while nothing gets done to help millions that need healthcare. Does anyone really think any of this would have happened if the people's choice for president, Hillary Clinton, was elected instead of Trump? NO WAY, our country would never be in the shape it is now, and odds are she would have kept Obamacare but fixed the parts that needed fixing.

I have to say this one final time—remember, if you hear Trump use words like "terrific" or "great" or "wonderful," watch out! Trump has a very bad habit of constantly using words like these to try to convince everyone that things are better with him as their leader. Most especially, watch out when he says something is "good for everyone." We all know when it comes to things like healthcare, there is no such thing as "good for everyone." He can't even get a majority to accept his plans, much less every American to agree with any one of them.

If everything stated in this book does not prove to you that Donald Trump should not be president, because he's not for We the People, he's for himself, then this should. In office as president for only the first twenty-four weeks, he spent a minimum of sixteen of those weeks at his own properties. Isn't the White House supposed to be the home of the president of the United States? It's no wonder nothing is getting done, the president is missing from the White House!

It's bad enough the president spends more time at his own properties than the White House, but after being in office for barely six months, he has already started his reelection campaign, even though the election is years down the road. This is more time and money not being used to help We the People, but used to try to get reelected. It's so unbelievable, it even shocked *me*. Trump spends most of his time not serving America, and now he's already spending presidential time kicking off his reelection campaign.

If ever there was a time for a new American Revolution, it's NOW! It's time for Congress and the Senate to save America from becoming Trump's country, which is where it is heading. This country has been through too much—too many lives have been lost to allow just one man to undo all the good others have done for centuries. Trump is not serving We the People, he's serving We the Trumps.

The tragic part of all this is Trump could have been a great president and done a lot to help the people in this country, but unfortunately, he grew up without a conscience. He doesn't know how to care for those less fortunate because he feels only wealthy people like him deserve to live the way he does. Without a conscience, he can *never* relate to the everyday struggles people go through because he's *never* in his entire life worried about paying even one bill, *never* had anything but the best healthcare in the world, *never* worried about giving his children anything but the best in life and *never* worried about putting his children through college. How can anyone who has *never* experienced what 99.99 percent of America has experienced possibly help them? His attempt to help We the People is like a young child performing heart surgery—it can't be done.

Trump's wealth will increase more than ever since he became president, and will continue to increase thanks to We the People paying $200,000 an hour so he can fly in the safest jet on Earth, be protected by the best security on Earth, and meet the most powerful people on Earth that will lead to priceless business opportunities. Trump's children, their children, their children's children are all set for life. They will *never* worry about having anything but the best of healthcare, *never* worry about things most Americans worry about on an almost daily basis—and all because We the Taxpayers are paying for it.

Should we be jealous of all this, or wish him and his family well? That depends on what he and his family will really do for Americans. So far, they have done nothing but criticize Obamacare, yet after more than half a year Americans still don't have the healthcare he promised them. Trump has spent most of his term trying to ban immigrants from countries that not even one terrorist has come from, causing hardship for millions of innocent men, women and children, while getting a gold medal from the country where almost all of the 9/11 terrorists were citizens. He has spent months trying to get a wall built that the cash-rich drug dealers laugh at, knowing they can go under, around or over, or find another way. In short, there is not one major thing Trump or his family has done to help Americans, while he and his family are building contacts for their future. Those contacts will earn them hundreds of millions of dollars, contacts they *never* could have ever made without Trump as president.

Trump said it himself, "I didn't know this would be so much fun!" Being president is a game to him, so he will do all he can to win because he doesn't like to lose.

Trump's goal is to be one of the wealthiest men in the world, with his name on as many buildings and businesses as he can get. He's in his seventies and knows he's not even close to having $2 billion, much less being one of the richest men in the world. By the way, one of the reasons he will not reveal his taxes is because he doesn't want anyone to know his real true wealth is barely a billion. He knows that the *only* way he can ever achieve his goal is by being president because without making the contacts only an American president can make there is no way he could ever gain the wealth needed to become one of the richest men in the world. This is why after just months, despite the fact that he really has not accomplished anything major for America, despite the millions of taxpayers' dollars he's wasted, he's already started to campaign for the next term, even though it's almost four years away. Instead of spending presidential time working on something to benefit the country and its people, he's using that time to raise money for himself. Guess who's paying for the fleet of cars and security taking him to the site where he's going to start raising money? The American taxpayers, of course.

Just when I think Trump can't do anything more selfish, he tops himself. One of his "promises" was that he was going to "work his ass off" as our president. With the fact that he has no political or military experience, you would think he would work his ass off learning all he could about being president. Instead, he took off every weekend during his first two months to get out of the cold Washington weather and travel to his mansion in warm, sunny Florida, promoting it so much that he was able to increase the membership fee at his club there from $100,000 to $200,000 per person. Then he flies to locations where he won the popular vote to *make speeches about himself*. Neither of these did anything to help the country or We the People; they cost taxpayers millions for Air Force One, plus millions more for security. Now he tops even that waste of presidential time and money by spending government time and resources to raise money for his next presidential campaign!

A man became president of the United States who has no political or military experience. Rather than try to educate himself, he instead spends 70 percent of his time on himself, NOT working for the country and its people, wastes millions of taxpayers' dollars, then goes even further by using government cars, security and taxpayer money to take him to a location so he can raise money for his next campaign. If all of this does not prove to you he is not fit to be president and does not prove he is out mainly for himself, then you truly have been brainwashed.

People have asked me, from knowing so much about Trump, if there is any way I could sum up in one sentence what we can expect from him as our president during a four-year term. By now everyone knows Trump is unpredictable, except for one thing. So, my answer is, after you have read this book twice so you will know the *real* Donald Trump, I don't need a full sentence to describe what to expect from Trump during a four-year term, I can do it in just two words—HE LIES!

I have mentioned "We the People" many times throughout this book because that is who the president of the United States is elected to serve. However, as I've consistently pointed out and for the final time, Trump was NOT elected by the 128 million Americans that went to the polls and voted. Trump was "officially" made President by seventy-seven electoral voters.

Therefore, by his actions as president of the United States of America, "We the People" have now become "We the Trumps." Those that would deny this only need to look to the facts.

Despite all the vastly educated people in Washington, Trump, his daughter and son-in-law combined have ZERO political or military experience whatsoever, yet they occupy the highest echelons of the White House.

Trump totally disregards our professional, experienced and educated intelligence agencies, putting America's very security at stake.

He sends out messages from his smartphone almost daily that he expects Americans to believe, which many times have nothing to do with the duties of America's president.

At a cost of $200,000 per hour, he uses Air Force One to benefit the Trump family personally, not We the People. Trump has no respect for the most honored office in American history, the office of president of the United States of America.

He uses his position as president to ensure that he

and his family have the connections that will gain them personal wealth in the hundreds of millions, even billions of dollars, both now and in the future. Just one example is, in a meeting with China's president, the Trump businesses gained preliminary approval in China for *six* trademarks, in scientific and technological services, construction, medical and veterinary services.

Any one of these would easily generate billions of dollars for Trump businesses. As president and having his daughter and son-in-law as White House advisers, he has a very distinctive edge to develop powerful business advantages like these that he or any other person would NEVER GET without the prestige of the presidency. Trump is using the power of America to get this business position.

Keep in mind that because of the conflicts of being President, he conveniently put his family members into the White House to plant the seeds for *billions* in future business when he leaves office.

This and much more is changing We the People, three of the most important words in American history, to WE THE TRUMPS, something unprecedented in American history.

Millions of Americans and their families struggle to pay their bills and worry about the security of their country because their own president fails to recognize reports from his own intelligence community. They worry that nothing for their benefit is getting done in Washington, they are faced with trying to get the same healthcare as their Congresspersons, and the better healthcare promised by their president is has not happened.

We the Trumps continue to enrich themselves, doing as they please, despite the division in America since Trump became president, the worst division since the Civil War, and despite the fact that there is far more not being accomplished in Washington than is being accomplished, all under the rule of We the Trumps.

For months, there have been thousands of hours spent dealing with the Trump/Russia situation. In fact, more time has been spent on that than any other topic, including healthcare.

Since his healthcare bill failed to pass *twice*, he went on-air to talk about the problems with Obamacare, blaming his fellow Republicans and others for his healthcare plan not passing. Since the day he started to campaign for president, he called Obamacare a disaster and told the world all that's wrong with it.

First, going on television and talking about what he's been saying for almost a year shows he's trying to cover up the *truth*—that he promised Americans a better healthcare system but has failed twice, simply because it was not good for Americans. We're lucky Congress is not passing something just because Trump wants it, or Americans would end up with something that could be far worse than what they now have.

Second, Congress may have had something worth signing if perhaps Trump had not played golf twenty times, not spent so much time and money flying to cities for pep rallies for himself, not spent his first two months in office going to his Florida mansion every weekend, not spent so much time talking about how great he is, etc., and had spent even half of this wasted time working on a healthcare bill that would help Americans while not asking others to do the work so he can just sign it. However, to continue to bring up Obamacare after he had seven months to create a new healthcare system shows once again he is a liar and is not fit to be president.

Trump had months to not only get a new healthcare system up and running as he promised, but to accomplish other important issues America needs resolved. He's now spent hundreds of millions of American tax dollars basically on himself. Seventy-five percent of the world feels he is a bad leader, affecting not only the reputation of the office of president but of America and its people. However, added to this is the fact that America has a president who has discredited his own intelligence community rather than standing up for them over Russia, a country which clearly tainted the American election so Trump would win. This was made even more clear by the fact that 75 percent of the population of many countries think Trump is a bad president while Russia has a 40 percent *approval rating* of Trump. There is clearly something un-American going on here that started when Trump brought his Miss Universe pageant to Russia.

For the president of the United States of America, while at a dinner party with world leaders, to go over to the president of Russia without his interpreter and carry on a *private* conversation for an hour is not only highly irregular but very suspicious.

Besides the fact that it's rude and insulting that an American president spent so much time with a country that's not even an American ally, it's made even more suspicious by all the unanswered questions surrounding Russia's influence on Trump's election and Russian connections to Trump's staff. An American president having a *totally private* conversation with the leader of a country that is an enemy, without even one additional American representative present, borders on treason.

Imagine an American president who has already raised months of unanswered questions about himself, his election as president and his staff, discussing who knows what with our enemy without even one other American present to verify what was said. With Trump known to lie so much, we can't believe anything he says about this meeting.

Trump has repeatedly broken American presidential traditions, such as dismissing a member of the press from a press conference, refusing to answer certain questions asked by member of the press, banning cameras from press conferences and accusing the press of reporting fake news without proof. He is limiting or banning free speech, one of our country's most important constitutional rights. However, all of this combined with something as serious as an American president having a private meeting with one of his country's greatest threats, denying the press and all Americans what could be serious and important information, goes well beyond anything any president has ever done.

America's president has used Air Force One many times for nonpresidential business. Trump omitted Saudi Arabia from the list of countries of banned immigrants *to protect us*, but it was only to protect future Trump business with the Saudis.

He has openly lied so many times, deceived Americans about so many important issues and limited free speech. No American president has ever committed such a serious attack on America's Constitution as to meet privately with one of America's greatest threats.

These and other serious issues written herein are things no true American president would ever do, and so far, he's only been in office for seven months. Just imagine the damage he can do if he is president for four years. WAKE UP AMERICA!

No one went through what I have with Trump. I can say without hesitation that the president of the United States of America LIES and lives in his own world, one that he likes to control. However, now as president he can no longer control things himself, which leads to massive internal confusion.

America does not want or need a president with these bogus credentials. Far too many have died to make America one of the fairest and most powerful countries in history. America does not need *one man* to erase so much of what America stands for and has accomplished, especially since he is *not America's choice for president.*

I have said this many times in the book, but since it's also being said again and again by Trump's brainwashed followers, I will address it a final time. Anthony Scaramucci, White House Communications Director for *ten days*, and one of Trump's lawyers, Jay Sekulow, both continued to lie to We the People by saying, "The People made Trump President, he's doing what they want and what they elected him to do."

First, as described at the beginning of this chapter is

a list of just some of what Trump promised Americans if he became president. The entire list scored a zero, meaning, so far, he's not accomplished even one of the things he promised Americans. Second, and one final time, We the People *did not elect Trump as our president*. I'm an American whose vote, like over 130 million other Americans' votes, did not count toward electing the president of the United States of America, so stop lying to us and leading us to believe that our votes elected Trump, when just seventy-seven electoral votes, made from an obsolete and outdated voting system, actually put Trump into the White House, *not* We the People. You are *lying* to Americans, or why else would my eleven-year-old son as well as many voting-age Americans I spoke with who heard you think that their votes actually elected America's president until I explained to them why it did not.

Congress, including many of Trump's own Republicans, along with the FBI and the other American intelligence agencies ALL want Russia sanctioned for interfering with our voting system. However, Trump thinks, as opposed to hundreds whose decisions are based on facts and research, that his one opinion should outweigh all others. Anyone feel the word *dictator* fits here?

Probably one of the most ridiculous Lies from Trump since he became president was "I Won! By the largest margin in the history of America." First, when it came to the extremely outdated centuries-old electoral college voting system, he had just seventy-seven more votes than Hillary; others had won by far larger margins than just seventy-seven people. When it came to actual Americans that voted, Hillary received almost 3 million MORE

VOTES THAN TRUMP. I'm sure everyone realizes just how many Americans that is who voted for Hillary over Trump. So the Truth here is Trump won by just seventy-seven individual votes on one hand and LOST by almost 3 million on the other hand, yet he continues to say he "won by the largest landslide in history."

One hundred, Three hundred, Five hundred, a Thousand—how many Lies, how many broken promises does it take before Americans have had enough from the one person in this country that people should trust?

Many have tried to take down Trump but have not succeeded. Seeing the true Donald J. Trump long ago, I came to the conclusion that there is only one person that can ever actually show the world the real Donald Trump, the one described in this book, the one person that is his worst enemy. That person is Trump *himself*.

I will leave you with Trump's own words of wisdom to his son Donald Trump Jr. In teaching him about business and life, Trump once told his son, "Don't ever trust anyone." Sometime later, Trump tested his son and asked him, "What did I tell you about who to trust?"

Trump Jr. replied, "I don't trust anyone, no one except you, you're my dad," to which Trump replied, "You failed. I said don't trust...ANYONE!"

For once, Trump Sr. got it right.

I rest my case.

"Why Aren't You Mad as Hell?"

My fellow Americans, why are you not *mad as hell?*

One of the many statements that stuck with me was when Trump promised Americans that, despite his love for golf, he would be *far too busy to play* and would instead be "working his ass off" for We the People.

In fact, he was so very busy he could only play golf NINETEEN TIMES during his first six months in office, compared to former President Obama who played golf just once in the same time frame. Trump flew to his mansion in warm and sunny Florida to get away from the cold Washington weather eight weekends *in a row*. Then there were all of the trips he took where people cheered him on as he talked about nothing except how great he was during the campaign. These trips accomplished nothing for Americans except the millions of tax dollars it cost for Air Force One and his security.

On his first trip overseas as president, Trump met the leader of Saudi Arabia—the country that produced the most terrorists who killed 3,000 people, destroyed the Twin Towers and damaged the Pentagon in 9-11—one of America's greatest tragedies—yet he did not include that country on his list of banned immigrants from "terrorist" countries. There he received that country's highest honor—a Gold Medal. He claimed he secured America billions of dollars' worth of business from that trip, when in fact that country needed the military equipment and they were going to buy it from us anyway, regardless of Trump making a trip there. Most of the president's time there was spent having dinner parties and celebrations and receiving his medal.

Then he caused an uproar and embarrassed America in front of the entire world by pulling out of the Paris agreement, basically denying that humans are not directly responsible for climate change due to our carbon emissions. We now join the only two other countries that are not signatories—Nicaragua and Syria.

Then there was the long-awaited trip to Poland and Russia. In Poland, there were once again more speeches full of self-praise, but nothing got accomplished. In Russia, we had the two most powerful leaders in the world, the two that could help the world more than any other two people on this Earth, and after all the time and money spent to get to Russia, our president's workday consisted of spending a little over two hours with Russia's president.

How many of you would like to take your family with you, fly in the most luxurious and safest jet in the world (a plane larger than most homes), be treated like a king wherever you went, have your workdays consist of getting gold medals, enjoy fancy dinner parties and ceremonies honoring you, and then meet with the leader of Russia, one of the most important countries to American foreign policy, and have the entire meeting consist of just two hours, with all of it costing American taxpayers millions of dollars for each trip, with nothing accomplished that actually helps Americans. Would you feel you were doing your job as president?

In his first six months, Trump had time to tweet over *five hundred times*, spent a total of almost *seven weeks* at his golf properties, saw his half-baked healthcare bill fail, had his travel ban shot down, and passed exactly ZERO pieces of major legislation.

This is what the president calls "working his ass off" while costing We the Taxpayers tens of millions of dollars for Air Force One and his security.

The question is, has the president actually accomplished *anything* that he promised all Americans he would do if elected?

In June 2017, there were a total of eight on-camera press briefings from the White House. So far in July there have been ZERO. When they do bother to conduct a briefing, it's off-camera, audio only, and conducted by the deputy press secretary, not her boss at the time, Sean Spicer. His last appearance happened only because his deputy wasn't in the White House that day! Sean Spicer can't be bothered answering questions from the American press, yet he has no problem being interviewed by the Christian Broadcasting Network, telling them how "engaged" the White House is with the press on a daily basis. Who does he think he is kidding? Why are press briefings so short and say almost nothing, and why won't they answer questions? That's their JOB.

Trump attacked Attorney General Jeff Sessions for recusing himself from the Russia investigation. Trump actually stated he would never have hired Sessions if he had known he would recuse himself. Hey Mr. President, the man is DOING HIS JOB. How about you do YOURS?

Where is the healthcare he promised everyone? Trump

calls Obamacare a disaster, yet spends 20 percent of his presidential time and taxpayer dollars playing golf and hobnobbing around the globe just to be treated like a king, having the best of everything and giving We the People absolutely nothing in return.

Where is the wall he promised Mexico would pay for?

Trump once said to me, "Imagine being president, you would have connections to every world leader, which could turn into billions for your businesses." There was no doubt in my mind that this comment referred to himself and his empire, as if he had *planned* on being president all along and just waiting for the right time.

Remember it's our taxpayer dollars, the money every American worked so hard for, that makes it possible for Trump and his family to fly around the world in the ultimate luxury and security, play golf, receive medals and awards and travel every weekend to his mansion in warm and sunny Florida. What have We the People received in return?

We the People should be mad as hell that we have a president using our hard-earned tax dollars and his presidential time to do nothing except get praise for himself and receive awards and presidential treatment, not because he is Donald Trump, but because he represents America.

While Trump and his family are enjoying a life only a few dozen people in the entire world ever experience, millions of Americans suffer because they do not have proper healthcare, and they suffer trying to figure out how to pay their taxes and take care of their families. There is something terribly wrong with this picture.

The president of the United States *should* be working his ass off for We the People because we've given him the life only one person on the planet every four years can have, thanks to We the People who pay for everything.

If ever there was a time for Americans to get mad, it's now! We the People have been changed to We the Trumps, putting his family in the White House with no experience whatsoever, while those with years of experience sit on the outside looking in. Trump and his family build connections and revenue for themselves while We the People pay the bills, and the Trumps travel throughout the world in ultimate luxury.

If you take a look at everything written in this book, take a pen and paper and write down all Trump has not done for this country and all he has received for himself and his family. There is no way it comes out any way other than WE THE TRUMPS. We the People are here just to pay for Trump to enjoy his life like none of us ever will.

Does this sound like I'm jealous? No, I am NOT! I am MAD. If Trump was really working his ass off like he promised, if America now had the healthcare system he promised, if we had a prescription system where I did not have to worry about paying for a prescription that cost $16,000 a month to sustain my life, then he would deserve everything he is getting.

However, for someone to live the way he has since becoming president, vacationing every weekend in Florida during his very first months in office rather than working the hardest to keep his promise of healthcare, etc., NOT traveling to areas of the country just to have people applaud him and praise him for accomplishing nothing for the people, NOT traveling to foreign countries to try and bring peace to the world yet spending only two hours of the entire trip meeting with the country we most need to mend relations with. All this proves he is not fit to be our president, and he is, as I've always said, thinking only of himself and his family, and WE THE PEOPLE are paying for it.

Why Americans aren't mad, I can't understand. Everyone works far too hard to give their families what they can, too many people suffer because they don't have the proper medical care or medicine, too many people die needlessly because they don't have adequate healthcare and medicine. Trump and Congress have a duty to care for all the American people.

Think about this, you work so hard and pay tax dollars so that our president and government can ensure that we have the best healthcare and medicine we need and more, yet in seven months the president has spent over a hundred million dollars on himself. You should be furious! If ever a president has used We the People, has taken advantage of We the People, and shows he doesn't care about We the People, it's now.

And as a final thought, forget all these words he says about how he is trying to make a greater America, that he has done more than any other president, because what I've just outlined here proves that it's nothing but lies, the truth is the truth—we don't have the healthcare promised, and, if the stock market is doing well, it is not because of Trump, it is because Americans have made it so by working to build this country. Many of the good and patriotic executives of companies throughout America have cared about their employees and done all they can to improve working conditions and to give people a decent salary, not anything that Washington or the president has done.

Every American should read this book so they know what's real. It cannot be any clearer, seeing what he has done for himself and his family and not for We the People. "We the Trumps" are in the White House, the first time We the People are not.

Anyone that thinks I am jealous of Trump is a 1,000 percent wrong, or that I am upset with Trump because it's a personal thing—you are a 1,000 percent wrong. I am fuming mad that the one man who is supposed to be our savior, supposed to bring good things to We the People, is doing just the opposite—abusing the greatest privilege any person on Earth could ever have, abusing the taxpayers' dollars that so many work so many thousands of hours for, so the president may live the way he does. Trump is someone who could help millions of people live a better life, have the healthcare and medications they need when they need them, saving thousands upon thousands of lives, yet he does not concentrate on any of that and instead spends more time playing golf and accepting awards than doing anything for We the People. Just imagine if you take all the days Trump has played golf, all the days he has traveled to other states to give himself praise and have rallies, all the days he has traveled overseas to accomplish little or nothing, all the hours he has spent sending Tweets and add up all those days and hours. Imagine what a good, true president could have accomplished in that time for We the People.

It's time Americans got mad—really mad—and got rid of anyone in Congress, and any president, who does NOTHING because there is no excuse for lack of a good healthcare system and proper medications—a prescription that can cost as high as $16,000 a month, so you are essentially being penalized for having cancer. It should not take months or years to create a healthcare system. Obama already put legislation in place, it just needs certain areas corrected and made better. Instead of improving Obamacare, Trump wants to throw it out and start all over again, wasting more time and money while people suffer and die from not having what they need. It's time Americans start a revolution—a revolution where the people's votes count and the electoral college is abolished because it is a joke, a revolution where Congress and the president have to live with the same healthcare system as the taxpayers. It's a joke that We the People cannot elect our own president, that a few hundred people no one even knows or even sees are the ones who actually elect the president of our country. Why are we living with something that was created during the 1700s when this country had but a tiny fraction of the people, and educated people, that it now has?

As I said before, no one thought more of Donald Trump than I did at one time, and I know he could have been a great leader and great president, but unfortunately, he grew up with so much wealth and power he never learned to care for anyone except himself. Not only is he without a conscience, but he is also without a heart. How else could he play golf, take a seventeen-day vacation after already spending many weekends at his mansion in Florida and taking trips for his own pep rallies while We the People sit on needles and pins waiting for a new healthcare system that will never pass Congress, no matter what rhetoric the president spouts on Twitter, unless it's good for all Americans.

My fellow Americans, I ask you again, *why are you not mad as hell?*

PS: Free copies of this are being mailed to certain members of Congress, the FBI and other important government agencies, plus key media groups so they are aware of important TRUTHS and FACTS as written herein.

Dedications

This is for my beautiful wife Suthanya, and my sons Steven and Michael Houraney, whom I treasure as much as life itself.

This book is also dedicated to every American who voted but did not have their vote counted in the 2016 U.S. presidential election because their government used a voting system created in the eighteenth century, denying them their right to select the next president of the United States by a margin of almost 3 million votes.

I also dedicate it to the mothers and fathers who sacrifice so much in order that their children may have a better life.

It is dedicated to my fellow Americans who work hard most of their lives, which has made America such a great country. From firefighters and law enforcement officers, toll collectors, plumbers and electricians, to waste collection workers, waiters and waitresses, to doctors and nurses, to construction workers and truck drivers and all the others that have made this country so great—this book is for you.

As well, it is dedicated to the men and women of the Armed Forces of the United States of America, who have risked and sacrificed their lives to protect us all and who are all true American heroes.

To my very special lifelong friends, Steven Flanagan and Captain Bill Behe.

And to the following who helped me get through the Trump years and keep the American Dream events alive, even after Trump tried to destroy them: Alex Toth, David "Billy Bob" Irvin, Victor Babinsack, Steven Goldberg, Natural Facet Company-Aaron, Joe Overcash, Ziad Ansari and Don Grissom.

Ultimately, this book is in loving memory of my dad, William George Houraney, Sr., who, due to terrible healthcare in the 1970s, died at just fifty-seven years old, denying us the chance to see him grow old with our mother and do the things with him one cannot do while growing up, and to my mother, who lost the love of her life far too soon but carried on helping all five of her children and always putting us first, and finally, to all mothers and fathers who put their children before themselves with the love only a parent can have.

Finally, I hope this book reflects the singular spirit of America. Our nation is a fortress of freedom and liberty because it would never settle for anything but the truth, which is what this book is all about.

A Heartfelt Thanks

I wish to give special thanks to some amazing people who have helped me as I fight cancer, as well as the severe pain from a bad auto accident I was involved in while at a stop sign and hit hard from behind, and terrible migraines that got so bad only trips to the ER could help.

To Dr. Richard Martinoff, my family doctor, who, besides being a terrific doctor for my wife and I, was always there when I needed him and first suspected I may have cancer. He sent me to a specialist who confirmed it and arranged radiation treatments.

To Doctor Ben Han, who through special pain medication made it possible for me to get through months of radiation treatment.

To Dr. Alexander Wang, DMD. Because so much medication had destroyed all my teeth, Dr. Wang made it possible for me to have full dental implants. He was so fast and efficient that what could have taken many days of pain took just hours each time, with very little pain.

To Dr. Todd Relkin, who helped me through the pain caused by the auto accident.

To Martin E. Hale, MD, my pain management doctor, for helping me obtain the proper cancer medication, without which I would be living in a hospital with pain medication administered by IV. By far one of the finest doctors I've ever had the honor of knowing.

To Dr. David Mishkel, my cardiologist, who helped me survive the heart problems that happened as a result of the cancer and the auto accident. Without him, I would have had a heart attack by now.

To Dr. Mitchell Rauch, a urologist who is helping treat my cancer.

To Dr. Daniel Lindeberg, for helping me get through a terrible gastric condition caused by the cancer.

To Dr. Shafi at Kessler Medicine, who is doing such a good job treating my lifelong injuries from the auto accident.

To Marc A. Kaufman, Esq., who handled the legal affairs when my wife and I were hit while at a stop sign, which caused me physical damage that became lifelong pain.

To IRA Pharmacy—Preveen and Lisa. When you are facing what I was, cancer, an auto accident and migraines, just as important as the best doctors is a pharmacy that makes sure you have the correct medications when you need them. Preveen and Lisa at IRA Pharmacy always made sure I had my much-needed medication.

To Dr. Michael Flischer, a wonderful doctor and longtime friend who delivered my son Michael just in time for me to fly to Las Vegas as our sold-out event at Caesar's Palace Resort waited for me to officially start their event! My first announcement on stage that night was . . . IT'S A BOY!

To West Boca Raton Hospital ER—Between my cancer, auto accident and lifelong terrible migraines, I've unfortunately spent a lot of time in hospital ERs. Most were terrible and had me wait up to an hour or more while I laid there in "terrible" pain. Then, even after seeing a doctor, I had another long wait to get medication for my pain. West Boca's ER was different. Within thirty minutes a doctor saw me and shortly thereafter gave me medication for the pain. When you feel like you are going to die because the pain is so bad and you have to wait so long, it's one of the worst experiences ever. It's made even worse if your wife and young child are with you and seeing you in such pain. However, when it's taken care of so efficiently, like they did at West Boca ER, it's a far better experience for all.

I was very fortunate to have known and also been friends with some terrific doctors who helped me get through the worst medical times of my life. However, despite a costly health insurance policy plus Medicare, the co-pays and medications that cost thousands, I've had to borrow money. However, it would have been even worse if not for at least *some* help from President Obama. How many people has Trump helped medically so far in his presidency?

Finally, a very special "Thank You" to both the following old friends and some terrific new friends who have helped me in many ways, for which I am forever grateful.

Victor Babinsack, website administrator

Doak Campbell, attorney

Joe V. Overcash, accountant

Paul Kurzweil, editor

Gary Rosenberg, cover and interior design

David "Billy Bob" Irvin, lifelong business associate and friend

Billie Behe, lifelong friend and writer

GEORGE HOURANEY AND
THE NATIONAL ARMED FORCES CLUB

If all the things George Houraney has done, he is especially proud of the National Armed Forces Club he created during the Vietnam War.

It started out when he sent a few hundred soldiers free calendars, photos, and stickers of their favorite race cars. *Free.* However, it didn't take long before it caught on within the military ranks, as next to their favorite girls, most military men love their cars.

The newly formed National Armed Forces Club was something that not only brought beautiful memories to the soldiers' nightmare war zone, but it helped to remind them of what they were fighting for.

Within months of when George started sending calendars and photos, thousands of requests started pouring in every week from military men—and even women—requesting the free calendars and photos.

It got to the point where it was costing George more money to fill the requests for calendars and photos than he was earning selling his merchandise at motorsports events and through the mail to regular customers. Although his messages said these items were free to any enlisted men or women, it also stated "while they last," which gave him a way out. As the sacks piled up in his office, they became too much to ignore—at least if you have a conscience. Besides using the money he received from selling his Corvette and Harley Davison, he also ended up using the profits he was making from his merchandise. But that didn't stop George—he kept on going.

This carried on far past the Vietnam War. During the Iraq and Afghanistan conflicts he ended up sacrificing what could have been profits for his company to make sure those who risked so much received something that made them feel at least a little better as they faced some of the worst terror on this earth.

Be sure to read the letters on the following spread, for they are part of American history. And keep in mind that some of the soldiers who wrote those letters to George never returned home . . . alive that is.

TO DONALD TRUMP

George Houraney was barely out of his teens at the time with very little income, and you were the same age, Donald Trump. With all the money you had—and being able to avoid the draft—what contribution did you make to assist our brave military men and women during the terrible Vietnam War and wars thereafter?

VIETNAM

ADE -- AN AMERICAN PATRIOT

Many people considered the Vietnam War, a battle plagued by antiwar protesters, to be, 'The War that shouldn't have been.' Thousands of young men and women died during this war, but were only recently recognized for their bravery by the *Vietnam Memorial* in Washington, D.C. When the surviving American Soldiers arrived home, weary, injured and forever changed, instead of being honored for serving their country by a ticker tape parade, they were met with country-wide antiwar sentiments.

ADE did what others did not do during the war -- we supported the brave men, boosted their morale and provided a touch of home, through the creation of the National Armed Forces Club. Recognizing that next to the special women in their lives, most men had an affinity for cars, we dispatched thousands of custom decals and free, colored photos of award-winning, motor sports champions to servicemen to be pinned up next to snapshots of their favorite girls.

We take great pride in having had the foresight to care when it mattered most. The following notes are a small representation of the thousands of letters of gratitude we received from U.S. soldiers stationed in Vietnam.

APPRECIATE YOU SENDING ONE TO ME. THANKS FOR REMEMBERING US OUT HERE ON THIS SIDE OF THE "POND".

ETRSN KEN FUJIWAMI
OPERATIONS DIVISION
USS REGULUS (AF-57)
F.P.O. SAN FRANCISCO 96601

Cpl. Gary W. _____
2ND ANGLCO - MARINE BARRACKS
BOX 46
FPO NEW YORK, N.Y. 09575

I read your recent offer in Car Craft Magazine and Commend you on your Endevor, it is good to know someone is thinking about the serviceman other than the hippies. please find my address enclosed for your Generous offer. I thank you very much

May God Bless you for this _____ ____, but wonderful thing you ____

____ to thank you for this offer. We servicemen have a hard time following our favorite sport while overseas. Companies like yours give us quite a needed lift. Thank you

Robert Carnahan I C 3
E Division
U.S.S. Bennington CVS-33
% F.P.O. San Francisco, Calif.
96601

I would like to become a member of your Armed Forces Club. I have heard that National Studios are doing this and I think this is really great. This is the type of thing that makes a guy think that everyone hasn't forgotten about him.

Thanks A Lot, hope to hear from you soon.

Spl James A. Rafko
US 54,955355
A Co 91st Engr B_n (CBt)
Fort Belvoir, Va. 22060

7 ___ Clay ___
___ GES
Box 2009
APO NY 09130

Dear Sir,

I am writing to you in regard to your article in the April issue in your magazine. I think what you are doing for us servicemen around the world is great for the morale of U.S. fighting men ...

It really helps moral to know that people
like you are behind us. In so many parts
back here that only don't care the slightest idea of
what we are fighting for. Sure they are a lot of war
mine saving their lives sometime, and I mean they'll be
a great many more. But this law are not wasted, for
soon we fight for the peace all off the world here to
offer, freedom! Again I would like to give thanks
you for your support of our in this U.S. around
from the men upon my homecoming.
Sincerely,
PFC Gregory R. Browne
PFC Gregory R. Browne
RA Purview   Vietnam
Co A 3rd Bn, 14th Int.
4th Infantry Division
RA SP 90288

It sure is nice to know that although our government may have forgotten about us to some extent,
we aren't forgotten by our rooting buddies
back stateside. Ever tried to soup up a M-48
tank?

Yours truly,

PFC Joseph A. Howell
US 67068?
A TROOP, 2/1 in the Army And is Stationed
APO San Fra in Viet Nam I know he

P.S. My hometown is Spartanburg
home of Dave Pearson, Cotton Owens
Lichfjohn, Rex White Eli Jinn

I have A Cousin who is
in the Army And is Stationed
Viet Nam I know he
would APPRECIATE the pictures
I just returned from there
myself I know that Anything
from home helps.

Thank you!
Jerry Wilton

His address is:
SP4 CHARLES R. Satterfield
US 53489430
HHC 1/46th Inf. 198 Ind. Bde.
APO San Francisco

I would like to become a member
Club. I have heard that National Studios are doing this ann-
think this is really great. Thsi is the type of thing that makes
a guy think that everyone hasn't forgotten about him.

Thanks A Lot, hope to hear from you soo

Sp4 James A. Rafko
US 54955355
A Co 91st Engr Bn (Cbt)
Fort Belvoir, Va. 22060

CPL THOMAS M   AS 2106888
MARINE BARRACKS USNS BOX 35
FPO NEW YORK, N.Y. 09597
Thanks for your generous offer. It gives
the car crazy serviceman a feeling that
someone cares.
Sincerely,
TM Thayer

SP4 JAMES J. Lynn
US 54964796
Co. C 504th MP Bn. (A)
APO SF 96294

Thank you again
for thinking of the
serviceman. It's a pleasure
to be over here fighting
for freedom for people
like you.
Jim Lynn

I would like to thank you,
in behalf of myself & the other 500,000
G.I.'s over here, for offering us an
offer like this. I'm in charge of a
motor pool & only fond of machines I
see are the ones the army puts out. So
I will enjoy the photos very much

Thanks
Sgt James L Putnam
97   B.H.C.
APO. San Francisco
96377

10 MAY 1968
Dear Sirs,
Please send me your special
Armed Forces packet of Car drag
racing photos as advertised in April
Car Craft magazine. May I add
that it is inspiring — morale building
since to us. That helps keep
our spirit high here on the line &
many men and enthusiasts like myself
feel the very same way. Thank you
very much.   Sincerely,
M. Potts U.S.N.

YOU'RE THE JUDGE

Join The Dream Panel Of Judges!

Your vote could decide which
of the world's most beautiful girls
will appear in the internationally famous
"American Dream Calendar."

DONALD J. TRUMP
AMERICAN DREAM
WORLD FINALS™

November 17-20, 1993
Crystal Ballroom

Also Enjoy:
• A Hilarious Comedy Challenge
• A Battle Of The Most Talented Vocalists
• The Hottest, One-Of-A-Kind
Automotive Designs

Donald Trump's invitation

You won't want to miss one single powerhouse competition:

Wednesday, November 17
Dream Girl Photo, Evening Wear
& Interview Competition
7:30 PM - 9:30 PM

Thursday, November 18
Dream Girl Photo, Evening Wear
& Interview Competition
7:30 PM - 9:30 PM

Comedy & Vocals Challenge
10:00 PM

Friday, November 19
Dream Girl Fashion Challenge
8:30 PM

Unveiling Of Hottest,
One-Of-A-Kind Car Designs
8:30 PM

Private Cocktail Reception
With The Dream Girls
9:30 PM*

Saturday, November 20
Hottest, One-Of-A-Kind Cars On Display
10:00 AM

DREAM WORLD FINALS
All Competitions
8:00 PM*

Winners' Reception & Dance Competition
10:00 PM*

RSVP "Dream"
Press 1 for Private Cocktail Reception,
Dream World Finals
& Winners' Reception.

Let us know if you'll be joining the
excitement & our judging panel.

* This invitation is limited to two adults and is not transferable.
Subject to availability. Schedule subject to change.

TRUMP'S
CASTLE
CASINO RESORT
Where service is king!

In addition to the Automotive Challenge, Music and Comedy, and Battle of the Bands events, there was the very popular International Model Competition. Here, Donald Trump poses with World Finalists at the event press conference.

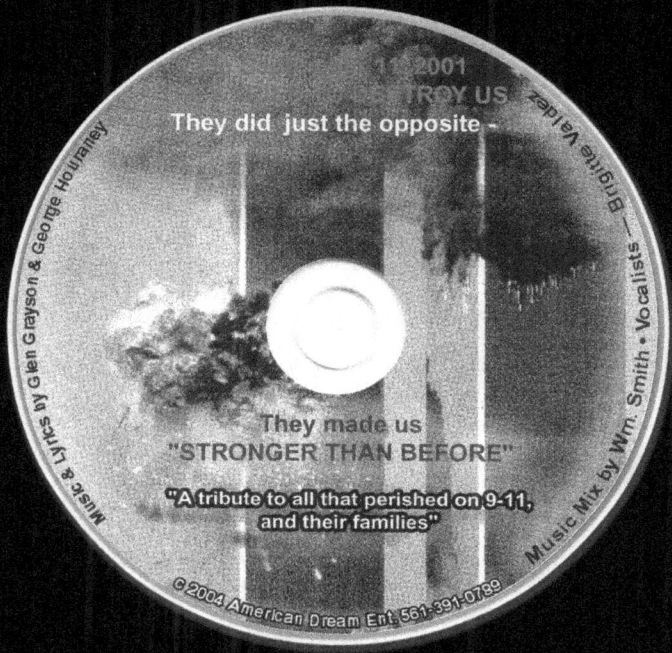

They did just the opposite –
11 2001 DESTROY US — Brigitte Valdez
Music & Lyrics by Glen Grayson & George Houraney
Music Mix by Wm. Smith • Vocalists
They made us
"STRONGER THAN BEFORE"
"A tribute to all that perished on 9-11, and their families"
© 2004 American Dream Ent. 561-391-0789

9/11 Tribute CD
Written, produced, and paid for by George Houraney and Glen Grayson.

The Triple Crown of Gaming™

The "Triple Crown of Gaming™"

Long overdue, for the 21st Century, Gaming finally has its own
"SUPER BOWL TYPE EVENTS" ... ©2015 American Dream Entertainment.

The event that could have saved Donald Trump's Atlantic City casinos.

In 2016, William George Houraney celebrated his 50th year of being in business with not even one legal action against his business and not a single bankruptcy. These are the designs Mr. Houraney created for official merchandise for the Donald Trump World Finals that thousands of people in more than thirty countries wore, bringing priceless PR for Trump's Casino.

www.ingramcontent.com/pod-product-compliance
Lightning Source LLC
Chambersburg PA
CBHW072111270326
41931CB00010B/1520